The Disobedient Writer

The
Disobedient
Writer

Women
and
Narrative
Tradition

NANCY A. WALKER

UNIVERSITY OF TEXAS PRESS
AUSTIN

Requests for permission to reproduce material from this
work should be sent to Permissions, University of Texas
Press, Box 7819, Austin, TX 78713-7819.

⊗ The paper used in this publication meets the
minimum requirements of American National Standard
for Information Sciences—Permanence of Paper for
Printed Library Materials, ANSI Z39.48-1984.

Library of Congress Cataloging-in-Publication Data

Walker, Nancy A., date.
    The disobedient writer : women and narrative
tradition / Nancy A. Walker. — 1st ed.
        p.   cm.
    Includes bibliographical references and index.
    ISBN 0-292-79095-3. — ISBN 0-292-79096-1 (pbk.)
    1. American prose literature—Women authors—
History and criticism.   2. English prose literature—
Women authors—History and criticism.   3. American fiction—Women authors—History and criticism.
4. English fiction—Women authors—History and
criticism.   5. Women and literature—United States—
History.   6. Women and literature—Great Britain—
History.   7. Authorship—Sex differences.   8. Sex role
in literature.   9. Narration (Rhetoric).   I. Title.
PS152.W35   1995
813.009'9287—dc20   94-30723

Contents

Acknowledgments

For various kinds of assistance with this manuscript—ranging from stimulating conversations and suggestions of sources to useful readings of portions of the manuscript itself—I would like to thank the following colleagues and friends: Margaret Anne Doody, Kay Pilzer, Roberta Rubenstein, Cecelia Tichi, Gay Welch, and Jack Zipes.

Permission to reprint previously published material has been granted as follows:

Material from my essay "Witch Weldon" in *Fay Weldon's Wicked Fictions*, ed. Gina Barreca, reprinted by permission of University Press of New England.

Material from my essay on fairy tales in *Santa Barbara Review*, vol. 2, no. 2, reprinted by permission.

Excerpt from "The Writer on, and at, Her Work" copyright © 1991 by Ursula K. Le Guin; first appeared in *The Writer on Her Work*; reprinted by permission of the author and the author's agent, Virginia Kidd.

Excerpt from "Lilith to Eve: House, Garden," in *Feminist Revision and the Bible* by Alicia Suskin Ostriker, reprinted by permission of Blackwell Publishers.

Excerpts from *The Handmaid's Tale* by Margaret Atwood. Copyright 1985 by O. W. Toad, Ltd. First American edition, 1986. Reprinted by permission of Houghton Mifflin Company. All rights reserved.

Excerpts from *Transformations*. Copyright 1971 by Anne Sexton. Reprinted by permission of Houghton Mifflin Company. All rights reserved.

Excerpts from Stevie Smith, *Collected Poems of Stevie Smith*. Copyright © 1972 by Stevie Smith. Reprinted by permission of New Directions Pub. Corp.

Excerpts from *Communication: The Autobiography of Rachel Maddux*, ed. Nancy A. Walker, reprinted by permission of the University of Tennessee Press.

Excerpts from Olga Broumas, *Beginning with O*. Copyright © 1977 by Olga Broumas. Reprinted by permission of Yale University Press.

The Disobedient Writer

Introduction # ACTS OF DISOBEDIENCE

T his book began with its final chapter. More specifically, it began in a course on the American novel that I taught in 1986. The course began with *The Scarlet Letter* and concluded with *The Handmaid's Tale*, which had just been published. As the class explored the obvious resonances between the two works, I thought about not merely the way in which Margaret Atwood reformulates Hawthorne's plot, setting, and motifs, but also the impetus for such a project—not only on the part of Atwood, but also on that of other women writers. What, in other words, is the relationship between women writers and the traditions of narrative? Such musings are hardly new, of course: Virginia Woolf articulated similar questions many years ago in *A Room of One's Own*, and dozens of scholars during the past two decades have investigated various aspects of this relationship in order to perform their own revision of literary history. We are thus able to see as never before the complex interrelation of factors that create what at any given moment scholars regard as the body of exemplary texts of our literary heritage—not the least of which is gender.

In her introduction to *The Other Side of the Story*, Molly Hite observes that "the notion that stories inevitably both obscure and encode other stories has been axiomatic to our understanding of narration since at least the eighteenth century" (4). The practice of appropriating existing stories in one's own work—borrowing, revising, recontextualizing—has a long and distinguished history that includes such unquestionably major works as Milton's *Paradise Lost* and the plays of Shakespeare. Before the advent of widespread literacy, folk literature relied for its very existence on a continuous reworking of narrative materials passed down from one generation to another. The human impulse to work changes on the inherited stories of a cultural tradition—to tell the story from a perspective or with narrative elements that make it more congenial to one's circumstances or goals—may if anything be abetted by the existence of such stories on the printed page, where they can be returned to again and again and ultimately transposed and transformed, as Shakespeare turned histories into tragedies and Milton turned biblical narrative into epic poetry.

Considerable evidence exists, however, to suggest that male and female writers have not participated in this appropriative and revisionary process in the same ways or for the same reasons. As axiomatic as the concept that stories "obscure and encode other stories" is the perception, which has gained force in recent decades, that women's relation to language, literature, education, and cultural traditions has been made problematic and complex by centuries of unequal access to power and agency within these systems. For women who are members of ethnic and racial minorities the distance from the center of these cultural systems has been exponentially greater. Nor are these insights solely the property of scholars of literature. The exclusion of women from language and the authority it confers has become a common trope in women's writing itself. Two examples stand out from the work of contemporary North American women writers: the prohibition against reading and writing for the women in *The Handmaid's Tale*, and the suppression of Nettie's letters to Celie in Alice Walker's *The Color Purple*. In other words, in the midst of the act of *claiming* language, these and other women authors metaphorically acknowledge their traditional exclusion from it.

Simultaneously, however, much standard literary history continues to be written in a manner that devalues women's part in the formation of literary tradition. Thus, in their 1991 history of American literature, *From Puritanism to Postmodernism*, Richard Ruland and Malcolm Bradbury hail Charles Brockden Brown as "the acknowledged father of the American novel" (63), while dismissing Susanna Rowson's earlier and highly influential novel *Charlotte Temple* as "none too interesting" (84), despite the fact that it helped to spawn the genre of the domestic novel, which occupied women as both readers and writers for much of the nineteenth century.[1]

The unexamined assumption that underlies statements such as those of Ruland and Bradbury (and I single them out not because their approach is unusual in literary histories but rather because of the recentness of their volume) is a tautology: Brown is the "father" of the novel in America because he has been declared to be so by scholars who have traced the development of a certain kind of novel to its headwaters and found him there. In different circumstances, with different preferences predominating, the novel as practiced by Rowson and her successors might have come to be viewed as "the" American novel, and the haunted heroes of Brown, Melville, and Hawthorne might have been regarded as players in an interesting but decidedly ancillary enterprise. Because of the way in which Western literary traditions have been formulated, however, most male writers who have appropriated and revised previous texts have worked within a tradition that included them and their experience, whereas women writers have more commonly addressed such texts from the position of outsider, altering them either to point up the biases they encode or to make them into narratives that women can more comfortably inhabit.

Women as writers—specifically as revisionist writers—will be my concern in the chapters that follow. But implicit in a discussion of women's imaginative encounters with a literary tradition of which they are not an obvious part is a consideration of women as readers of this tradition, for prior to resisting the authority of the assumptions or narrative necessities of a text must come an understanding of its putative power and an ability to read through it to possibilities of altered meaning. As British fiction writer Angela Carter states in "Notes from the Front Line," "Reading is just as creative an activity as writing and most intellectual development depends on new readings of old texts" (69). What Carter intends, and what her own writing strikingly exemplifies, is what I am calling a "disobedient" reading, a reading that resists sexist and racist formulations and that results in a new text that attempts to overturn these formulations while remaining sufficiently referential to the original to make clear its point of origin. Thus Carter, in *The Passion of New Eve*, signals in her title as well as in numerous narrative elements that she is working variations on the Genesis story of creation, and Atwood's *The Handmaid's Tale* reveals in its language, plot, and setting its encounter with the Bible, traditional fairy tales, and *The Scarlet Letter*.

The revisionary tendency in women's literature did not, of course, originate in the twentieth century. In "The Reenchantment of Utopia and the Female Monarchical Self," Rachel Trubowitz posits that Margaret Cavendish, arguably the first woman writer of note in English, intended her 1666 *Blazing World* as a "canny revision of the utopian social paradigm" (229), which "reenchants" and "feminizes" the utopian genre (230). Cavendish's utopian vision creates a world ruled by women, in which both church and state are governed as matriarchies; her work is thus a precursor to Charlotte Perkins Gilman's *Herland* (1915), which was itself a response to the popular utopian genre at the turn of the century.

Appropriating a literary genre in order to revise or even reverse its assumptions, ideologies, or paradigms is one of several ways in which a writer may alter an inherited tradition, and such a method is by no means the exclusive property of women. Indeed, literary history—particularly the history of fiction—is frequently constructed by successive writers turning to their own purposes the patterns and materials created by other writers. And yet it is also true that women's relationship to such an inheritance has normally been fundamentally and dramatically different from that of men. As Florence Howe puts it in her introduction to *Tradition and the Talents of Women*, "We now understand—as Virginia Woolf did before us—how difficult it has been, and still often is, for a woman writer to find her form and language, since readers, regardless of their gender, have grown accustomed to the works and tradition of male writers, especially to their themes" (17).

This difficulty can lead to several consequences: silence; acquiescence to the models of the tradition; or the disobedient, deliberate reconstituting of a genre to accord with women's experience and vision. Gilman's *Herland* does not, in fact, represent such a disobedience to the utopian genre; Gilman's vision of an all-female society is itself radical, but she works no fundamental changes on the utopia as a fictional form and must introduce male characters as a means of explaining and justifying the very separatism she depicts. Caroline Kirkland, on the other hand, does reformulate the genre of frontier exploration in *A New Home—Who'll Follow?* Kirkland not only retells the story of settling the American wilderness from an interior, domestic perspective, she also overturns the usual heroic self-justification of such stories to show the self-interest and intolerance that she saw as embodied in the much-celebrated individualism of nineteenth-century America.

Even more fundamental than genre, which is a concern of the literate, are cultural mythologies, which, though extant for centuries in written form, emerged from an oral tradition that reflected the dominant values of Western culture and disseminated them in stories available to the nonliterate as well. In "Diving into the Wreck," Adrienne Rich writes of the "book of myths/in which/our names do not appear." The names of women *do* appear in the biblical story of creation and in European fairy tales—the two sets of mythologies that I focus on first in this book—but to point to Eve, Sleeping Beauty, or Cinderella is not to contradict Rich's message that women tend to be without individual agency in such stories. They are, instead, emblematic of approved or unapproved female behavior, and as emblems they have a prescriptive function that is the target of the writers who revise such stories. So pervasive are the Genesis story and the classic fairy tales that contemporary authors need make only passing references to them in order to call up their outlines in the minds of readers. One recent case in point is Joyce Carol Oates's novel *Black Water* (1992), a thinly veiled version of the Ted Kennedy/Chappaquiddick incident. Not only does Oates revise the public accounts of Senator Kennedy's dishonorable abandonment of the submerged car and its female occupant by telling the story from the drowning girl's perspective, she also casts it as a tragic version of the story of the young girl who has found her "prince." Like Cinderella, Kitty Kelleher feels singled out, sought after by the senator, "as if, as in the most improbable of fairy tales, the man had made this impromptu trip to Grayling Island expressly to see *her*" (139). The reference to fairy tales both heightens the fictive, fatally misguided quality of Kitty's elation and points to the unreality of the "happily ever after" of the tales themselves.

Writers who appropriate such "public domain" stories as biblical narrative and folk tales do so both with the expectation that their readers will be familiar with the stories they use and, somewhat paradoxically, without intervening very directly in issues of a literary canon. That is, they may challenge the authority or force of widespread social narratives having to do with women's nature or role, but they are not responding to specific, identifiable authors who are part of a privileged literary history. To rework a specific text by a specific author, as Atwood reworks *The Scarlet Letter*, is to exercise a different kind of disobedience, one that questions the singularity and ownership of certain themes, plots, tropes, and narrative strategies. Such revisions are a way not only of subverting the traditional text, but also of laying claim to it, entering into dialogue with it on an equal plane.

Two studies of women writers' encounters with literary tradition signal in their titles purposes consonant with mine. Molly Hite's *The Other Side of the Story* (1989) and Gayle Greene's *Changing the Story* (1991) take different, productive approaches to the work of twentieth-century British and North American writers. Hite, beginning with Jean Rhys, whose *The Wide Sargasso Sea* is a celebrated instance of narrative revision, and moving to discussions of works by Doris Lessing, Alice Walker, and Margaret Atwood, proposes that these writers reorient "the dominant stories of a given culture" (3) by "emphasizing conventionally marginal characters and themes" (2), as Rhys tells the story of *Jane Eyre* from the point of view of Bertha, making Brontë's "madwoman" a pivotal person instead of merely a peripheral image. By making explicit and central the stories that were formerly implicit and marginal, Hite demonstrates how these writers "*re*-center the value structure of the narrative" (2). Greene's *Changing the Story* focuses specifically on metafictional novels that deal with the development of the woman artist: Lessing's *The Golden Note-book*, Margaret Drabble's *The Waterfall*, Margaret Laurence's *The Divin-ers*, and Atwood's *Lady Oracle*. Metafiction, which simultaneously calls attention to the conventions of fiction—and thus to itself *as* fiction—Greene posits, "draw[s] attention to the conventionality of the codes that govern human behavior, . . . [and] reveal[s] how such codes have been constructed and how they can therefore be changed" (2).

Hite and Greene share the assumption, with which I concur, that fiction reflects the author's concern with social realities, and that to "change the story" is not merely an artistic but also a social action, suggesting in narrative practice the possibility of cultural transformation. By concentrating on works written since the late 1960s, both authors suggest that this narrative re-vision is a relatively recent phenomenon among women writers. While it is true that the impetus for and the freedom to question and resist tradition have increased dramatically in recent decades, as the sheer number of women writers has become a circumstance worthy of note, I would argue that this tendency has existed for much longer. Indeed, it might well be the case that part of the project of a woman's writing at all has necessarily been to come to terms with the fact of her own cultural marginalization in a literary tradition defined largely as male. It is certainly the recognition of this position outside a literary establishment that occasioned Anne Bradstreet's well-known comment in the seventeenth century about whether a needle or a pen better suited her hand, and a similar consciousness informs Kate Chopin's "Elizabeth Stock's One Story," a discussion of which opens the first chapter of this book. Even, that is, when not addressing a particular text or genre (as Margaret Cavendish addressed the utopian genre), women writers have frequently revealed in their work an awareness of working against instead of inside cultural heritage.

To the extent that a narrative is referential to a prior narrative in its own construction, it calls attention to its own fictive and conditional character. Put another way, it becomes *a* narrative rather than *the* narrative, a construct to be set alongside other constructs. Thus this revisionary kind of narrative is closely allied to metafiction. Whereas metafiction calls attention to the conventions of creating fiction—its mechanisms of plot, character, and voice—the narratives I am addressing accomplish a similar end by calling attention to the elements of another version of the story. Atwood's narrator in *The Handmaid's Tale*, for example, tells us frequently that her story is a "reconstruction," which on one level refers to the fact that, being denied materials with which to write, she is recording the events after the fact, from memory, but which on another level invites the reader to consider what other stories here receive "reconstruction": most obviously *The Scarlet Letter*, but also "Rumpelstiltskin," in which the girl must agree to give away her first-born child, and other fairy tales. When writers such as Ursula Le Guin and Lynne Sharon Schwartz retell the Genesis story of Adam and Eve, they need not name the central characters, so familiar are the outlines of the story; yet this very familiarity ensures that the biblical account will resonate with the revision as two possible versions of the story, neither possessing sole authority.

It is precisely the issue of authority that distinguishes the revisionary strategies of the works I consider in this study from the numerous instances in which an author borrows the plot of a familiar work to use as the framework for his or her own. Such borrowing, like productions of *Hamlet* in contemporary dress, suggest continuity rather than disruption and propose that certain human dramas have a timeless quality that allows them to be replayed in different eras with undiminished relevance. Thus, for example, Upton Sinclair's 1950 novel *Another Pamela; or, Virtue Still Rewarded* retells Samuel Richardson's 1740 novel, setting it in California in the 1920s but employing Richardson's epistolary method to create episodes that, as the jacket blurb has it, are "as true to life today as they were two hundred years ago." Such uses of traditional narratives—of which there are countless examples—endorse instead of challenging the assumptions of the original.

Revisionary, "disobedient" narratives, on the other hand, expose or upset the paradigms of authority inherent in the texts they appropriate. Margaret Homans has pointed out, for example, that Gloria Naylor's obvious use of Dante's *Inferno* in her novel *Linden Hills* (1985) allows for a subversive reenactment that tells rather than submerging the story of the woman in the cave, "a female figure, violated yet surviving, a subtle ironist who takes it as her task to expose to view the underworld of male domination, letting its horrors speak for themselves" ("The Woman in the Cave," 402). Similarly, Kay Pilzer has demonstrated that Jane Smiley's 1991 novel *A Thousand Acres* reformulates Shakespeare's *King Lear* to give narrative authority to the female characters and thus to ex-

pose and question the patriarchal patterns that Shakespeare and his contemporaries took for granted. At its extreme, revisionary narrative ex-
plodes the concept of authority altogether. As Jack Zipes says of some
recent revisions of traditional fairy tales, "The end goal of the postmod-
ernist fairy tale is not closure but openness, not recuperation but differ-
entiation, not the establishment of a new norm but the questioning of all
norms" ("Recent Trends," 33).

Part One of *The Disobedient Writer* focuses on reworkings of biblical
and fairy-tale narratives, addressing two pervasive sets of stories in the
Western cultural tradition. Part Two to some extent reverses the process.
Instead of examining multiple revisions of the same stock of cultural narratives, this section deals with two nineteenth-century American wom-
en's texts that revised dominant cultural mythologies: the masculine story
of frontier exploration and settlement, and the feminine story of domesticity and sentiment. At the same time that the European fairy tale
was being domesticated for childhood acculturation to a middle-class
ideal, complete with gender roles, the persistent efforts at national self-
definition had produced some equally persistent mythologies that would
later affect the criteria for developing an American literary canon. Caroline Kirkland's 1839 *A New Home* "domesticates" the account of west-
ward expansion, focusing on the process of community development instead of on the divine mandate to subdue and civilize the wilderness and
using satire to undercut the capitalistic complacency of masculine empire
building. By 1853, as Elaine Showalter notes in *Sister's Choice*, Kirkland
believed that a uniquely indigenous American literature had emerged in
the work of such writers as Catherine Sedgwick, Harriet Beecher Stowe,
and Susan Warner, whose "themes were domestic, local, and vernacular"
(12). But by the time one could speak of American literature as a distinc-
tive entity, these writers had been largely dismissed by standards that
devalued these very qualities. In the following year, 1854, the popular
newspaper columnist known to her readers as "Fanny Fern" published
her autobiographical novel *Ruth Hall*, which, in its depiction of a woman's self-sufficient rise to success as a writer, resisted the sentiment and
domesticity of the popular mid-century novel. Scorned by contemporary
reviewers for its author's irreverence toward men and their institutions,
Ruth Hall likewise disappeared from consideration until the 1980s.

Despite reiterated calls for a distinctively "American" literature (and
despite an academic enterprise premised on the existence of that literature), scholars in recent years have increasingly called into question the
validity of claims to such a nationalistic concept. Peter Carafiol, in *The*

American Ideal, puts the matter perhaps most bluntly: "'America,' like divine providence, has been an assumption demanding illustration, not a thesis that required proof" (11). Similarly, the notion of "American literary history," with its accompanying suggestion of a fixed and orderly canon of representative works, may now be regarded as a convenient fiction subject to the influences of political ideologies and aesthetic preferences. Ruland and Bradbury argue that, while "all literary histories are critical fictions," the recurring need for a "usable" past has made American literary history "more fictional than most" (xv). Yet such fictions have considerable ideological power, as do the various mythologies devised to give cohesion to the otherwise formless and chaotic enterprise of founding a nation comprising competing interests. Such stories, promulgated by political and religious rhetoric and reaching the general public through advice manuals, newspaper editorials, children's literature, and advertising, take on authority quite apart from the reality of social experience.

The cultural ideology that differentiated sharply the nature and role of male and female in nineteenth-century America, while never uniformly descriptive of lived experience, provided the narratives according to which travel, exploration, and individual accomplishment were the province of men, and the settled world of home and family was women's particular responsibility. The privileging of the public over the domestic as the source of "the" American story would ensure that the authors whom Caroline Kirkland saw as the creators of a truly American literature would be considered peripheral to the literary tradition as developed by successive generations of scholars. Kirkland and Fanny Fern, in resisting the public versus private narrative in their own work, demonstrated their understanding of these stories and also of their susceptibility to alteration.

The fact that Kirkland's *A New Home* and Fern's *Ruth Hall* are both barely fictionalized autobiography (though the latter is framed as a novel) carries its own significance. As Chopin's character Elizabeth Stock knows instinctively, when a woman encounters a tradition that does not include her, and in which all of the stories seem already to have been written, there remains to be told one's own story. Moreover, because the concepts of individual selfhood and subjectivity have been problematic for women, merely to present publicly one's life is a disobedient act. And to present autobiography as the story of frontier life or independent career success, as Kirkland and Fern, respectively, do, is to revise these options to include women. Part Three deals with autobiography, both the formal autobiography, in chapter 4, and Atwood's use of the autobiographical form of the journal in *The Handmaid's Tale,* in chapter 5.

To write autobiography is to compose an image of the self to present to one or more others, and because of the consciousness of self-presentation—of the life on the page as a more or less deliberate construct—the autobiographer shares in the task of the writer of fiction. At the same time, however, autobiography is the insertion of the self into historical narrative, a claim to be counted as significant in a particular time and place. For a woman to do this at all is to revise traditional concepts of who counts, who is worthy of a life story. Margaret Halsey, in her 1977 *No Laughing Matter: The Autobiography of a WASP,* has no doubt at all that hers is a story that should be told. She intends it as a cautionary tale for those who would insist on the inevitability of white Anglo-Saxon Protestant dominance of American sociopolitical thought and practice. The ideals of self-sufficiency and virtue in public life that Benjamin Franklin extolled in his *Autobiography,* and of which he proposed himself as an exemplar, have in Halsey's view become perverted in the twentieth century into egotism and abuse of authority. Thus, as Franklin writes with optimism about personal and national progress, Halsey believes it is time for WASP culture to "climb down" from its sense of superiority. Whereas Halsey intended *No Laughing Matter* as a public document, Rachel Maddux sought to present herself to one other person in a lengthy letter when she was twenty-eight years old. Published fifty years later, in 1991, *Communication* similarly challenges the Franklinesque notion of self-sufficiency, as Maddux realizes that her effort at self-revision has left her isolated and vulnerable.

Atwood's *The Handmaid's Tale* brings together many of the threads developed in the preceding chapters. Not only does Atwood revise *The Scarlet Letter,* she also uses the motifs of the classic fairy tales as part of her dystopian projection, and the novel takes the form of a journal as Offred recalls her days as a Handmaid in Gilead. But Atwood approaches revision on several levels. Biblical language is revised within the text by both the leaders of the Republic of Gilead and the narrator, each for their own purposes. The fundamentalists who are ideological descendants of Hawthorne's colonists alter biblical texts as a means of enforcing their authority, while Offred devises an ironic version of the Lord's Prayer that resists the authority of both religious doctrine and the rulers of Gilead. And the very possibility of a stable, knowable history—whether personal or public—is challenged by Offred's repeated reminders that her account is a "reconstruction" and by the doubts about authenticity expressed in the "Historical Notes" section at the end of the novel.

My intention in the pages that follow is suggestive rather than comprehensive. By selecting texts by both well-known authors and those whose work is just now being recognized or retrieved, I want to demonstrate that the revisionary impulse has been widely shared by women writers in different periods and genres—that it is, in fact, an integral part of writing as a woman in the Anglo-American tradition. Narratives are essential to our sense of place in a human continuum, and one of the strategies that women have employed to mark out their own places is to challenge the authority of existing narratives by telling them anew out of their own necessities. The result is a body of literature—of which the works I deal with here are but a fraction—that is characterized by wit, irreverence, and freshness of vision. In *The Tongue-Snatchers*, Claudine Herrmann describes the condition against which such women write: "In the immense totality of culture, woman appears to have been placed between parentheses, emerging unexpectedly in connection with other things, when she can't be stopped, traversing texts like a shadow, to be eliminated as quickly as possible so that one may go on, without wasting time, to more important matters" (6). The disobedient reader as writer is no longer a shadow on the text, but rather makes the text a shadow of her own.

PART
ONE

Engaging Mythologies

One

IN THE BEGINNING: REVISITING THE GARDEN

1

Man does, they say, and Woman is.
Doing and being. Do and be.
O.K., I be writing, man.
I be telling.
URSULA LE GUIN,
"THE WRITER ON, AND AT, HER WORK"

In Kate Chopin's stark tale "Elizabeth Stock's One Story," written in 1898, the title character, "an unmarried woman of thirty-eight" (37), has "always felt as if [she] would like to write stories," but whenever she tries to think of a plot, she finds that "some one else had thought about [it] before [her]" (38). Living in the small town of Stonelift, Elizabeth Stock is surrounded by other people's stories; not only is the town so small that "people were bound to look into each other's lives" (39), but Elizabeth is the town postmistress, daily handling the mail that comes in and out of Stonelift by train. When she attempts to use, as an author, these daily dramas, for example, writing about "old Si' Shepard that got lost in the woods and never came back," she is discouraged by her Uncle William, who tells her, "this here ain't no story; everybody knows about old Si' Shepard" (38). Elizabeth had better, Uncle William thinks, "stick to [her] dress making" (38). The only story Elizabeth Stock can tell, then, is her own, and it is the unpublished manuscript of her own story, found by an unnamed and unsympathetic frame narrator, that becomes Chopin's story.

"Elizabeth Stock's One Story" is a paradigmatic story of the woman writer. Written a year before the publication of her controversial novel *The Awakening*, Chopin's story shows her keen awareness of the gendered nature of writing. Elizabeth is told by Uncle William to give up the pen in favor of the needle, as Anne Bradstreet had feared being told more than two centuries before, and when she persists in trying to think of a story that has not been told before and that "everybody" doesn't already know, she recounts "turning and twisting things in my mind just like I often saw old ladies twisting quilt patches around to compose a design" (38). After she wrote her "one story" and was hospitalized in Saint Louis with consumption, the narrator tells us, "she relapsed into a silence that remained unbroken till the end" (37). The statement by the condescending (perhaps male?) narrator that Elizabeth was "much given over to scribbling" (37) even recalls Hawthorne's comment about the "d——d mob of scribbling women" earlier in the nineteenth century, and Chopin's use of the "found manuscript" device recalls Hawthorne's use of it in *The Scarlet Letter*. Indeed, the narrator's dismissive tone may remind us of the dismissive attitude of the scholars of Gilead in the "Historical Notes" section of Margaret Atwood's *The Handmaid's Tale*: just as they call into question the authenticity of Offred's taped "manuscript," so Chopin's narrator declares that he has found among Elizabeth Stock's "bad prose" and "impossible verse" only "the following pages which bore any semblance to a connected or consecutive narration" (37).

But what is Elizabeth Stock's "one story" about? When Elizabeth finally sits down "quiet and peaceful" on an autumn day, what story does she choose to tell? Ostensibly, she wants to tell of "how I lost my position" as postmistress; actually, she tells the story of a proud, independent woman whose sense of responsibility to others brings about both her professional and her physical downfall. She announces herself with dignity: "My name is Elizabeth Stock. I'm thirty-eight years old and unmarried, and not afraid or ashamed to say it" (38). Though she self-effacingly claims to have lost her job "mostly through my own negligence" (38), she actually becomes the tragic heroine of her story, braving an ice storm to take an important postcard to the town's leading citizen. The exposure to the elements causes her to become ill, and someone in Stonelift reports her for reading other people's postcards, although she claims it is "human nature" to "glance at" a postcard and believes that "if a person had anything very particular and private to tell, they'd put it under a sealed envelope" (39).

As a writer, Elizabeth Stock composes her one story in private and then is silent, her life remaining a "sealed envelope," its contents disclosed only to the dismissive narrator. Yet in addition to setting Elizabeth against a literary tradition of which she cannot be a part, Chopin also suggests that her entire relationship with language is problematic. Most obviously, it is an act of reading—the postcard—that puts her job in jeopardy, and when she receives the letter that dismisses her from the position of postmistress, she cannot trust herself to understand what it says and must ask Vince Wallace, her would-be suitor, to interpret it for her. When Elizabeth does read, it is a novel from her local library; she has not been educated to have sophisticated tastes in literature, and when she tries to think of plots for stories, she plays with the formulas of popular fiction: "I tried to think of a railroad story with a wreck, but couldn't. No more could I make a tale out of a murder, or money getting stolen, or even mistaken identity" (38). Education—and hence literature—is the province of men. The person who takes her job at the post office is a "poetical-natured young fellow" (43), and one of her regrets at losing her job is that she cannot continue to pay for the education of her nephew Danny, who was "full of ambition to study" (44).

Elizabeth Stock (her name suggests a storehouse of untold stories) is thus one of the vast number of silenced women, like Virginia Woolf's "Shakespeare's sister." But what about women like Kate Chopin herself, who wrote in the face of the fact that so many of the stories had already been told? How does the woman writer deal with the accumulated weight of canonical texts in which the tradition of her own voice is the merest whisper? In place of Harold Bloom's "anxiety of influence," the situation is more nearly the anxiety of absence. In her foreword to *On Lies, Secrets, and Silence*, Adrienne Rich writes of such an absence of tradition:

> *The entire history of women's struggle for self-*
> *determination has been muffled in silence over and*
> *over. One serious cultural obstacle encountered by*
> *any feminist writer is that each feminist work has*
> *tended to be received as if it emerged from nowhere;*
> *as if each of us had lived, thought, and worked with-*
> *out any historical past or contextual present. This is*
> *one of the ways in which women's work and thinking*
> *has been made to seem sporadic, errant, orphaned of*
> *any tradition of its own.*
> (11)

Elizabeth Stock, in her limited though emblematic way, is aware that many people before her have written stories, have created a tradition of literature, and she is unable to find an original way to add to or affect that tradition. Instead, her brief autobiography provides us with a description of her exclusion.

Such exclusions are themselves, of course, a part of literary history. What is not written, or is written and not published, or is published and ignored becomes a telling part of the formation of culture. Paul Lauter makes a similar point in *Canons and Contexts* when he argues for the importance of the historical context of a work of literature, because "writing by marginalized groups—women or 'minorities'—is for a number of reasons more directly implicated in the immediate problems of historical change" (120). In this context, it is important to set Kate Chopin apart from her character Elizabeth Stock as representing two poles of response for the woman who would be a writer. Elizabeth is overwhelmed and silenced by a literary tradition to which she can find no point of entry; Chopin, in contrast, wrote *The Awakening* as a way of altering the course of that tradition.[1]

2

One foot in the door of the Unknown, the other still holding open its place in the Book of Old Plots.
GAIL GODWIN, *VIOLET CLAY*

My concern in this study is with some of the ways in which women writers have worked against, revised, and reinterpreted some of the literary traditions they have known. My primary focus is on fiction by North American women, although other genres and nationalities are represented as well. The centrality of fiction and autobiography in such a study owes much to the sense women have had that their lives, both in and out of literature, have been plots constructed by people other than themselves. The traditional stories—what Gail Godwin refers to in *Violet Clay* as "the Book of Old Plots" (57)—include not only those in the standard literary canon, but also those whose force is at least as culturally pervasive: fairy tales, myths, the Judeo-Christian Bible. Perhaps more than any other contemporary woman writer, Margaret Atwood uses such narratives in her own poetry and fiction—appropriating, parodying, revising, and recontextualizing. In a 1978 essay, she muses about the "ancestresses" that any female character she might create would have:

> *Old Crones, Delphic Oracles, the Three Fates, Evil*
> *Witches, White Witches, White Goddesses, Bitch*
> *Goddesses, Medusas with snaky heads who turn men*
> *to stone, Mermaids with no souls, Little Mermaids*
> *with no tongues, Snow Queens, Sirens with songs,*
> *Harpies with wings, Sphinxes, with and without se-*
> *crets, women who turn into dragons, dragons who*
> *turn into women, Grendel's mother and why she is*
> *worse than Grendel; also . . . evil stepmothers, comic*
> *mothers-in-law, fairy godmothers, unnatural mothers,*
> *natural mothers, Mad Mothers, Medea who slew her*
> *own children, Lady Macbeth and her spot, Eve the*
> *mother of us all.*
> ("THE CURSE OF EVE," 219)

While most of these traditional stories have been authored by males, women writers have at times sought to engage earlier genres or texts authored by females. Such is the case, for example, with Fanny Fern's 1854 novel *Ruth Hall*, which emerged from but revised the sentimental or "domestic" novel of the mid-nineteenth century. Nor is such revision or resistance always a response to the burden of a constraining tradition. Particularly when the woman writer is allowed awareness of her own tradition, she may alter it not to win freedom from it, but rather to honor its nurturing power. Such, for example, is the argument that Michael Awkward makes in *Inspiriting Influences* regarding the black female novelists who followed Zora Neale Hurston in the twentieth century. What Awkward perceives as "textual affinities" among *Their Eyes Were Watching God*, Toni Morrison's *The Bluest Eye*, Gloria Naylor's *The Women of Brewster Place*, and Alice Walker's *The Color Purple* result, he believes, not from a "common sexual and racial oppression, but, rather, most frequently occur as a function of black women writers' conscious acts of refiguration and revision of the earlier [Afro-American] canonical texts" (4).

Several studies have focused, as does Awkward, on the ways in which certain literary traditions have been constructed. They address not merely the shape those traditions have taken in literary histories and anthologies, but also the factors that have caused them to be perceived—sometimes erroneously—in certain ways rather than in others. Janet Todd, for example, in *The Sign of Angelica: Women, Writing, and Fiction, 1660–1800*, argues that women were actively engaged in the development of the novel in England during the Restoration and the early eighteenth century, but that their contributions to a then-fluid form were omitted from consideration once the form became more defined in the hands of Richardson, Fielding, and others. Thus, standard histories of the novel have begun with these latter figures, obscuring our view of the earlier female practitioners. Cushing Strout, in *Making American Tradition: Visions and Revisions from Ben Franklin to Alice Walker*, writes of thematic "resonances" among American writers during the nineteenth and twentieth centuries and suggests that literary tradition is created when "writers themselves . . . respond in their work to previous writers" (5)—primarily male writers in Strout's study. Gayle Greene's *Changing the Story: Feminist Fiction and the Tradition* concentrates on four twentieth-century British and Canadian women writers (Doris Lessing, Margaret Drabble, Margaret Laurence, and Margaret Atwood), proposing that their "feminist metafictions" demonstrate that the making of literary tradition is "a process wherein fiction performs complex negotiations with the works of the past, negotiations which are both appropriations and subversions" (7). And Elaine Showalter, in *Sister's Choice: Tradition and Change in American Women's Writing*, undertakes a literary history of American women that takes into consideration not only the diversity of women's experience but also the intertextuality of their work.

What these otherwise disparate studies have in common is the understanding that while editors, critics, teachers, and scholars have an important role in determining what successive generations of readers understand to be the literary heritage of a culture, it is the writers themselves who are most central to this enterprise, and that what and how they write is often closely connected to their sense of their relation to literature itself, as heirs to and readers of previous texts. It is such an understanding, informed by psychoanalytic theory, that led Bloom to form his theory of the "anxiety of influence," in which one generation of writers seeks to assert its separation from the previous one. Because Bloom's theory is predicated solely on male writers, scholars who work with women writers, such as Annette Kolodny and Deanna L. Davis, have found it problematic as a universal paradigm.[2] Indeed, when women writers have, unlike Chopin's Elizabeth Stock, been conscious of a prior tradition of women writers that could nurture and potentially include them, their tendency has been not to be competitive, as in Bloom's model, but instead to view themselves as part of a community and a continuum.

Two studies of different groups of women writers make this point ably. In *American Women Regionalists 1850–1910*, Judith Fetterley and Marjorie Pryse argue that the group of writers they term "regionalists" (as opposed to "local colorists") "frequently knew each other and admired each other's work. . . . Stowe clearly influenced Jewett, and later Jewett clearly influenced Cather" (xii). Moreover, Fetterley and Pryse find that the work of these writers embodies the values that also characterize their nurturance of one another's talent. In Stowe's story "Uncle Lot," for example, "the values Stowe explores . . . more closely resemble the values of domesticity, stability and community than the values of separation and 'rugged individualism' associated with life on the frontier" (xiv). Similarly, in *Friendship and Sympathy: Communities of Southern Women Writers*, Rosemary M. Magee describes the "communities" of support and encouragement that successive generations of writers—from Eudora Welty and Katherine Anne Porter to Kaye Gibbons and Lisa Alther—have created for each other from their position on the "periphery" of the southern literary establishment. These later writers continue to "struggle to find their bearings and to articulate the place of their work in modern American letters" (xvi–xvii).

But despite compelling evidence that some women writers have provided for themselves and each other a sense of belonging in what Lorna Sage calls (borrowing from Henry James) "the house of fiction," the scholarship of recent decades has provided ample proof that the more common story has been one of isolation, exclusion, and silencing. Indeed, one wonders how Kate Chopin might have reacted had she read (as perhaps she did) the statement by the editor of an 1890 edition of Elizabeth Barrett Browning's poems: "Let us acknowledge that authorship, as a career, is undesirable for a woman." Having thus acknowledged what he clearly believes to be common wisdom, Browning's editor is then obliged to spend several pages in elaborate explanation of why "Mrs. Browning" may be considered an exception, concluding that her obvious intellectual achievements are "rather masculine" (xii). In this manner he unsexes the poet, only to call her a short while later "an honor to her sex" (xiii)—not, we note, an honor to literature, but instead an anomaly.[3]

Nearly fifty years after Kate Chopin wrote "Elizabeth Stock's One Story," the Canadian-born writer Elizabeth Smart published her extraordinary prose-poem *By Grand Central Station I Sat Down and Wept*. Smart's 1945 text counterpoints Chopin's story in illuminating ways; feeling herself similarly excluded from language and literature, Smart's narrator refuses silence, appropriating the literary tradition and bending it to her own purposes. Whereas Elizabeth Stock's story is a (fictional) autobiographical fragment left in a desk drawer, *By Grand Central Station* is a long public lament based on Smart's long love affair with the English poet George Barker, with whom she had four children while he remained married to another woman. The story is thus an account of simultaneous inclusion and exclusion: the lover—the poet—becomes a metaphor for all literature, for the Word itself, by which the narrator is denied legitimacy. As Lorna Sage puts it in *Women in the House of Fiction*, "Being jilted by Lit. is Smart's theme. Or to put it more elaborately, *By Grand Central Station* is the story of a love-affair with the high style (poetry and tragedy) which came to a sticky end in the low-mimetic mode" (54).

Whereas Elizabeth Stock merely believes that all the stories (except, of course, her own) have been written, Smart's narrator adopts a more adversarial stance: "The texts are meaningless, they are the enemy's deception" (40). Literature—the texts—is gendered as masculine, confronted symbolically as it is embodied in both lover and father. As an excuse to be together, the narrator and her lover pretend a "necessary collaboration at the typewriter," but the meeting paralyzes her:

> He has a book to be typed, but the words I try to
> force out die on the air and dissolve into kisses whose
> chemicals are even more deadly if undelivered. My
> fingers cannot be martial at the touch of an instru-
> ment so much connected with him. The machine sits
> like a temple of love among the papers we never fin-
> ish, and if I awake at night and see it outlined in
> the dark, I am electrified with memories of danger-
> ous propinquity.
> (29)

Emotion is thus pitted against intellect—feminine against masculine—as it is also in a later scene with her father:

> As I sat down in the swivel chair in my father's of-
> fice, with his desk massively symbolic between us, I

> *realized that I could never defend myself. What was*
> *my defence but one small word which I dared not ut-*
> *ter, because jazz singers and hypocritical preachers*
> *and Dorothy Dix had so maligned it. . . . [My fa-*
> *ther] could spread his mind out before you like the*
> *evidence of a case. But if he saw emotion approaching*
> *he smiled painfully, rocking in his swivel chair, hop-*
> *ing it would pass.*
> (69)

The word she dares not use is, of course, "love," but in a more general sense she is excluded from language itself, represented as it is in the solid objects of typewriter and desk interposed between her and the masculine world of narratives.

Words represent authority. Apprehended while traveling illicitly with her lover, Smart's narrator writes, "I sat in a little room with barred windows while they typed" (53). "It is all written down. There are fourteen sheets and six copies of each. They fly over the continent like birds of ill omen, and will lie in files to blackball me from ease" (56). Not only in her present, but also in the past the narrator sees language and literature as the province of men. Traveling home to Canada, she thinks of earlier settlers: "And over the fading wooden houses I sense the reminiscences of the pioneers' passion, and the determination of early statesmen who were mild but individual, and able to allude to Shakespeare while discussing politics under the elms" (65). In religion as in history, women seem to her to be excluded from language: "Who were the female saints, I say, and how did they manage to fill their beds with God? How can any woman from this empty world construct communication with heaven?" (109).

Yet paradoxically, Smart's narrator uses language that is richly allusive to the English literary tradition; indeed, she plunders the Bible, Shakespeare, and the metaphysical poets, echoing and altering their language to mingle it with the mundane language of everyday life, claiming that which has sought to exclude her. Rather than, as Sage proposes, descending from the "high style" to the "low-mimetic" as the love affair comes to an end, she mixes the two levels of discourse all along, as if to suggest that the language of the literary tradition is not by itself adequate to represent her experience. At times she counterposes the high style of poetry to mundane rhetoric, as when the Arizona police question her about cohabiting with her lover:

> *What relation is this man to you? (My beloved is*
> *mine and I am his: he feedeth among the lilies). . . .*
> *Did you sleep in the same room? . . . In the same*
> *bed? (Behold thou art fair, my beloved, yea pleasant,*
> *also our bed is green). . . . Were you intending to*
> *commit fornication in Arizona? (He shall lie all*
> *night betwixt my breasts).*
> (53 – 54)

The language of "Song of Solomon" is clearly insufficient to answer the legalistic queries of secular authority; the two exist on different planes, and the romance of the past is made to seem insubstantial alongside the reality of adultery, despite the depth of her love.

Smart's narrator's rebellion goes beyond mere language. At several points she inserts herself into the literature of the past to usurp the role of male hero. She compares herself to Macbeth (20) and outdoes Christ: "I was raised for this event from more than a three-day burial, and would have built memorials to last longer than 2000 years" (73). Most important, she is God-like, her own creator. Like Elizabeth Stock, but on a far grander scale, she has established herself by telling her own story. At the end, her poet-lover's notebook page is "as white as my face after a night of weeping. It is a sterile as my devastated mind" (127), while *her* pages are filled, as her body is with her unborn child. If Smart's narrator equates the poet-lover with literature itself, both lover and literature prove fickle and inadequate, opening the way for her own self-creation.

The two most frequently cited sets of statements about the difficulties of women writers working against the inherited literary tradition bracket the publication of Smart's *By Grand Central Station* and were themselves published forty-two years apart. These are, of course, Virginia Woolf's *A Room of One's Own* (1929) and Adrienne Rich's "When We Dead Awaken: Writing as Re-Vision" (1971; in *On Lies, Secrets, and Silence*). Woolf spends much of her long, eloquent essay searching the past for clues to women's exclusion from the tradition, and one of her conclusions is that "there was no common sentence ready for her use." The prose of Johnson and Gibbon, of Thackeray and Dickens and Balzac "was a sentence that was unsuited for a woman to use. . . . All the other forms of literature were hardened and set by the time she became a writer" (79–80). Thus, Woolf goes on, it was to the newer form of the novel that women turned in the eighteenth century.

Whereas Woolf's project is primarily historical and investigative,

Rich's is exhortatory. "Re-vision," she says, "the act of looking back, of seeing with fresh eyes, of entering an old text from a new critical direction—is for women more than a chapter in cultural history: it is an act of survival" (35). Rich here writes of the act of reading, the need for women to verse themselves fully in "the assumptions in which we are drenched" (35), but she could equally be addressing the act of writing, for it is only by understanding how previous texts have arisen from and sustained certain belief systems that subsequent writers can resist and revise them. And the project, as Rich articulates it and as Elizabeth Smart's method in *By Grand Central Station* illustrates, is radical. For Rich, "nothing can be too sacred for the imagination to turn into its opposite or to call experimentally by another name. For writing is re-naming" (43).

Resisting or altering traditional literary forms is not without its perils, especially for the woman writer. Two examples from nineteenth-century American literature represent a pattern that held largely true from the time women entered "the house of fiction" until quite recently. Fanny Fern's 1854 novel *Ruth Hall* and Kate Chopin's 1899 novel *The Awakening* met similar fates: the novels—and most particularly their authors—were widely denounced for violating norms of "ladylike" fiction. Fern's satiric portraits of characters based on her father and brother, her exposure of religious hypocrisy, and her heroine's devotion to career rather than marriage were deemed improper departures from the morally righteous formulations of the domestic novel. Chopin's depiction of Edna Pontellier, a woman who rejects the conventional duties of an upper-middle-class wife, moves out of her husband's house, and indulges in an extramarital affair, drew criticism of a morally indignant kind; even Edna's death at the end of the novel did not save her creator from the scorn of the literary establishment.

In earlier centuries, merely to write at all—regardless of subject matter—was sufficient to draw such scorn to a woman. Writing of the late seventeenth century, Janet Todd comments that "the writing lady could be equated with the Amazon, the whore or the witch [the three central images used by men to characterize the autonomous woman], indulging in improper verbal freedom as well as or in place of a sexual one" (33). Todd is not alone in perceiving that a woman's artistic forthrightness has traditionally been equated with sexual indiscretion. In 1819, Stendhal was even more blunt: "The publication of a book is fraught with difficulties for anyone but a harlot; the vulgar, being able to despise her as they please for her profession, will praise her to the skies for her talent and will even go into raptures about it." Having already, that is, declared herself beyond respectability, the "harlot" may take no new risks by becoming known as a writer. Although Stendhal was ostensibly sympathetic to the plight of women, he nonetheless had the effect of perpetuating the very circumstances he claimed to deplore. French novelist Claudine Herrmann, quoting this passage in her book *The Tongue-Snatchers (Les Voleuses de langue)*, comments on the "normative tone" of Stendhal's remarks and continues: "No one explains better than an enlightened man just how necessary it is to find ways of despising a woman and just how criticism may be made to reflect on her person rather than on her works" (27). Stendhal becomes in Herrmann's view similar to Woolf's "Professor von X," who, in *A Room of One's Own*, is the composite of all the "men who have no apparent qualification [to write about women] save that they are not women" (27).

The recurring message in titles such as Herrmann's *The Tongue-Snatchers* and Alicia Ostriker's *Stealing the Language* is that women as writers commit a subversive—even an illicit—act. To possess language is to possess the power to name—"no small power," as Paul Lauter comments (118)—and thus to define. In Rich's words, "the very act of naming has been till now a male prerogative" (*On Lies, Secrets, and Silence*, 35). In envisioning a culture in which language is forbidden to those not supposed to have power, Atwood in *The Handmaid's Tale* draws on centuries of cultural recognition of the power of language, and her frequent evocation of biblical language in that novel recalls for us the most significant origin in Western culture of the power of naming: Adam's naming of the creation in Genesis—including the double naming of his female companion, first as "woman" and then as "Eve." Thus the act of naming is inextricably tied to the act of creation itself.

3

And the rib, which the Lord God had taken from man, made he a woman, and brought her unto the man.
GENESIS 2: 22

Because the Genesis story as popularly understood, with its establishment of the woman as both secondary and sinfully disruptive, has acquired such authoritative force in Western culture, it is not surprising that a number of writers have turned their revisionary impulses upon it.[4]

Among the many rewritings of the Genesis story of creation, the best-known in American literature is Mark Twain's "The Diary of Adam and Eve," first published in 1905. Twain's version of the story assumes significance in a discussion of women's re-visions of the biblical story in part because of the canonical weight of his work, but more importantly because Twain's story so clearly demonstrates how the refashioning of a traditional text emerges from and represents its own cultural context.

It seems at first glance remarkably progressive for Twain to have given the naming power to Eve rather than to Adam, but instead of signifying Eve's authority, her assigning of names serves to reinforce the common nineteenth-century stereotype of the meddlesome, talkative female. "I get no chance to name anything myself," Adam complains to his diary. "The new creature names everything that comes along, before I can get in a protest" (272). Particularly annoying to Adam is Eve's penchant for renaming what he has already named. Having settled on the "musical and pretty" name "Garden of Eden" for their surroundings, Adam finds it "high-handed" of Eve to have renamed the area "Niagara Falls Park." Unwittingly perhaps, Twain has made his Eve a revisionist; what contemporary readers would have understood is that Adam's name for the Garden is "right," whereas Eve's is "wrong." Further, when it is Eve's turn to speak, we learn that her motivation for being quick to name the creation reinforces her stereotypical subordination:

> When the dodo came along he thought it was a wild-cat—I saw it in his eye. But I saved him. And I was careful not to do it in a way that could hurt his pride. I just spoke up in a quite natural way of pleased surprise, and not as if I was dreaming of conveying information, and said, "Well, I do declare, if there isn't the dodo!"
> (284)

Eve's feminine project is thus to support Adam's masculine ego; hers may be the superior knowledge, but she must use it to reinforce his sense of superiority.

Twain's Adam and Eve are a pair familiar in nineteenth-century American literature: the efficient, garrulous, interfering wife and the lazy, dreaming husband who seeks to avoid her insistent domesticity. This couple is embodied in Washington Irving's "Rip Van Winkle," Harriet Beecher Stowe's Sam Lawson and his wife, and Mr. and Mrs. Skiddy in Fern's *Ruth Hall*; it is a literary, gendered representation of the tension between restless individualism and the moral and behavioral strictures of settled middle-class culture. In Twain's own work, this tension is represented most fully in the contrast between Huck Finn and women such as the Widow Douglas and Aunt Sally. Twain's Eve annoys Adam with her "sivilizing" tendencies. She puts up "Keep off the grass" signs and implores Adam to stop going over Niagara Falls in a barrel, while Adam echoes Huck in his feeling that he is "too much hampered" by her, as he attempts repeatedly to escape an increasingly settled Garden.

After the Fall, Twain's re-creation of the Genesis account becomes a love story that reinforces traditional gender characteristics and roles. Drawn closer together by expulsion from the Garden and the subsequent birth of children, Adam and Eve continue to misunderstand and disagree with each other—Adam refers to "the lack of harmony that prevails in our views of things"—but their relationship derives from the sentimental romance. Eve writes that "if he should beat me and abuse me, I should go on loving him," and Adam has the last line of the story at Eve's grave: "Wheresoever she was, *there* was Eden" (293–294). In humanizing the Genesis story by means of humor and the diary format, Twain does so in terms that reinforce Victorian concepts of gender differences.

Several decades before Twain wrote "The Diary of Adam and Eve," Gail Hamilton (pseudonym of Mary Abigail Dodge) used elements of the Eden story in her humorous essay "My Garden." Originally published in the *Atlantic* and included in her collection *Country Living and Country Thinking* (1862), "My Garden" is not as closely modeled on the Genesis story as is Twain's piece, but Adam and Eve are clearly in the background. Hamilton's essay is a mock lament about the female narrator's failure as a gardener, but it is clear that she writes more generally of the woman as creator, as the narrator directly claims the right to speak in a female voice. She begins "My Garden" by poking fun at readers' different expectations of male and female writing:

> *When any one tells a story, we wish to know at the outset whether the story-teller is a man or a woman. The two sexes awaken two entirely distinct sets of feelings, and you would no more use the one for the other than you would put on your tiny teacups at breakfast, or lay the carving-knife by the butter-plate. Consequently it is very exasperating to sit, open-eyed and expectant, watching the removal of the successive*

swathings which hide from you the dusky glories of
an old-time princess, and, when the unrolling is over,
to find it is nothing after all, but a great lubberly boy.
Equally trying is it to feel your interest clustering
round a narrator's manhood, all your individuality
merging in his, till, of a sudden, by the merest
chance, you catch the swell of crinoline, and there you
are. Away with such clumsiness! Let us have every-
body christened before we begin.
(31)

Having challenged authors to reveal their sexes, Hamilton accepts her own challenge: "I do, therefore, with Spartan firmness, depose and say that I am a woman" (31).

Hamilton next conflates gardening and writing, both of which she perceives as male prerogatives:

I am aware that I place myself at signal disadvantage
by the avowal. I fly in the face of hereditary preju-
dice. I am thrust at once beyond the pale of masculine
sympathy. Men will neither credit my success nor la-
ment my failure, because they will consider me poach-
ing on their manor. If I chronicle a big beet, they will
bring forward one twice as large. If I mourn a de-
ceased squash, they will mutter, "Woman's farming!"
(31)

The "Eden" of the unnamed Eve-narrator is three acres of land in the country where she plans to grow flowers, fruit, and vegetables. Her initial vision of this Eden is a utopian one in which "feathery asparagus and the crispness of tender lettuce waved dewy greetings" (33). But this Eve, like the one in Genesis, is not the first person to arrive in the Garden—the Adam figure is already there: "Halicarnassus was there before me" (33). To be second, Hamilton makes clear, is to be secondary, and to acquire an insurmountable handicap:

It has been the one misfortune of my life that Halicar-
nassus got the start of me at the outset. With a fair
field and no favor I should have been quite adequate
to him. As it was, he was born and began, and there

> *was no resource left to me but to be born and follow,*
> *which I did as fast as possible; but that one false move*
> *could never be redeemed.*
> (33 – 34)

As the one "born" second, like Eve in Genesis, Hamilton's narrator must "follow" the first-born male. The land is "his creation," she remarks later (39).

Like Twain, Hamilton gives her Eve figure the power of naming, but for a different reason. Whereas naming the creation is part of Twain's stereotypical portrait of the talkative, meddlesome woman, Hamilton has her narrator use the botanical names of the seeds she intends to plant in order to show that such erudition is considered inappropriate for a woman. When the narrator proudly shows Halicarnassus the seeds of *Lychnidea acuminata* and launches into a lyrical description of its heroic Greek origins, he undercuts her eloquence by pronouncing that "it grows wild almost. It's nothing but phlox" (35). When the narrator tries again with *Delphinium exaltatum*, Halicarnassus's response is described as "profane": "What are you raving about a precious bundle of weeds for?" (36). And indeed the narrator's Latinate phrases and rhetorical flourishes do her no good, for most of what she plants fails to thrive. She cannot even serve as the agency of the Fall, because the apples are attacked by cankerworms.

To underscore the fact that her Eve-like narrator's exclusion from generativity in the Garden is metaphoric of her exclusion from the creation of literature, Hamilton includes in "My Garden" a passage in which her narrator ruminates about the fact that she does not have the proper ancestry to be an author. Her great-grandfather was a barber, and she cannot think of an author with that particular professional ancestry. "Shakespeare's father was a wool-driver, . . . Defoe's a butcher, Milton's a scrivener, Richardson's a joiner, Burns's a farmer" (41–42). With a barber as an ancestor, she feels she lacks the credentials to join the ranks of these male authors, and so laments, "My whole life long have I been in search of a pedigree" (41).

Throughout "My Garden" Hamilton uses a biblical rhetoric that establishes the Eden story as a primary inspiration for her essay. Contemplating the bounty she believes her gardening will provide, for example, the narrator muses that "our table shall be garnished with the products of our own soil, and our own works shall praise us" (38). Her cucumbers fail because of what she feels is their "innate depravity" (45), and when a series of such failures effectively drives her from the garden, she is consoled by "the victory which I gained over my own depraved nature" (53). She has learned to see her neighbor's flourishing garden with "sincere joy" rather than with jealousy (53), although, as she goes "quietly down into the valley of humiliation and oblivion," she wishes that people would refrain from asking her about her garden lest it put too great a strain on her "Christian character" (54). Yet the very hyperbole and the mocking tone of Hamilton's essay make the narrator's "humiliation and oblivion" a very different matter from Elizabeth Stock's silence. While Hamilton makes pointed comments about the relationship between women and the literary tradition, the Genesis story serves as a convenient and familiar trope rather than an oppressive sentence.

Two more recent feminist revisions of the Eden story, however, testify to the pervasive power of the traditional story and the need to challenge the power relationships that it inscribes. In "Beyond the Garden," Lynne Sharon Schwartz presents the story from the unnamed Adam's perspective. Schwartz's Adam, like Twain's, is initially bewildered by Eve, who has the power of language and who shares that power with his father: "Like his father, she had words at her command, piercingly direct words" (36). Eve thus becomes identified with the God-like authority of Adam's father, of whom he is terrified. Adam's insecurities increase when he watches Eve give birth to their first child: "Why had his father given this great power to her? Could she possibly be the preferred one? Was it because he was made of dust and she of firmer stuff?" (37). Like Hamilton, Schwartz associates language with generative power and posits that Eve's possession of both is threatening to Adam. But whereas in the 1860s Hamilton imagined Eve's creativity undermined and thwarted, Schwartz's 1991 version instead records Adam's smugness when he discovers that he had been an indispensable part of the creation of children—"She could never have done it without him" (37).

With his fragile ego bolstered by this knowledge, Schwartz's Adam initiates the "separate spheres" ideology that was the middle-class ideal in Hamilton's day. Adam devotes his energies to inventing machines to probe and subdue the earth, while "in his new arrogance, he was willing to cede to [Eve] the domestic sphere, so lacking in grandeur" (37). The increasingly paternalistic Adam must remain dominant even in the domestic realm, however: "even there, it was his part to invent the machinery and hers to operate it, under his guidance. . . . The solution had been there all along—to treat her as his father had treated him" (37–38).

Ironically, in "Beyond the Garden" it is Adam's ego and his desire to live up to the image of his all-powerful father that provides a way out of paternalism and the traditional separation of roles. Because he invents but does not use the domestic "machinery," he finds himself entirely and uncomfortably dependent on Eve, "waiting for her to prepare his food and stitch his clothes, keep his worldly affairs in order and educate the children in his own image" (38). Schwartz's Adam cannot even empty an ice cube tray. To overcome his feeling of powerlessness, Adam learns to do what Eve does and begins to assume "domestic" responsibilities. The result is to effect a kind of reconciliation between Eve and Adam: "She still could not countenance what he sanctioned in his sons, and she would never care much for his father's threats and bravado, but since he was the only helpmeet there was, she accepted him, even welcomed him, and grew spirited and beautiful once again" (38). In this, the last sentence of "Beyond the Garden," Schwartz performs her most radical revision by giving over the point of view to Eve, who in effect has the last word.

Ursula Le Guin's story "She Unnames Them," first published in *The New Yorker* in 1985, takes a far more subversive approach to the issues of language and naming. In this brief revision of the Adam and Eve story, which Alicia Ostriker calls a "counter-parable" (*Feminist Revision*, 81), Eve assumes the power to *remove* the names that have labeled the parts of the creation and in the process negates the human (and God-like) authority to confer names, erasing the boundaries that names create. Like Twain and Schwartz, Le Guin uses humor as a means of presenting the biblical drama in human terms and undermining its mythic power. The first part of the story describes the reactions of the various living creatures to having their names removed; the yaks acquiesce only after long deliberation, whereas swine, asses, and chickens "all agreed enthusiastically to give their names back to the people to whom—as they put it—they belonged" (192–193). When Eve assumes her narrative "I" in the second half of the story, the reader first learns that she has been the agent of this process and understands part of her motivation: "They seemed far closer than when their names had stood between myself and them like a clear barrier" (193). The absence of names has a leveling effect: "My fear of them and their fear of me became one same fear. And the attraction that many of us felt . . . was now all one with the fear, and the hunter could not be told from the hunted, nor the eater from the food" (193–194).

This second part of the story takes on elements of a situation comedy as Eve goes home to Adam in order to return her own name to him and his father; "I could not now," she says, "in all conscience, make an exception for myself" (194). Eve hopes for a confrontation that will produce real communication with Adam—"talk was getting us no-where"—but he is preoccupied and scarcely notes her presence, failing to notice that she has said good-bye and asking her when dinner will be ready. Finally, having renounced her name (whether "woman" or "Eve" is not made clear), the narrator leaves to make a fresh start, learning a new language: "My words now must be as slow, as new, as single, as tentative as the steps I took going down the pathway from the house" (194). To reject the language of the patriarchy is to reject its power, and by the end of the story the narrator's language has begun to challenge our expectations of meaning as she walks "between the dark-branched, tall dancers motionless against the winter shining" (194).

In *Feminist Revision and the Bible*, Alicia Ostriker discusses the enor-mous outpouring of biblical revision in post–World War II women's po-etry, noting both the "explicit anger" that motivates and characterizes much of it and the tendency of other poets to employ "comedy, shame-less sexuality, an insistence on sensual immediacy and the details belong-ing to the flesh as holy, an insistence that the flesh is not incompatible with the intellect." Exemplifying the anger is Stevie Smith's commentary on the story of Eve:

> *What responsibility*
> *It has in history*
> *For cruelty.*

Diana George's poem "The Fall" provides an example of the more co-medic revisionary approach. Here, the fruit to which Eve succumbs "was no apple, people," but instead a banana, "sidekick and brother/of the snake" (*Feminist Revision and the Bible*, 81). If, Ostriker concludes, "the Bible is a flaming sword forbidding our entrance to the garden, it is also a burning bush urging us toward freedom. It is what we wrestle with all night and from which we may, if we demand it, wrest a blessing" (*Femi-nist Revision and the Bible*, 79–86).

In her article "(M)other Eve: Some Revisions of the Fall in Fiction by Contemporary Women Writers," Madelon Sprengnether similarly com-ments on the impulse that women writers have to reconsider the Eden story:

> *If it is true that stories are created out of other stories*
> *in the infinite regress of culture, then it is no surprise*
> *that women writers should make use of one of the*

> *most powerful among them to deal with their own*
> *versions of the origins of consciousness. Because the*
> *Fall purports to explain basic facts of the human con-*
> *dition, it offers a convenient point of departure for fic-*
> *tion that seeks to do the same.*
> (320)

Sprengnether argues that women's fictions that resist the "biblical master plot" (299) posit the Fall as the daughter's loss of the mother, so that absence becomes a key ingredient of the daughter's formation of a self-concept. The revised Edenic plot that Sprengnether identifies in Rumer Godden's *The Greengage Summer* (1958), Joan Chase's *During the Reign of the Queen of Persia* (1984), Jamaica Kincaid's *Annie John* (1983), and Marilynne Robinson's *Housekeeping* (1980) also works against the Freudian construction of the woman as split by the son into "asexual mother (Mary)," "erotic object (Eve)," and "the threat of death, . . . frequently marginalized and scapegoated in the figure of woman as witch" (305). Rather than fragmented by the needs of others, woman becomes in these revisionary fictions a being activated by desire for the absent "other," such desire being the locus of creativity.

Sprengnether's reading of *Housekeeping* sets it against the "oedipal master plot that sustains" the biblical one (299), but Robinson's novel is also a cultural document that depends for much of its force on American mythologies concerning home, domesticity, and individualism.[5] The Freudian theory of ego development may "sustain" the biblical narrative by making woman (Eve) inferior and sinful, but quite apart from psychoanalytic theory, the Genesis story has particular resonance for a nation envisioned from the beginning as the "new Eden." Marilynne Robinson has acknowledged repeatedly that the Bible served as one inspiration for her novel. In an interview for the American Audio Prose Library (reprinted in *Belles Lettres*), when asked what text she was "meditating on" when she wrote *Housekeeping*, Robinson responds, "The Bible, unquestionably" (37). She not only grew up in a traditionally religious environment, in which "there was a numinous sense around biblical language" (37), she also studied the Bible in religious studies courses at Brown University. In the same interview, Robinson links the Eden story to her novel: "An idea of Eden that may lurk behind the book is that at some point there will be wholeness and composure and completeness in a way that is not compatible with the existence of time or experience in time" (38).[6] In an interview with Sanford Pinsker, Robinson addresses the concept of an individual revising tradition for her own needs. Of her character Ruth, Robinson says:

> *Ruth has certain urgent problems that have to do*
> *precisely with her own experience. Anything like a*
> *received history or received tradition would be held*
> *very much in doubt. Her test of all reality, the mean-*
> *ing of all utterance is, after all, polarized around cer-*
> *tain obsessive experiences. She does use her own tra-*
> *dition—the Bible, for example—but she pries it loose*
> *from its traditional significance and rearranges it, re-*
> *interprets, for her own use.*
> (PINSKER, 126)

Housekeeping is, as Sprengnether notes, a novel that deconstructs its own title (318). Or rather, it deconstructs our conventional understanding of what housekeeping is or should be—an understanding that can itself be traced to the story of Eden: harmonious, timeless coexistence amidst abundance. The novel develops a pattern of leaving rather than staying, transience instead of permanence. The forced expulsion of Adam and Eve from the Garden in Genesis is transformed in Robinson's novel into the self-willed act of going away. The narrator, Ruth, describes her grandfather as having "escaped this world" (3) even though he died in a train wreck. He was fond of travel literature, "journals of expeditions to the mountains of Africa, to the Alps, the Andes, the Himalayas, the Rockies" (4), and, fittingly, he takes a job with the railroad, which, ironically, requires that he settle in the town of Fingerbone, Idaho, until his train plunges off the bridge crossing the lake that neighbors Fingerbone.

The grandfather is connected to Edenic images as Robinson's narrator describes the paintings he created as a young man. In one of them, "Every tree bore bright fruit, and showy birds nested in the boughs, and every fruit and bird was plumb with the warp in the earth. Oversized beasts, spotted and striped, could be seen running unimpeded up the right side and unhastened down the left" (4). But this surreal ideality, created out of "ignorance or fancy" (4), is, like the grandfather's questing spirit, terminated by the train accident, and the grandfather's death also removes the only male character from the novel. In her interview with

Pinsker, Robinson notes that the railroad accident was the first scene of the novel that she wrote, and "poof! there went grandfather" (121), leaving only female characters.

Grandfather's widow, left to raise three teenaged daughters, is the most nearly conventional housekeeper in the novel. "Her bread was tender and her jelly was tart, and on rainy days she made cookies and applesauce" (11–12). Yet "she conceived of life as a road down which one traveled" (9), and in the mornings her daughters "pressed her and touched her as if she had just returned after an absence" (12). Most important, the four women occupy a space not governed by the linear, goal-oriented questing of the American dream, but guided by natural rhythms: "With [Grandfather] gone they were cut free from the troublesome possibility of success, recognition, advancement. They had no reason to look forward, nothing to regret. Their lives spun off the tilting world like thread off a spindle, breakfast time, suppertime, lilac time, apple time" (13). Though idyllic, their life during these years is somehow insubstantial, as Robinson suggests in the image of the thread, and, once grown, all three daughters leave—Molly to become a missionary in China, and Helen and Sylvie to marry men who remain shadowy figures in the novel (of Sylvie's husband there is not even a snapshot).

The most dramatic departure in *Housekeeping*—in part because of the matter-of-fact way in which it is narrated—is Helen's suicide by driving a borrowed Ford from a cliff into Fingerbone Lake seven and a half years after leaving Fingerbone. Helen has returned with her daughters, Ruth and Lucille, and, after installing the girls on her absent mother's porch, she recapitulates her father's accidental death by drowning. Because the act can only seem without motive to Ruth, who tells us the story, it remains unmotivated and gratuitous except within the pattern of leave-taking that the novel has established and that it will continue to develop.

The girls' grandmother, having watched her husband and her daughters become absences, takes care of the two girls, but has lost faith in the power of a household to "hold" people. "She whited shoes and braided hair and fried chicken and turned back bedclothes, and then suddenly feared and remembered that the children had somehow disappeared, every one" (24–25). The grandmother dreams that "she had seen a baby fall from an airplane and had tried to catch it in her apron, and once that she had tried to fish a baby out of a well with a tea strainer" (25). If the house in Fingerbone is a version of the Garden—significantly, there is an apple orchard on the property—the rituals and utensils of housekeeping are insufficient to keep or hold its inhabitants.

This family history, driven by the tension between leaving and staying, keeping and repudiating, is prelude to the appearance of Sylvie, Ruth and Lucille's aunt, who comes to care for them after their grandmother's death, when their two unmarried great-aunts prove unequal to the task. In one of many ironic juxtapositions in the novel, the great-aunts, Lily and Nona, who value order and predictability above all else, turn the care of the two girls over to the transient Sylvie—"'An itinerant.' 'A migrant worker.' 'A drifter'" (31). And from this point on Sylvie redefines housekeeping as Robinson revises what Maureen Ryan, in "Marilynne Robinson's *Housekeeping*: The Subversive Narrative and the New American Eve," terms "a central myth of canonical American literature" (81). This myth embodies the premise that true (male) selfhood requires the repudiation of "civilization," which becomes the enemy and is figured as female in such characters as Dame Van Winkle, Huck Finn's Aunt Sally, and Tom Wingfield's mother in *The Glass Menagerie* (81). Ryan argues that Sylvie and Ruth, by leaving home at the end of *Housekeeping*, reenact the journey of the classic male hero, with the significant variation that instead of seeking isolated individualism they wish to preserve their relationship with each other—to remain a "family."

Robinson invites such a reading with her many allusions to classic nineteenth-century texts. Sylvie's preference—and increasingly Ruth's—for the natural over the artificial recalls Thoreau's *Walden* (their house, too, is beside a lake) and Huck Finn's preference for life on the raft over life on the "civilized" shore. Sylvie and Ruth's trip as mentor and pupil across the railroad bridge recalls Jim and Huck's travels down the Mississippi. Joan Kirkby has pointed to *Housekeeping*'s "resonances" with the scenes of housekeeping in *Walden* and in the poetry of Emily Dickinson. Robinson has acknowledged Dickinson and Melville as two of her important literary influences (*Belles Lettres*, 37) and has joked that "if *I* would write a book with only female characters that men would read, then I could have *Moby-Dick!*" (Pinsker, 122).[7]

Yet as much as Robinson's novel is clearly marked by her fondness for classic nineteenth-century texts, *Housekeeping* is most revolutionary in its more subtle reworking of the Genesis story. The "New American Eve" of Maureen Ryan's title is the female counterpart of R. W. B. Lewis's "American Adam," but in a far more radical way Robinson challenges the authority of the Creation story by recasting its central figures as women and giving Ruth the power to be its author—its creator. Late in the novel, Ruth muses about the generations of nameless women who did not tell their own stories:

> *If we imagine that Noah's wife, when she was old,*
> *found somewhere a remnant of the Deluge, she might*
> *have walked into it till her widow's dress floated*
> *about her head and the water loosened her plaited*
> *hair. And she would have left it to her sons to tell*
> *the tedious tale of generations. She was a nameless*
> *woman, and so at home among all those who were*
> *never found and never missed, who were uncommem-*
> *orated, whose deaths were not remarked, nor their*
> *begettings.*
> (172)

In contrast to Noah's wife, Ruth tells the story of generations—specifically the succeeding generations of women in her family, to whom
men are, at most, incidental parts of the drama. Ruth's grandmother
thinks of her husband that "it had never seemed to her that they were
married . . . she had never really wished to feel married to anyone" (17).
The years between Ruth's grandfather's death and the eldest daughter's
departure for a mission in China were "years of almost perfect serenity"
(13) as the four women lived by themselves in the Garden. Of her own
father, Ruth remarks, "I had no memory of this man at all" (14), and
Sylvie's husband is equally a nonentity. Although Sylvie had come back
to Fingerbone "to stand where Helen had stood in my grandmother's
garden and marry someone named Fisher" (15), by the time she returns
to Fingerbone to live with her nieces it is known that "she had simply
chosen not to act married," and the great-aunts "saw in Sylvie a maiden
lady" (43), which suggests a recaptured virginity.

   In addition to this matrilineal succession of generations—or rather as
part of it—Sylvie gives birth to Ruth, an event that occurs on two levels.
Most overtly, Sylvie creates Ruth in her own image, fostering in her
Sylvie's own penchant for unrooted transience even as Lucille increasingly yearns for a more "normal" life and ultimately goes to live, appropriately, with her home economics teacher. As the differences between the two sisters become more pointed, Ruth begins to think of
the world of goals and ambitions and rules as the "other world," while
she, like Sylvie, remains "unimproved and without the prospect of
improvement":

> *It seemed to me then that Lucille would busy herself*
> *forever, nudging, pushing, coaxing, as if she could*

supply the will I lacked, to pull myself into some
seemly shape and slip across the wide frontiers into
that other world, where it seemed to me then I could
never wish to go. For it seemed to me that nothing I
had lost, or might lose, could be found there, or, to
put it another, way, it seemed that something I had
lost might be found in Sylvie's house.
(123 – 124)

What is to be found in Sylvie's house, in addition to the absent mother, is the possibility of perpetual redemption and rebirth, which is rendered metaphorically by two dead apple trees in the orchard. "Every spring," Ruth tells us, "the waters are parted, death is undone, and every Lazarus rises, except these two" (124). But even in this post-Edenic garden, there is hope of regeneration, for "if ever a leaf does appear, it should be no great wonder. It would be a small change, as it would be, say, for the moon to begin turning on its axis" (124). It is this world of spontaneous regeneration that does not require the agency of a deity that Ruth increasingly wants to inhabit with Sylvie.

Images of a more literal birth recur throughout the novel as well. When Sylvie first comes to the house in Fingerbone, Ruth recalls that "as she sat there in a wooden chair in the white kitchen, sustaining all our stares with the placid modesty of a virgin who has conceived, her happiness was palpable" (49). That this pregnancy will result in the virgin birth of Ruth becomes clear later in the novel, when Sylvie takes Ruth on her initiation journey into solitude at the ruined house across the lake. Following Sylvie down to the boat, Ruth automatically imitates Sylvie's posture and gait, "as if I were her shadow," and thinks to herself, "we are the same. She could as well be my mother. I crouched and slept in her very shape like an unborn child" (145). As Sylvie pulls the boat into the water, the birth is enacted: "I crawled under her body and out between her legs" (146). Later, ashore near the ruined house, Ruth imagines a regeneration such as that which could visit the dead apple trees in her grandmother's orchard: "What flowering would there be in such a garden?" (152). It is this infinite possibility of rebirth that directly counters the finality of the Fall and the expulsion from the Garden, and which thus challenges the authority of the biblical story. The ultimate redemption is figured in maternal, not paternal, form: "there will be a garden where all of us as one child will sleep in our mother Eve, hooped in her ribs and staved by her spine" (192).

In narrative strategy and style, Robinson addresses the arbitrariness and fictive qualities of all stories. Ruth narrates *Housekeeping* as though from beyond the grave, and she sometimes assumes the stance of the omniscient narrator in describing scenes she could not have witnessed. The ending of the novel is deliberately ambiguous about the fate of Ruth and Sylvie after they have set fire to the house in Fingerbone and started to walk across the railroad bridge. "Since we are dead," Ruth says at one point (217), but it seems equally likely that they are dead only metaphorically—dead to the "other world" that Lucille presumably still inhabits. The fact that the "other world" believes they drowned in the lake ("LAKE CLAIMS TWO," proclaims the headline of a newspaper article that Sylvie keeps pinned inside her lapel [213]) gives them a kind of freedom that Robinson uses as narrative freedom for Ruth. "We were never found, never found, and the search was at last abandoned," says Ruth (213), referring to the search of the lake for their bodies; but the statement points as well to the elusive nature of truth and warns against uncritical acceptance of any story—including that which Ruth tells in *Housekeeping*. Ruth has earlier suggested that it is a human tendency to make up stories about oneself to tell to strangers. She notes that in bus stations people "will tell you long lies about numerous children who are all gone now, and mothers who were beautiful and cruel." Even if they are telling the truth, she says, "they have the quick eyes and active hands and the passion for meticulous elaboration of people who know they are lying" (157)

Robinson employs several rhetorical devices to simultaneously underscore Ruth's power as storyteller and call attention to the fictive, contingent potential of all narrative. *Housekeeping* seems to be a primarily chronological narrative with Ruth as first-person narrator performing the autobiographical act of telling her story after the polite introduction "My name is Ruth" (3). Yet at several points it is clear that she is relying not on memory but on imagination—creating scenes she could not have witnessed and imagining events that have not happened. Such passages are signaled by the word "say," which has the meaning of "imagine," but which is at the same time a command to speak, as though she conjures another voice to counterpoint her own. Early in the novel Ruth in this way imagines her grandmother hanging out clothes in the early spring, before Fingerbone has recovered from the winter: "Say there were two or three inches of hard old snow on the ground" (16). Beginning with images of deadness, the passage moves to regeneration, as the wind blowing the sheets on the line "announced to [the grandmother] the resurrection of the ordinary" (18). The passage in which this annunciation occurs ends in the fruitful garden of the Fingerbone house, where the grandmother harvests potatoes and thinks (so Ruth imagines), "What have I seen, what have I seen. The earth and the sky and the garden, not as they always are" (19). Ruth's grandmother comes to seem the agent of rebirth as Ruth describes her wearing "vestments" (19).

Other passages invoked by "say" resurrect Ruth's dead mother, Helen. Standing by the lake on a spring day, Ruth imagines that her grandfather's train, "as if in a movie run backward," emerges from the water with all its passengers alive and well, and her imagination continues resurrecting her relatives: "Say that this resurrection was general enough to include my grandmother, and Helen, my mother. Say that Helen lifted our hair from our napes with her cold hands and gave us strawberries from her purse" (96). Shortly thereafter, Ruth again imagines her mother into life: "Say that my mother was as tall as a man, and that she sometimes set me on her shoulders, so that I could splash my hands in the cold leaves above our heads" (116). In the penultimate chapter, Ruth revives her mother for the final time in order to imagine how her story would have been different had Helen returned that Sunday night rather than driving into the lake, and she concludes that it is her mother's absence—her existence only in a child's memory—that creates her numinous quality. Had they returned to the apartment in Seattle, "her eccentricities might have irked and embarrassed us when we grew older. We might have forgotten her birthday, and teased her to buy a car or to change her hair. We would have left her finally" (197), as Helen and her sisters left their own mother.

Marilee Lindemann has commented that "the true house to be kept" in *Housekeeping* is "the house of the imagination, which obliterates the distinctions between past losses and future possibilities by according them equal degrees of mental 'reality'" (118). While it is true that as narrator—as creator—Ruth has the power to give life to her dead mother, at the same time Robinson's language makes clear that such rebirth is merely a story—something that is "said." In a passage remarkably reminiscent of Virginia Woolf's intuition of some "pattern" behind the "cotton wool" of everyday life in "A Sketch of the Past," Ruth remarks that "everything that falls upon the eye is apparition, a sheet dropped over the world's true workings" (116).

A related narrative strategy is the use of the negative. As the novel progressively negates conventional notions of housekeeping, all the while making repeated references to houses and the ways in which they are or are not kept, so too the use of words of negation creates tension between presence and absence, or in Woolf's terms "being" and "non-being." To say that something is *not* is to suggest that it might have been; the shadow remains even while substance is denied, moving the narrative in two directions at once. As Ruth and Sylvie's isolation from the town of Fingerbone increases, for example, Ruth notes that after the flood, "the restoration of the town was an exemplary community effort in which we had no part" (74). When Lucille finally leaves to live with Miss Royce, Ruth "walked up and down Sycamore Street—not looking for her, of course, but acting as if I were" (140). This oppositional language, like Ruth's imagined alternatives to the story she is telling, speaks to the arbitrary and mutable nature of all narrative, and Robinson employs both with particular force in the final pages of the novel, in which there is "an end to housekeeping" (209). Following the transforming experience of crossing the bridge in the dark, Ruth's narrative voice becomes that of a disembodied spirit as she and Sylvie, in their transient life, pass through Fingerbone on the train. Unable to see the house, they are nonetheless able to see the garden, where "someone has pruned the apple trees," and Ruth imagines that it might have been Lucille, "fiercely neat, stalemating the forces of ruin" (216).

Possible realities collide as *Housekeeping* concludes, resisting closure. "If Lucille is there" in Fingerbone, Ruth tells us, "Sylvie and I have . . . thrown the side door open when she was upstairs changing beds, and we have brought in leaves, and flung the curtains and tipped the bud vase" (218). But this is Ruth's construction of Lucille's imagination as it in turn creates Ruth and Sylvie, and finally the two wanderers exist—or do not exist—only in Lucille's mind. In the final paragraph, Ruth imagines Lucille at a restaurant in Boston, where the rest of the family is dimly present through the absence of negation:

> *Sylvie and I do not flounce in through the door. . . .*
> *We do not sit down at the table next to hers. . . . My*
> *mother, likewise, is not there, and my grandmother in*
> *her house slippers with her pigtail wagging, and my*
> *grandfather, with his hair combed flat against his*
> *brow, does not examine the menu with studious*
> *interest.*
> (218)

Alone in the restaurant, Lucille "does not watch, does not listen, does not wait, does not hope, and always for me and Sylvie" (219). Thus *Housekeeping* ends far from Fingerbone, far from home and garden, with the characters suspended in the realm of pure imagination, where any future is possible.

At one point in *Housekeeping*, Robinson alludes openly to the fact that the traditional literary canon is linked to convention and conformity rather than to the free self-creation that Ruth and Sylvie represent. As Lucille becomes increasingly determined to "improve" herself by adhering to the practices that will ensure acceptance by her peers and the school system, she serves as Robinson's parody of the march to the "American Dream." She exercises and brushes her hair and, like Benjamin Franklin and Jay Gatsby, keeps a diary of these improving activities. She also reads, "with what rigor, what hard purpose," books that include *Ivanhoe, The Light That Failed, Wuthering Heights*, and *Little Men*, "and anything else she took to be improving" (132). As Lucille seeks to *be* improved by reading classic texts, Ruth sets out to improve the texts themselves by revising them to give her a central role—not least as the daughter of Eve, or, perhaps, as her predecessor Lilith, a disruptive force refusing subordination to Adam.

Indeed, as her freely moving presence hovers around the figure of Lucille, Ruth resembles the figure of Lilith in Ostriker's poem "Lilith to Eve: House, Garden," in which Lilith is a subversive servant with the superior knowledge of the oppressed:

> I am the woman outside your tidy house
> And garden, you see me
> From the corner of your eye
> In my humble cleaning lady clothes
> Passing by your border of geraniums
> And you feel satisfied
> You feel like a cat on a pillow
>
> I am the woman with hair in a rainbow
> Rag, body of iron
> I take your laundry in, suckle your young
> Scrub your toilets
> Cut your sugar cane and
> Plant and pick your cotton
> In this place you name paradise, while you

Wear amulets and cast spells
Against me in your weakness

I am the one you confess
Sympathy for, you are doing a study
Of crime in my environment, of rats
In my apartment, of my
Sexual victimization, you're raising money
To send my child to summer camp, you'd love
If I were not so sullen
And so mute

Catch me on a Saturday night
In my high heels stepping out and you shiver
I have the keys to your front door
In my pocket.
(*FEMINIST REVISION AND THE BIBLE,*
92–93)

Ostriker's Lilith has the curious freedom of the marginalized to live a life invisible to those in power, her "mute" presence a mask for her acute perceptions of those for whom she is merely a sociological problem. By permitting Ruth and Sylvie to "step out" of the conventional narrative frame and make the ending of the novel a new beginning, Robinson makes their invisibility a sign of presence rather than absence, just as Ostriker's "Lilith" poems give body and contemporary presence to that legendary figure.

Two   # TWICE UPON A TIME

1

*And he thrashed her and thrashed her, so that she
began to hate stories and from that time on forswore
listening to them.*
"HOW A HUSBAND WEANED HIS WIFE FROM
FAIRY TALES"

The epigraph is the last line of a Russian tale included in *The Virago Book
of Fairy Tales* (1990), edited by Angela Carter. The wife has invited her
thrashing by interrupting a storyteller, a guest at her husband's inn, after
he has repeated one line over and over. The tale is a variation on the story
of Sheherezade: the wife will allow as guests at the inn only those who
can entertain her with storytelling, a practice her husband resents because
it limits the pool of potential clients for his inn. The wife's disobedience
to the injunction that she not interrupt the story is the excuse he needs to
exercise his authority and punish her—not only with a beating, but also
with the removal of stories from her life. The tale thus deals with the
punishment of a disobedient woman, but it also suggests the persistence
of tradition, for when the wife interrupts after the guest has repeated
again and again the same line about an owl alighting in a garden and
drinking water, the guest says, unconvincingly, "That was only the beginning; it was going to change later" (228). With no indication of any
alteration in the story of the water-drinking owl, the reader shares the
wife's skepticism about the promised "change."

For all of their fluidity as an oral form, the fairy tales of the European

tradition are, at the same time, remarkably fixed in their essential elements, and for all of their emphasis on transformations—frog into
prince, sleeping beauty into wide-awake princess—the possibilities for
female exercise of power are extremely circumscribed in the versions that
have appeared in print since the seventeenth century. Physical attractiveness exerts considerable force, occasioning rescue and leading to marriage, but beauty is available only to the young; older women tend to be
cast as jealous stepmothers or witches. The inexorable march of time
thus marks out the same fate for all women. And if this is so for the
characters, Angela Carter suggests that a similarly paradoxical situation
exists for the female-identified originators of such stories. Carter points
out that in both the French and the English traditions, the figure of the
storyteller is "Mother Goose," an old woman spinning (yarn and tales)
by the fireside. She is pictured this way as early as the seventeenth century in the collection assembled by Charles Perrault. The identification
of the female figure with the origin of the fairy tale—in a form, unlike
the novel, so obviously fictional—devalued both, as Carter explains:

> Obviously, it was Mother Goose who invented all
> the "old wives' tales," even if old wives of any sex
> can participate in this endless recycling process, when
> anyone can pick up a tale and make it over. Old
> wives' tales—that is, worthless stories, untruths,
> trivial gossip, a derisive label that allots the art of
> storytelling to women at the exact same time as it
> takes all value from it.
> (VIRAGO, XI) [1]

But if, from the standpoint of "literature," the fairy tale occupies a low
status in light of its identification with women, children, and popular
culture, it nonetheless exerts considerable cultural force, a force that has
been the subject of much attention and debate in recent years. For Angela
Carter, fairy tales constitute a sustaining heritage of heroines. Although
women, she writes, "bear at least an equal part [with men] in the transmission of oral culture, they occupy centre stage less often than you
might think" (xiii); and thus in Carter's view the search for fairy-tale
heroines constitutes "a wish to validate my claim to a fair share of the
future by staking my claim to my share of the past" (xvi).

For others, however, the qualities associated with the best-known of
the fairy-tale heroines—qualities such as innocence, passivity, helpless-

ness, and vulnerability—make them dubious and even pernicious as models for female self-concept and behavior. As Marcia K. Lieberman points out, "Millions of women must surely have formed their psycho-sexual self-concepts, and their ideas of what they could or could not ac-complish, what sort of behavior would be rewarded, and of the nature of reward itself, in part from their favorite fairy tales" (187). Lieberman's analysis of the common patterns in popular European fairy tales reveals a set of expectations for young women that features—and potentially fosters—competition, jealousy, and materialism. The beauty contest, for example, is a "constant and primary device" in the stories (187). Girls compete on the basis of what they look like, not what they are capable of: "The beautiful girl does not have to *do* anything to merit being cho-sen; she does not have to show pluck, resourcefulness, or wit; she is chosen because she is beautiful" (188). The reward for being chosen is marriage: "Marriage is the fulcrum and major event of nearly every fairy tale" (189). Further, marriage brings with it financial reward. Cinderella is just one of many women for whom marriage means a dramatic im-provement in material circumstances. A clear scheme thus emerges from repetition in one tale after another: she who possesses physical beauty is eligible to be chosen for marriage and financial security.

Resulting logically from such a scheme are the sharp differentiations of male and female spheres and, more significant, the isolation of the heroine even within her female world. It is these lessons that Louise Ber-nikow remembers absorbing from her childhood fascination with Dis-ney's *Cinderella*:

> *I carry her story with me for the rest of my life. It is a story about women alone together and they are each other's enemies. This is more powerful as a lesson than the ball, the Prince or the glass slipper. The ech-oes of "Cinderella" in other fairy tales, in myth and literature, are about how awful women are to each other. The girl onscreen, as I squirm in my seat, needs to be saved. A man will come and save her. Some day my Prince will come. Women will not save her; they will thwart her. There is a magical fairy godmother who does help her, but this, for me, has no relation to life, for the fairy is not real and the bad women are.*
> (18)

Competition for the single prize, as Bernikow perceives, isolates women from one another, making them enemies rather than allies; isolation becomes an expectation that carries over from the fairy tales to relationships in real life.

The power of the fairy-tale paradigm, as Bernikow also suggests, is not limited to the tales themselves, but resonates in narrative more generally. The seductive image of the Prince, she proposes, is the downfall of Flaubert's Madame Bovary. A belief in princely salvation "poisoned Madame Bovary's imagination"; "all she got was a false prince—a lover who did not lift her from the ordinariness of her life" (25). In a manner more ironic than tragic, Margaret Atwood incorporates elements of the fairy tale in *The Handmaid's Tale*. As in "Cinderella," women are divided and isolated by competition, with the prize being pregnancy rather than the Prince. The Aunts, as they indoctrinate the Handmaids into the passivity of forced adultery, are derived from the figure of the evil stepmother, and the wives of the Commanders figure as Snow White's jealous stepmother, their biological function usurped by the younger Handmaids.

In his introduction to *Don't Bet on the Prince*, Jack Zipes wisely cautions against a reductive approach to fairy tales that would see in all of them the same formulas and stereotypes. Zipes points out that if one looks at the complete collection of Grimm tales, for example, it is possible to find active, heroic girls and women who succeed by their wits. While this is true, it is also the case that these are not the tales that have had the widest cultural dissemination—most recently, by Walt Disney film adaptations.[2] Whether such tales as "Cinderella," "Snow White," and "Sleeping Beauty" have achieved such wide popularity by chance or because their plots endorse—and are endorsed by—prevailing cultural assumptions about woman's nature and role must remain a matter of speculation, of course, but one measure of their pervasive cultural presence is the extent to which they have been the subject of feminist revision.[3] Fairy tales and feminist revelations of their destructive potential have reached even music videos. Julie Brown's *The Homecoming Queen's Got a Gun* satirically subverts the image of Cinderella by first identifying the homecoming queen with that fairy-tale figure and then having her engage in a shooting spree that contradicts the passive nature of both the homecoming queen and Cinderella.[4]

Before dealing with particular reworkings of specific tales and motifs, we must recognize that revision is part of the very nature of the fairy tale, as it is of other oral forms. Stories told by one generation to the next are frequently altered or embellished according to the teller's memory or talents, or in order to suit a particular cultural context. Even when committed to print, such stories are, unlike stories attributed to a specific author, perceived as common property, subject to variation. Indeed, sometimes the version of a tale known best in modern times is quite different from the tale as it circulated for centuries. Such is the case, for instance, with "Cinderella," which, as Jane Yolen demonstrates in "America's Cinderella," did not emphasize its heroine's passivity until the Perrault version of the late seventeenth century. The characterization was successively modified further by the Brothers Grimm and Walt Disney. Similarly, the language of the tales has been altered over time, particularly as part of the effort to present "cleaner," more refined, and less earthy versions. Such alterations were especially common in the nineteenth century, as Angela Carter points out, largely as a result of class consciousness. "Removing 'coarse' expressions was a common nineteenth-century pastime, part of the project of turning the universal entertainment of the poor into the refined pastime of the middle classes, and especially of the middle-class nursery" (*Virago*, xvii).

The feminist revisions of traditional fairy tales with which this chapter deals also arise from particular cultural contexts, and they have most recently been fueled by an increased awareness of the power of stories to influence girls' and women's choices and aspirations. One of the best-known of such studies is Rachel Brownstein's *Becoming a Heroine: Reading about Women in Novels* (1982), in which Brownstein argues that the life patterns of fictional heroines exert a powerful influence on female readers' sense of their own possibilities. Even before that, Karen E. Rowe demonstrated the dissemination of fairy-tale motifs into romance magazines and even the stories in mainstream women's magazines,[5] and Madonna Kolbenschlag's *Kiss Sleeping Beauty Goodbye: Breaking the Spell of Feminine Myths and Models* (1979) and Colette Dowling's *The Cinderella Complex: Women's Hidden Fear of Independence* (1981) identified behavioral patterns that, while not caused by fairy tales in any direct way, mirrored the very values that gave the tales wide currency. Identifying patterns of thought and behavior with their fairy-tale equivalents is one way to resist the power of traditional plots. A second way is to change the story by rewriting it in one's own terms, as have Angela Carter, Fay Weldon, Anne Sexton, Margaret Atwood, Jill McCorkle, and others.[6]

2

I really didn't notice that he had a funny nose.
And he certainly looked better all dressed up in fancy
clothes.
He's not nearly as attractive as he seemed the other
night.
So I think I'll just pretend that this glass slipper feels
too tight.
JUDITH VIORST, " . . . AND THEN THE
PRINCE KNELT DOWN AND TRIED TO PUT
THE GLASS SLIPPER ON CINDERELLA'S FOOT"

Writers have approached the rewriting of fairy tales in several ways.[7] One of these, which is illustrated by the foregoing Judith Viorst poem, is to demythologize the tale by recasting it in human terms. What if, Viorst asks, seen in the cold light of day rather than in a ballroom, the Prince just does not measure up to his idealized image? Might Cinderella simply remove herself from the fantasy, refuse to play the game? If a woman can be passed over because she is not sufficiently beautiful, surely a man can be dismissed on the same grounds. This is the method used by Gail Godwin in *Violet Clay*, when her title character imagines what could happen after the marriage that concludes the Gothic romance—the contemporary equivalent of the fairy tale. Violet imagines the heroine growing bored after redecorating the castle, seeking fulfillment in painting and pregnancy as the hero turns out to be an ordinary man from whom she is ultimately divorced, and left wondering whether she would be happier if she were "perpetually eligible for infinite rescues, infinite salvations, infinite new starts" (22). In both cases, fantasy is revealed *as* fantasy, leading only to disillusionment.

At the other extreme of a revisionist continuum is the impulse to write entirely new tales that share the stylized characterizations, simple plot lines, transformative acts, and interactions between human beings and animals of the traditional tales, but that feature dramatically different power relationships and outcomes, granting particular agency to women. Although the enormous outpouring of such "alternative" tales dates from the 1960s and the 1970s in both England and America, as Zipes points out in *Don't Bet on the Prince*, the beginnings of such an alternative tradition can be found in the Victorian period, practiced by such authors as Mary De Morgan, Mary Louisa Molesworth, and Evelyn Scharp.

These authors were among dozens of writers who revived the fairy tale as a legitimate genre in nineteenth-century England after nearly two centuries of its suppression by a Puritan ideology that denigrated the imaginative and fanciful in favor of a stern attention to morality and duty. While the literary fairy tale flourished in France and Germany during the seventeenth and eighteenth centuries, in England such tales were considered unsuitable for the developing minds of children, which should be focused on the practical realities of the actual world rather than on fairies and magic. Not until the romantic poets, such as Blake, Keats, Wordsworth, and Shelley, established the realm of the imagination as a counter to an increasingly industrialized and regimented nineteenth-century society did both old and new fairy tales emerge to amuse and instruct young readers—and to lodge their own protests against utilitarian modes of thought and behavior.

Further, the Victorian tales constitute in part the reclaiming of a women's literary tradition. As Nina Auerbach and U. C. Knoepflmacher state in their introduction to *Forbidden Journeys: Fairy Tales and Fantasies by Victorian Women Writers*, "Women writers of the Victorian era regarded the fairy tale as a dormant literature of their own" (11). Charlotte Brontë's *Jane Eyre* is permeated by fairy-tale motifs, most notably those of "Beauty and the Beast," which is the tale that has been the most frequent subject of revision during the last hundred years. For women to once again become the creators of tales—whether original or revised—required an acknowledgment of the origins of the traditional tales, as Auerbach and Knoepflmacher point out: "Not until the Romantic fascination with primitivism, childhood, and peasant folklore redirected collectors like the Grimms to female informants such as Dorothea Viehmann, did the genre's rich mythical veins again become accessible, and its female origins become fully apparent to a dominant literary culture" (12).

While many of these tales were heavily didactic, encouraging conformity and obedience, others challenged the assumptions of Victorian culture—including those having to do with gender roles—and some even made subversive use of the tropes of traditional tales in a manner approaching metafiction. Zipes, in his introduction to *Victorian Fairy Tales: The Revolt of the Fairies and Elves*, refers to the second category as "utopian" tales, inasmuch as they propose a reality antithetical to the rigidity of Victorian culture. Both male and female authors of fairy tales, he points out, "created strong women characters and placed great emphasis on the fusion of female and male qualities and equality between men and women" (xxv). Further, these tales function as social critiques: "All the formal aesthetic changes made in the tales are connected to an insistence that the substance of life be transformed, otherwise there will be alienation, petrification, and death" (xxvi).

Both a strong female character and a critique of a regimented culture are central to Mary De Morgan's "A Toy Princess" (1877). Although the tale purports to be set "more than a thousand years ago, in a country quite on the other side of the world," it is clearly meant to address Victorian codes of civility; the people are "so very polite that they hardly ever spoke to each other" except to say "Just so," "Yes, indeed," "Thank you," and "If you please" (165). When a princess from another country marries the king of this restrained land, she brings with her a native capacity for showing emotion, but finds it stifled in this repressive environment. After giving birth to a daughter who inherits her tendency to laugh and cry, she dies, leaving her daughter to grow as unhappy as she had been among these silent people. When the queen's fairy godmother sees how miserable the young princess is, she whisks the child away to be raised by a happy fisherman's family and substitutes for her a life-sized toy princess who is capable only of uttering the four approved phrases. Years later, when the fairy godmother learns that the king intends to retire and turn the kingdom over to the fake princess, she reveals the trick and offers the real, thinking and feeling princess to the kingdom, whose council votes its preference for the empty, mechanical young woman. Tabaret, the fairy godmother, speaks to the country's favoring of passive, silent women when she says scornfully, "When you had that bit of wood-and-leather Princess, you could behave well enough to it, but now that you have a real flesh-and-blood woman, you none of you care for her" (173–174). The real princess leaves happily to marry a young fisherman and live in a cottage by the sea.

Whereas De Morgan stays close to the traditional form of the fairy tale in "A Toy Princess," using it to satirize an obsessively polite culture, Evelyn Sharp and Edith Nesbit mock the stock tropes and motifs of the traditional tales in a manner similar to the work of Anne Sexton, Fay Weldon, and Angela Carter nearly a century later. Sharp's "The Spell of the Magician's Daughter" (1902) employs this method as a means of making fun of the didacticism and preachy language of cautionary tales for children. Firefly, the youngest of four daughters of a magician, does not apply herself to her father's instruction in the elements of witchcraft, unlike her sisters, who "thought it would be good fun to turn people into frogs and toads, and to go to the christenings of Princes uninvited"

(361). Thus, when a boy she meets in the woods requests of her a spell that will remove an annoying giant from his country, she finds "herself in an awkward fix, which is what may happen to any of us if we do not learn our lessons properly" (362–363). But in fact the spell that Firefly makes up eventually does rid the country of the giant; despite her inattention to her lessons, she has cast a "real" spell because, her father tells her, "you took it straight from your head and your heart" (365). Intention and sincerity, in other words, prove to be more effective than behavior. The boy in the woods turns out to be a prince, whom Firefly marries when they are grown, but she wins this prize because of her cleverness and perseverance, not because of her beauty. Further, she marries him in spite of the sexist attitude he displays when they first meet, dismissing her as an ally against the giant because of her sex. "It is a pity," he says, "that you are only a girl," to which she responds, "I do not think it is a pity at all, . . . I would *much* rather be a girl, thank you" (362). Early in the story Firefly, uninterested in her witch's training, flippantly declares that she will choose marriage rather than a career of casting spells—"If I must do something, . . . I will marry the King's son" (361)—but at the end, Sharp suggests that she has both marriage and a career: "So the magician's youngest daughter did marry the King's son. . . . But there's no doubt that she also became a witch, for to this day she can do what she likes with the King's son" (372). Not only has Firefly asserted the worth of being female; Sharp suggests that she has converted the prince to her way of thinking.

Edith Nesbit's "The Last of the Dragons" (ca. 1900) similarly emphasizes female agency. Nesbit overturns, in both language and plot, the mythic story of the princess who is rescued from a dragon by a prince, thereby depriving the old tale of authority by pointing to its status as a mere story "told in royal nurseries at twilight" (353). The princess in Nesbit's story "knew what she had to expect" when she turned sixteen: "The dragon would not eat her, of course—because the prince would come and rescue her" (353). But she nonetheless resists the ritual, even though her father protests that "it's always done, my dear"; she believes that "it would be much pleasanter to have nothing to do with the dragon at all" (353). More important, she is less than enchanted by the prospect of a prince: "All the princes I know are such very silly little boys" (353), and she suggests reversing the procedure by rescuing the prince, because she knows that she handles a sword "better than any of the princes we know" (354). When this "strongest and boldest and most skilful and most sensible princess in Europe" (354) is assigned a prince who is more philosopher than hero, she convinces him to merely pretend to go through with the ritual rescue, not least because, as the "last of the dragons," it is an extremely endangered species. Kindness prevails over heroism as the young couple befriends the dragon instead of killing him, and Nesbit uses this turn of the plot to metaphorically tame the giant of industry. When the dragon is first roused from his cave, the noise he makes "sounded as if a rather large cotton-mill were stretching itself" (355), but by the end of the story the dragon is fitted out to convey children to and from the seashore, and is about to be transformed into the first airplane.[8]

Nesbit's revised tale is strikingly contemporary, and to it could be applied Zipes's description of the more recent feminist fairy tale: "the aesthetics . . . are ideological, for the structural reformation depends upon a non-sexist (and non-racist, I might add) world view that calls for a dramatic change in social practice" (*Don't Bet on the Prince,* 13). Jeanne Desy's 1982 story "The Princess Who Stood on Her Own Two Feet" is a good example of the alternative tale. Desy's story features a princess, a wizard, talking animals, and magic spells, but the princess stands "on her own two feet" both literally and figuratively by refusing to marry a prince who does not respect her and overcoming the stigma of being taller than her suitors. Also common in the alternative tale of both the turn of the century and recent decades is humor, which Desy uses to undercut the solemn authority of the traditional tale. Writing that the prince "strode" to the door, for example, Desy adds parenthetically, "he never walked any other way" (43); and of Mirabelle, the Wizard's talking cat, she writes that Mirabelle "never had been much of a conversationalist" (47).

These stylistic interventions with conventional language and tropes mark the writer's active engagement with—and disobedience to—textual traditions that enclose women in scripts not of their making. In *The Madwoman in the Attic,* Sandra Gilbert and Susan Gubar use the Grimm version of "Little Snow White" as a paradigm of the woman who "plots" (writes). To scheme the death of her silent stepdaughter, Snow White, the stepmother must be figured as evil, a witchlike character trying to kill the innocence—and hence the inaction—that Snow White represents. But paradoxically, authority remains vested in the (male) voice of approval in the mirror; the standard by which both mother and daughter are judged resides outside of themselves, so that neither can claim true authorship. Gilbert and Gubar suggest that even after Snow White is rescued from her coffin, only a certain unruliness can save her from continued textual entombment: "[I]f Snow White escaped her first glass coffin by her goodness, her passivity and docility, her only escape from her second glass coffin, the imprisoning mirror, must evidently be through 'badness,' through plots and stories, duplicitous schemes, wild dreams, fierce fictions, mad impersonations" (42). Only by cracking "the Queen's looking glass," in other words, can women writers break the power of the voice of authority that issues from it.

Both male and female writers of the twentieth century have directly or indirectly revised popular fairy tales. Donald Barthelme's 1967 novel *Snow White* is a celebrated case in point, and writers as disparate as Milt Gross and James Thurber have produced versions of "Little Red Riding Hood." But there is particular significance in feminist reworkings of such tales, because the versions of the tales against which they work were themselves deliberately shaped by male writers such as Perrault and the Brothers Grimm to deliver certain prescriptive messages concerning women. Zipes makes this point in his introduction to *The Trials and Tribulations of Little Red Riding Hood.* Whereas in the oral versions of this folk tale Little Red Riding Hood escapes the advances of the wolf— which are as much sexual as they are life-threatening—by her own cunning, Perrault recast the little girl as innocent and fearful and appended a lengthy moral tag following her demise that warns young girls against trusting strangers. Zipes locates Perrault's version of the tale in a late-seventeenth-century context of increased concern about proper behavior, noting that it "is a projection of male phantasy in a literary discourse considered to be civilized and aimed at curbing the natural inclinations of children" (13). When, in turn, the Brothers Grimm undertook to present their own version of the tale in the early nineteenth century, they found the French version "too cruel, too sexual, and too tragic," and "adapted it to comply with the emerging *Biedermeier* or Victorian image of little girls and proper behavior" (14). The young heroine is presented in the Grimm version as disobedient, for which she must be punished, but her actual life is saved by a male hunter; thus, "what had formerly been a frank oral tale about sexuality and actual dangers in the woods became . . . a coded message about rationalizing bodies and sex" (17).

In the 1972 feminist revision of "Little Red Riding Hood" by the Merseyside Fairy Story Collective, the transformations of the tale emphasize the wisdom of the grandmother figure (here a *great*-grandmother), the young girl's capacity for maturation, and a matrilineal transmission of magic and power. Significantly, the girl is given a name, Nadia, so she is known by her identity as well as by the red cloak she wears. Initially, Nadia is a distressingly fearful child; rather than disobedient, as in the

Grimm version, she is timid and cautious, even refusing to join her schoolmates in making fur jackets for the winter because she is afraid of the sharp knives used to cut the fur. Yet when she sees her great-grandmother courageously fending off the wolf with a burning branch, she is inspired to plunge a knife into his heart, and great-grandmother and granddaughter together use his fur to line the red cloak. The cloak itself becomes both an emblem of the girl's new power and, because it once belonged to the great-grandmother, a representation of the empowering of one generation of women by another. Finally, the revised tale addresses concerns such as those of Louise Bernikow about women as each other's enemies in fairy tales: Nadia's great-grandmother instructs her to lend the now-magic red cloak to other fearful girls so that they too can be brave.

Anne Sexton's poem "Red Riding Hood," in her 1971 book *Transformations*, works its revision in a very different way. Instead of altering the plot and characters of the tale, Sexton is faithful in outline to one of the Grimm versions, in which a woodsman cuts open the wolf to free the swallowed-but-alive girl and her grandmother. Sexton's "transformation" takes place in the language and the framing of the tale, both of which bring it into the middle of the twentieth century as if to underscore the story's continued power. The style is breezy, tough, and slangy, a strategy that, as Alicia Ostriker comments, "remind[s] us that such stories were once crackling with energy for their listeners" (232). The young girl's red cape is "her Linus blanket," a contemporary reference to the comic strip "Peanuts" that points to her traditional dependence and helplessness, and the "wolf dressed in frills, / a kind of transvestite" seems to her "no more dangerous / than a streetcar or a panhandler." Despite Sexton's adherence to a traditional plot, her language continually questions the tale, as when, noting that Red Riding Hood is taking wine and cake to her sick grandmother, the poet stops to query, "Where's the aspirin? The penicillin? / Where's the fruit juice?" More significantly, the descriptions of the wolf make him curiously androgynous. Introduced as a transvestite, after swallowing the two women he is described as pregnant, appearing "to be in his ninth month," and the hunter who frees Red Riding Hood and the grandmother does so with "a kind of Caesarean section." The wolf is thus both predator and mother, and the final horror of Sexton's poem is that the two women retain no memory of being swallowed and then set free, so that by implication it could all happen again, just as the tale is told over and over.

Sexton's framing of the story of Red Riding Hood reinforces this sense of repetition and continuity, for the wolf is only one of the "deceivers" with which the poem deals. Preceding the fairy tale are accounts of several others—all women—including the poet's speaker herself. A suburban matron shops in a supermarket while plotting to meet her lover in a church parking lot; a pair of female con artists cheats an elderly woman out of her life savings. The speaker confesses that, although she is outwardly "quite collected at cocktail parties," in her head she is "undergoing open-heart surgery." Her second confession prepares thematically for the story of Red Riding Hood, and especially for its sense of doomed repetition. Deceived by the notion that "nothing haunts a new house," the speaker builds a summer home, only to be haunted by her past, unable to "move to another city/where the worthy make a new life" (73–79).

Transformations, which includes sixteen revisions of classic fairy tales, is one of the most thoroughgoing and ambitious modern reworkings of the stories. Sexton's speaker describes herself in the first poem in the collection, "The Gold Key," as a "middle-aged witch," "ready to tell you a story or two." This witch, intrinsically disobedient and disruptive, announces her intention to "transform the Brothers Grimm" (1–2). The speaker reminds us of her narrative freedom by altering the tone in which she recontextualizes the tales—sometimes sarcastic, at other times harsh or sympathetic. As Ostriker accurately observes, "while the tales themselves are fixed . . . the teller is mobile. She emits an air of exhilarating mental and emotional liberty, precisely because she is distanced from the material she so penetratingly understands" (*Feminist Revision*, 234). The sense of exhilaration is evident in Sexton's description of *Transformations* to her friend Brian Sweeney: "I take the fairy tale and transform it into a poem of my own, following the story line, exceeding the story line and adding my own pzazz. They are very wry and cruel and sadistic and funny" (Middlebrook, 336–337).

In *Stealing the Language*, Ostriker makes the point that mythology—in which she includes folktales, legends, and Scriptures—has a "double power" for the writer who would use it to his or her own ends:

> *It exists or appears to exist objectively, outside the self. Because it is in the public domain, it confers on the writer the sort of authority unavailable to someone who writes "merely" of the private self. Myth*

> *belongs to "high" culture and is handed "down"*
> *through the ages by religious, literary, and educa-*
> *tional authority. At the same time, myth is quintes-*
> *sentially intimate material, the stuff of dream life, for-*
> *bidden desire, inexplicable motivation—everything in*
> *the psyche that to rational consciousness is unreal,*
> *crazed, or abominable.*
> (213)

It is the "crazed" and "abominable" elements of the fairy tales that seem most to interest Sexton in *Transformations*. Even when her tone is wry or humorous, she reminds us forcibly of the brutality and violence in versions of the tales not air-brushed by Disney—or even by the Brothers Grimm. Middlebrook, in her 1992 biography of Sexton, suggests that some of the character of the poems in *Transformations* can be traced to the psychotherapy she was undergoing when she wrote them in 1970, an experience that brought her once again face to face with "her personal struggle with the living dead" (337). Middlebrook further suggests that the material of fairy tales might have been especially appropriate to one in therapy, with its emphasis on childhood experience: "Fairy tales deal with the struggle of children to overcome giants, ogres, and witches, often to satisfy the wishes of kings and queens by undergoing terrible ordeals" (337).

Whatever their origins, the poems in *Transformations* accomplish a double work. At the same time that Sexton transforms the tales by giving them a hip, twentieth-century immediacy, she preserves or even restores their folkloric horror. "Cinderella," for example, becomes the sudden rags-to-riches story, similar to that of "the plumber with twelve children / who wins the Irish Sweepstakes," or the charwoman enabled by an insurance windfall to move "from mops to Bonwit Teller." But Sexton's rendition of the tale pits earthy violence against the vacuousness of Cinderella's "happily-ever-after" life. Cinderella's stepsisters cut off parts of their feet in an attempt to make the slipper fit (an element that makes logical the tale's origin in China, with the first recorded Chinese version dating from the ninth century), and when they show up at the wedding, their eyes are pecked out by birds. Cinderella and the Prince, "like two dolls in a museum case," have "their darling smiles pasted on for eternity. / Regular Bobbsey Twins" (53, 57). Snow White, whom Sexton refers to as a "dumb bunny" when she accepts the poisoned apple from the Queen, ends up in a similarly doll-like, artificial state, "rolling her china-blue doll eyes open and shut / and sometimes referring to her mirror / as women do" (8–9). Meanwhile the jealous queen has danced herself to death, "her tongue flicking in and out / like a gas jet" (9).

Transformations concludes with Sexton's rendition of "Sleeping Beauty," here titled "Briar Rose" (the original Grimm title), which opens and closes with accounts of father-daughter incest. The prefatory stanza recapitulates the process of a woman recapturing childhood memories through hypnosis, "swimming further and further back," until she is two years old sitting on her father's lap. The father's affection turns menacing in the final lines, as the father entreats the child to "come be my snooky / and I will give you a root" (107). The threatening tone of the preface has distinct echoes in the tale itself: following the curse of the thirteenth fairy, Briar Rose's father takes extraordinary measures to safeguard her, so that "she dwelt in his odor. / Rank as honeysuckle" (109), and when, after a hundred years of sleep, the prince awakens Briar Rose with a kiss, she emerges as from a nightmare, calling "Daddy! Daddy" (110). Thereafter Briar Rose is afraid to go to sleep, and the savior prince is obscured in her imagination by the predatory father:

> It's not the prince at all,
> but my father
> drunkenly bent over my bed,
> circling the abyss like a shark,
> my father thick upon me
> like some sleeping jellyfish.
> (112)

The final lines of "Briar Rose" suggest that the tale's heroine is doomed by this memory to remain always in childhood, "this life after death" (112). When we consider also the doll-like states of Cinderella and Snow White at the end of Sexton's versions of their tales, it seems clear that a central message in Transformations is the power of fairy tales to proscribe female maturation, by trapping women in either doll-like compliance or unresolved nightmares.

In her 1977 collection of poems, Olga Broumas acknowledges the influence of Sexton by using quotations from Transformations as the epigraphs for two of her own revisions of fairy tales, "Cinderella" and "Rapunzel." But the seven poems in which Broumas addresses the tales in

Beginning with O push the stories farther from their traditional outlines. As Ellen Cronan Rose has observed:

> *If Sexton's rewriting of the Grimms' fairy tales suggests that the socialization of women in patriarchy distorts our natural development, Broumas's force us to consider the possibility that lesbianism is not deviant but a natural consequence of the undeniable fact that a woman's first love object, like a man's, is her mother.*
>
> (221)

Broumas's revisions reverse the central gender relationships of the traditional tales. Men are not rescuers, but rather intruders; women are lovers and nurturers of each other instead of jealous competitors. Her Cinderella is a "hand-picked" woman "whose small foot conveniently / fills the slipper of glass," but she lives in "a house of men / who secretly / call themselves princes," and is "Apart from my sisters, estranged / from my mother." Although some might think this Cinderella privileged—"I am the one allowed in / to the royal chambers"—she instead feels alone in an alien world. Unlike other women who have been singled out for inclusion in a male world—"the woman writer, the lady / umpire, the madam chairman"—Broumas's Cinderella feels herself "A woman co-opted by promises," who is forced

> to bear witness, falsely
> against my own kind, as each
> other sister was judged inadequate, bitchy,
>   incompetent,
> jealous, too thin, too fat.

In place of her falsely won privilege, Cinderella would prefer a return to her former fireside: "Give / me my ashes" (57–58).

A similar theme informs Broumas's "Snow White." Whereas the traditional tale features intergenerational jealousy, Broumas imagines three generations of women sleeping peacefully together until the husband / father disrupts the peace by returning from war. Three years into the marriage, Snow White realizes that her "Blond, clean, / miraculous" husband is an "alien instrument," whereas she and her mother are "two halves / of a two-colored apple." The conclusion of the poem imagines a return to the mother; instead of an occasion for jealousy, the mirror is here representative of the mother-daughter bond, as Snow White tells her mother, "I'm . . . your fairest, most / faithful mirror" (69–71).

Broumas's version of "Little Red Riding Hood" restores the sexual implications of early versions of the tale, but from a lesbian perspective. The "red hood" is here the "mantle of blood" of the newborn girl, which becomes in turn the necessary disguise for her female-identified sexuality. Heeding her mother's injunction to "Stick to the road and forget the flowers, there's / wolves in those bushes," Red Riding Hood opens her hood "only at night, and with other women," using the gift her mother has given her for both concealment and connection (67–68). Instead of Sexton's sexless, doll-like princesses, the heroines of Broumas's revised tales are lusty participants in sexuality who challenge cultural restrictions, such as the two women in "Sleeping Beauty" who kiss each other in public, taking "unspeakable liberties" (62).

Jill McCorkle's retelling of the Sleeping Beauty tale, like the poems of Sexton and Broumas, demonstrates the cultural persistence of such narratives. In contrast to Sexton's "wry and cruel and sadistic" rendition or Broumas's tale of women awakening women, however, McCorkle's story "Sleeping Beauty, Revised," in her 1992 collection *Crash Diet*, features a wide-awake heroine who is well aware that her life is not that of the fairy-tale princess, even though she sometimes wishes for a prince. The divorced mother of a small son, the narrator anticipates her first date since the divorce as a possible new beginning, but realizes quickly that such dreams are illusions. Her date arrives looking "tall and fresh-looking, crisp as a stalk of celery . . . the kind of man I always wanted to date in college" (200). Yet even though "he looks like someone (a good guy or prince) out of one of [her son] Jeffrey's books," she is aware of the insubstantiality of the princely image: "I kept expecting him to turn to the side and become the flat straight edge of a picture page" (201), and following his barely concealed flirtation with the young, attractive waitress at the restaurant, she imagines "his picture ripped from a story book—a two-dimensional prince" (212). At the restaurant, she is conscious of being the outsider, looking in on the fairy tale as he observes the waitress: "He looks like he's in a trance, like the Prince when Cinderella enters the ballroom, the Prince when he finds Snow White in her coffin, the *Prince* when he makes his way to Sleeping Beauty's bedside" (208).

Indeed, McCorkle's narrator emerges as a realist in a world in which others are ensnared in fantasy. Early in the story, she muses about one of Jeffrey's baby-sitters, who is dreamily engaged to be married and has chosen a china pattern named "Eternal." The young woman names the pattern in "a hypnotic way that suggested she wouldn't wake up until that first time she found her Eternal on the top shelf coated in dust. The happy ending comes if she can look at the dishes and laugh, and wonder why young couples don't ask for something like a washer and dryer, a car battery that never dies" (198). The narrator has a similar urge to awaken the women in the restaurant who announce their belief that flag burners should receive the death penalty: "Rewrite the fairy tales *and* the Constitution, I want to yell, go for the Gettysburg Address. Rewrite the Bible" (207). Even though she joins her date in imagining ways to rehabilitate the evil characters in fairy tales, she resists his view that the traditional tales are "horrible"—"There are bad things that happen all over; why should fairy tales be excluded?" (203). The stories are, to her, just stories, and when they are finished, "you just turn the page and start all over" (213).

The central character in Margaret Atwood's "Bluebeard's Egg," in contrast, has married her prince and only gradually becomes aware that he may be a modern equivalent of Bluebeard. McCorkle and Atwood both use fairy-tale motifs to underscore the attractions of fantasy for vulnerable women, but whereas McCorkle revises "Sleeping Beauty" to give her narrator an ironic distance from it, Atwood uses the Bluebeard motif to provide a sinister undercurrent for a story about a woman beginning to doubt her husband's devotion and fidelity.

Near the end of Atwood's story her central character, Sally, receives the assignment from her teacher in "Forms of Narrative Fiction" to write a new version of the story of Bluebeard "set in the present and cast in the realistic mode," or, as the teacher puts it, with "no real magic" (154). This assignment is precisely the one that Atwood herself fulfills in writing "Bluebeard's Egg"; the story of a modern marriage invokes and parallels the traditional story of Bluebeard, except that without magic there can be no rescue and hence no happy ending. In the version of the tale that Perrault and the Brothers Grimm both write, the maiden is saved from Bluebeard's "bloody chamber" by her brothers, but the version the teacher reads to Sally's class predates these and features a clever (and magic) young woman who outwits Bluebeard and brings her two slain sisters back to life. In Atwood's story, Sally is still

with her Bluebeard, wondering what will happen next and possessing
no magic.

As Barbara Godard points out in "Tales within Tales," part of Atwood's project here is to draw attention to the process by which stories
are told and retold on a variety of levels: "In the fictional world, Sally as
reader is decoding various versions of the Bluebeard story from the
quoted world, to recode them in the modern day version which is to be
her class exercise" (71). In this sense, "Bluebeard's Egg" focuses on "the
processes of construction, the constant fictionalizing we engage in as human beings" (76–77). Yet it is the reader of Atwood's story, not Sally
herself, who is able to make the full connection between the traditional
versions of the Bluebeard story and her own marriage.

Sally views her husband, Ed, as charmed, "a child of luck, a third son
who, armed with nothing but a certain feeble-minded amiability, manages to make it through the forest with all its witches and traps and
pitfalls and end up with the princess" (132–133)—who is Sally herself.
But Sally is Ed's third wife, and it bothers her that she does not know
what went wrong with the first two marriages so that she, like the clever
third sister, can avert disaster. "What if," she thinks, "he wakes up one
day and decides that she isn't the true bride after all, but the false one?
Then she will be put in a barrel stuck full of nails and rolled downhill,
endlessly, while he is sitting in yet another bridal bed, drinking champagne" (134).

The fact that Ed is a heart specialist connects him immediately to
blood and human organs and recalls the dismembered bodies of women
in Bluebeard's secret chamber. The analogue for Bluebeard's bloody
chamber is the room in Ed's clinic containing the latest in high-tech
heart-monitoring equipment. As the girl in the story of Bluebeard is
forbidden to enter the secret room, so Ed is initially reluctant to show
Sally this room, and once there, she finds it oddly sexually charged and
unsettling—"clearly a dangerous place": "It was like a massage parlour,
only for women. Put a batch of women in there with Ed and they would
never want to come out. They'd want to stay in there while he ran his
probe over their wet skins and pointed out to them the defects of their
beating hearts" (145).

Until the evening of the dinner party, when she sees Ed fondling her
best friend, she imagines him to be the pursued rather than the pursuer;
teasing him about his "bloody chamber," she says that the women in
"that little dark room of yours" will "gobble you up . . . chew you into

tiny pieces" (147). But his familiarity with her friend Marylynn calls into question her assessment of him—unlocks the door to her uncertainty—and so the story ends.

3

I am all for putting new wine in old bottles, especially if the pressure of the new wine makes the old bottles explode.
ANGELA CARTER, "NOTES FROM
THE FRONT LINE"

Princes, toads, princesses, beggar girls—we all have to place ourselves as best we can.
FAY WELDON, *WORDS OF ADVICE*

While many contemporary women writers have felt sufficiently haunted by the paradigms of the more popular fairy tales to have engaged them in their writing, few have undertaken so far-ranging an engagement as have the British fiction writers Fay Weldon and Angela Carter. Fairy-tale references, motifs, plots, and characters permeate much of the fiction of these two women, both of whom have been repeatedly noted for the wit and irreverence of their work. Yet the differences between them are equally instructive about the feminist project of disobedient revision. Weldon, for all her outrageous humor, her sometimes extravagant use of exaggeration, and her occasional forays into futuristic settings (as in *The Rules of Life*), is essentially a realist writer, conscious of and concerned with revealing the grim, gritty problems that exist "down among the women," as the title of one of her novels so tellingly puts it. Even the grotesquely fanciful plot of her best-known novel, *The Life and Loves of a She-Devil*, is merely the logical extension of a woman's desire to be as alluring as her husband's mistress. Weldon's characters' fascination with fairy tales, in other words, is a mark not of their eccentricity, but of their ordinariness. Carter, in contrast, is a fabulist. Her fiction, although it is at least as referential to literary tradition as is Weldon's, features transformations of time, gender, and reality that re-create a world different from elements of the one she observes. In Weldon's fiction, fairy tales are among the many cultural scripts that her characters resist, revise, or are ensnared by; Carter goes inside the tales to "make the old bottles explode."

There are at least two reasons why fairy tales hold a natural appeal for Weldon. One has to do with class, the other with gender. The contemporary England about which she writes seems nearly as rigidly class-bound as the postfeudal world of the fairy tale, with the haves and the have-nots separated by a gulf that is both economic and ideological. Thus intones her narrator at the beginning of the story "Pumpkin Pie" (*Moon over Minneapolis*, 1991): "The rich have got to come to some accommodation with the poor—and by that I don't mean provide housing (though I can see that might help) but 'to accommodate' in its old sense: that is to say recognize, come towards, incorporate, compromise" (81). "Pumpkin Pie" is reminiscent of the Cinderella story—without the fairy godmother or the rescuing prince. Instead of being converted into a coach (à la Disney), the pumpkin is here converted into a pie that similarly becomes an instrument in the class war. The tale is told by a wry, scolding narrator, a contemporary Mother Goose, who warns her listeners to "pay good attention" and later asks, "Are you still listening? Or have you turned the music up" (81).

The Cinderella figure in "Pumpkin Pie" is Antoinette, the Latino maid at the Marvin household. As "a dumpy 45-year-old Latino with a scar down the side of her face," she "wasn't right for opening doors and smiling" (85), so she is kept in the kitchen to fix Thanksgiving dinner for the Marvins and their guests. The dinner—including the pie—must be strictly nonfat because of Mr. Marvin's heart condition and Mrs. Marvin's ostensible adherence to the Pritikin diet, but when the fat-free pie burns because Antoinette must sneak home to handle a family emergency, she substitutes a traditional pie made with whole eggs. As cholesterol is a slow poison, no one drops dead at dinner, but Weldon's narrator finds the danger sufficient to issue a moral to the story: "The pumpkin pies of the poor taste as good if not better than the pumpkin pies of the rich; so if you can't make your own, do without, and let the hired help stay home for a change. Or you'll find cholesterol in your pie and a knife in your back, and a good thing too" (88).

Yet despite this warning to the rich, Weldon's narrator recognizes that real life is more complex than the fairy tale, with its sharp dichotomy between good and evil. Midway through the story, she stops to assess her listener's awareness of this complexity: "Whose side are you on, I wonder? . . . The rich or the poor? Have I loaded the scales? No. You wish I had, but I haven't" (85). The narrator thus signals her position as storyteller, with the power to make choices, revise, control the reactions of her listeners.

Weldon's characters not only tell stories, they are surrounded by them, both sustained and oppressed by them. "There is more to life than death," says the narrator in *Down among the Women* (1972); "there is, for one thing, fiction. . . . Give yourself over entirely to fiction, and you could have eternal life" (159). Myths, including fairy tales, allow Weldon's women to dream, even while those dreams reveal themselves as false. "Myths," says the narrator in *Down among the Women*, "are not true. Myths simply answer a need" (158).

Nowhere in Weldon's fiction is the need for myths and fantasy more clearly demonstrated than in the character Gwyneth in *Female Friends*. Gwyneth "retreats from the truth into ignorance, and finds that the false beliefs and half-truth, interweaving, make a fine supportive pillow for a gentle person against whom God has taken an irrational dislike" (45). She raises her daughter, Chloe, on old wives' tales and aphorisms: "Red flannel is warmer than white"; "Marry in haste, repent in leisure" (45). The greatest falsehood that Gwyneth tells herself is that she has only to declare her love to Mr. Leacock, her employer, and her Prince will come to her. "Gwyneth believes she has only to speak the words and Mr. Leacock will be hers; and forever procrastinates, and never quite speaks them. . . . And so [women] grow old in expectation and illusion, and perhaps it is preferable to growing old in the harsh glare of truth" (108). Illusions and stories may insulate women from painful truth, but they also separate women from one another as, in the fairy tales, they foster competition for male approbation. Chloe, as narrator of *Female Friends*, comments on the lack of sisterly solidarity among her friends: "Our loyalties are to men, not to each other": "Well, morality is for the rich, and always was. We women, we beggars, we scrubbers and dusters, we do the best we can for us and ours. We are divided amongst ourselves. We have to be, for survival's sake" (249).

The most extreme instance of the power of female jealousy in Weldon's fiction is *The Life and Loves of a She-Devil* (1983), a novel saturated with fairy-tale motifs. Mary Fisher is a princess in a tower—both a fictional creation and a creator of fictions. The popular romances she writes are the modern equivalent of the fairy tale; or, as the narrator, Ruth, puts it, "She tells lies to herself, and to the world" (1). Ruth, in turn, is compounded of Cinderella's jealous stepsisters and an evil fairy who contrives to bring Mary Fisher down from her tower. The style of the novel is incantatory, the language of spells—"I sing in praise of hate, and all its

attendant energy" (3)—and the plot hinges on transformation, that staple
element of the fairy tale, by which frogs become princes. Ruth, aided by
the modern magic of plastic surgery, transforms herself from a six-foot-
two, unattractive woman into the image of the delicate, lovely Mary
Fisher and regains her husband, Bobbo, who remains more frog than
prince.[9]

One of Weldon's purposes in *She-Devil* is to deflate the notion of ideality that is the goal of fairy tales and myths, and the perfection of pre-
lapsarian Eden is one of her targets. Ruth and Bobbo live "exactly in the
middle of a place called Eden Grove," a suburban development "planned
as paradise" (4). The emptiness and artificiality of this "paradise" are
immediately evident, not only in the deceit that characterizes their marriage, but also in the social interaction among the neighbors, which is a
thin defense against nothingness:

> *My neighbors and I give dinner parties for one an-*
> *other. We discuss things, rather than ideas; we ex-*
> *change information, not theories; we keep ourselves*
> *steady by thinking about the particular. The general*
> *is frightening. Go too far into the past and there is*
> *nonexistence, too far into the future and there you*
> *find the same.*
> (5)

Bobbo, deep into his affair with Mary Fisher, tells Ruth that "it is a good
life," although he is increasingly absent from Eden Grove and therefore
"does not say so as often as he did" (5). Ruth, for her part, finds "this
centerless place" barely tolerable, observing wryly that it is "a better
place to live than a street in downtown Bombay" (4).

Ruth is thus a dissatisfied Eve in a trumped-up Eden, and it is appropriate that her first major act of rebellion is to burn down the house in
Eden Grove, tellingly located at "No. 19 Nightbird Drive" (4). Hers is a
willing departure from the Garden, not an expulsion, and it is the beginning of her quest for self-transformation—a quest undertaken out of
hate, not love, because love, Ruth remarks, "is a pallid emotion. Fidgety
and troublesome, and making for misery" (12). As Ruth undergoes the
lengthy process of physical transformation into the image of Mary
Fisher, she takes on a succession of false identities, becoming in turn
Vesta Rose, Polly Patch, Molly Wishant, and Marlene Hunter as she

manages the ruin of Bobbo and Mary Fisher in order to assume her place in the High Tower.

Although *The Life and Loves of a She-Devil* has been read by many as a triumph of the unattractive, betrayed wife over the forces of idealized romance, a consideration of the fairy-tale elements that inform the novel leads to a much bleaker reading that embodies an even stronger indictment of the romance tradition. Weldon both extends and inverts the Cinderella story to demonstrate the awful power of the ideals of romantic love and physical beauty. Initially, certainly, Weldon means for her readers to feel sympathy for her narrator. As a child, the unlovely Ruth has two lovely stepsisters, and she is early on abandoned by both her stepfather and her mother. Her marriage to Bobbo is occasioned by her accidental pregnancy, and she is as unwanted as a wife as she had been as a child. Her drive to assume the physical image of Mary Fisher requires that her body be mutilated, which recalls the versions of the Cinderella story in which Cinderella's stepsisters cut off parts of their feet to try to make the glass slipper fit. However, in the end, the process of self-invention requires that Ruth be no longer a woman but an artifice; further, by taking Mary Fisher's place as the author of romances (though she refuses to publish them), she is engaged in perpetuating the same notions of romantic ideality that had caused her, as Ruth, to be shunned. The last lines of the novel invite us to read beneath the wicked comedy of *She-Devil*: "I am a lady of six foot two, who had tucks taken in her legs. A comic turn, turned serious" (278). Serious, indeed. By enclosing Ruth in the fairy-tale plot, Weldon has ensured that she will end as a replica rather than a person, as artificial as the doll-like figure in Sexton's "Snow White."

Far more triumphant, though no less in thrall to cultural notions of feminine attractiveness, is Gabriella Sumpter in Weldon's *The Rules of Life* (1987). Having led a thoroughly self-centered life, Gabriella narrates her story from the grave in the year 2004, thanks to the discovery by the priests of the Great New Fictional Religion that the stories of the recently departed can be captured on tape. Gabriella is thus a kind of ultimate Sleeping Beauty, one who cannot be awakened but who can tell her story—a woman who, at the time of her death at the age of sixty-one, was "still capable of inspiring erotic love": "My step did not have time to falter, my spine did not curve; my eyes had wrinkled but barely dimmed: my teeth, with considerable help from my dentist, Edgar Simpson, remained white, firm, even, and above all *there*" (15). Despite the pleasure that Gabriella has derived from her erotic encounters, she finds death (sleep) preferable to life, for life is painful, and "the briefer the experience the better" (15). In fact, her "great achievement" is that she has not married or borne children, which reverses the fairy-tale trajectory toward marriage to the prince.

Like many a fairy-tale heroine, Gabriella is orphaned and left to find her own way in life. Her mother, a "poor, pretty, inconsequential thing" (36), is killed by a wasp sting, and her father, a largely unsuccessful gambler, dies when their house burns down. Gabriella is rescued—and immediately bedded—by a doctor's assistant, but, in another of Weldon's inversions of fairy-tale plots, this experience neither ruins her nor serves as a cautionary tale for the reader, but instead launches her happily on a life of erotic pleasure. As Gabriella puts it, "One of the great rewards of my life has been the discovery that there is always a better lover than the last" (55).

This portion of *The Rules of Life* engages and subverts some of the earliest versions of "Little Red Riding Hood," especially the versions collected by Perrault in which the suggestion of seduction by the wolf was meant as a warning to gullible young girls. The color of the girl's red cape has thus been linked by some to the blood of forced sexual encounter. Weldon reverses the moral purpose of the tale and prepares for Gabriella's delight in her first sexual experience by recalling an episode from Gabriella's childhood. At a children's mass that she attends, the priest tells a parable about a party at a castle to which only those children were admitted who were dressed in spotless white. A little girl who stains her dress by eating blackberries (like Eve and the forbidden fruit) is excluded from the "endless bliss" of the castle, and the priest warns his young listeners not to "be like the little girl who in her wilfulness stained her purity" (24). At the age of five, Gabriella has already made up her mind on the issue of purity, especially because she senses that the priest, "with his little piggy eyes and his soft mouth," would like to get his "fat white hand" under her dress, and she deliberately spills ink on her white dress. If "purity" leads to the likes of the priest, "I [want] to be stained" (24).

In an even more sweeping way than *Female Friends* or *The Life and Loves of a She-Devil*, *The Rules of Life* turns on the concept of fiction itself, of which fairy tales are a part. In the futuristic world of this short novel, technology and skepticism hold sway, and the dominant ideology is the "Great New Fictional Religion." The fact that the deity of this religion, the "Great Screenwriter in the Sky," is known to have had "many a bad idea in his time" (13) prevents its adherents from taking much of anything at face value; the priest of this religion who serves as the primary narrator of the novel can foresee the advent of the *Revised Great New Fictional Religion*, which would hold the Great Screenwriter to higher standards than his current B-grade movie tendencies.

The most *un*virtuous Gabriella Sumpter has in fact practiced the only virtue possible for one with such a second-rate deity: she has, according to the narrator, followed the script the Screenwriter has written for her. "Virtue," he comments, "lies in consenting to the parts allotted to us, and . . . just as some can't help being victims others can't help being oppressors, and . . . the best we can do is to help the Great Plot of life go forward, with all its myriad, myriad subplots" (21). Life itself is thus a scripted fiction within which, as Gemma says in *Words of Advice*, "we all have to place ourselves as best we can." Gabriella has played the role of mistress to a succession of men; beginning as a potential beggar girl, she has risen to the role of princess, though never marrying the prince in question.

At the same time, however, Weldon provides ample evidence that Gabriella's story is a tale no more true than any fairy tale. Gabriella herself signals her own unreliability by referring to her story as "fiction" and warning the priest who transcribes her tape that there are no rules in fiction, thus granting herself the freedom of the storyteller. "I have," she remarks, "or had in my life, no particular appetite for truth" (17). Further, the priest several times doubts the accuracy of the tape recording, acknowledging that the "Technology of Truth" is "in its infancy, not its maturity" (16). Finally, the story of the dead is refuted by the living. Timothy Tovey, said by Gabriella to have been the most devoted of her lovers, denies to the priest having seen her in the twenty years before being summoned to her deathbed. "Did she tell you the truth?" Tovey inquires of the priest, and answers his own question: "I doubt it" (77). The closest Gabriella has come to royalty is to have lived, as Tovey's mistress, in a house "in the keeping of the Royal Family to dispose of as they want" (17).

Yet unlike Ruth, in *She-Devil*, who ends by inhabiting another woman's story, tower, and even her body, Gabriella is her own creation. In the tale she tells she is, unlike Red Riding Hood, unafraid of the wolf, and in the end she chooses the role of a Sleeping Beauty who does not wait for the kiss of a prince, but instead captivates the priest who transcribes her story, as if to prove her claim to the part of the irresistible princess.

There may be no rules in fiction, but there are rules in life, Gabriella Sumpter maintains as she distills the "valid rules" from her experience.

In a similar spirit of instruction, Gemma passes along "words of advice" in Weldon's novel with that phrase as its title. Like Gwyneth's aphorisms and Gabriella's rules, Gemma's "words" are suspect, arising as they do from the fairy tale that she inhabits as an antidote to reality. *Words of Advice* tells of three women—Gemma, Elsa, and Janice—who must extricate themselves from the mythologies on which they have patterned their behavior and expectations. Instead of palimpsestic images, as they are in *The Rules of Life*, fairy tales are in this novel used overtly as elements of the plot. Elsa tells fairy tales to her brothers and sisters and comes to see herself in terms of the tales; Gemma tells Elsa her own life as a fairy tale in order to save her from ignorance; and Janice awakens from her grim existence as the discarded wife. Transformations abound amid resonances of Rapunzel, Red Riding Hood, Rumpelstiltskin, and Sleeping Beauty.

Young Elsa, secretary to and mistress of Victor, Janice's estranged husband, is compounded of Red Riding Hood, Rapunzel, and the heroine of "Rumpelstiltskin," and narrowly escapes the fates of all three. Arriving at the home of Hamish and Gemma for the weekend, Elsa finds herself consigned to a high room, where she is expected to type inventories of the antiques that the wealthy Hamish will sell to Victor. No more able to type well than she is to spin straw into gold, Elsa is rescued by Hamish-as-Rumpelstiltskin in exchange for sexual favors; here, that is, Rumpelstiltskin not only demands the girl's first-born child, but intends to father it as well. Simultaneously, Elsa as Red Riding Hood is willingly pursued by Victor-as-wolf, a reference that Weldon confirms by several times echoing the language of the tale. Following their predinner lovemaking, for example, Victor prepares to leave Elsa, "*the better to* change for dinner" (9; emphasis added).

Elsa's youthful innocence is counterpointed to Gemma's cynicism. Whereas nineteen-year-old Elsa is vulnerable to the snares set for fairy-tale heroines, Gemma has willfully constructed her own history to resemble a fairy tale to replace the unglamorous truth that she has married the frog instead of the prince. Gemma recognizes in Elsa the naïveté of her own youthful self; what she does not recognize until the end of the novel is that she is just as ensnared in fiction as is Elsa. Early in the novel, Gemma signals their similarity when she says to Elsa, "I have a story to tell. It's a fairy tale. I love fairy tales, don't you?" When Elsa responds that she does, Gemma says, "I thought you would" (20). The tale Gemma then tells concerns the betrothal of Mr. Fox to Lady Mary, who, on the eve of their wedding, discovers Mr. Fox eating human flesh and carries home as evidence a finger with a ring on it. Her brothers kill Mr. Fox to save her from a horrible fate.

The tale is one that Gemma heard on the train on her way to London as a young girl, and she believes that the hearing of it predestined her to fall in love with a Mr. Fox. "Fairy tales," she tells Elsa, "are lived out daily" (21), and the story of her own life that she tells Elsa intermittently during the rest of the novel is as fabricated as the tale of Lady Mary and Mr. Fox that she heard on the radio—fabricated to explain her missing finger, her inability to walk, and the loss of her prince, Mr. Fox. Only at the end does Hamish tell the truth that frees both Gemma and Elsa: Mr. Fox, his business partner, was a homosexual; rather than being severed by Mr. Fox, Gemma's finger was caught in an elevator door and subsequently amputated; and the paralysis of Gemma's legs is emotional, induced by her realization that she has been betrayed by the prince and has married the frog. Stripped of her fairy tale, Gemma is able to walk and exhorts Elsa to run away from fairy tales: "Run, Elsa! Run for all you're worth. Don't fall. Please don't fall, the way I did. . . . You must run for me and all of us" (233).

Victor's wife, Janice, is in thrall to the more prosaic cultural mythology of the ideal wife, as defined by Victor. She is to be Snow White, the eternal virgin, "someone as pure and helpful as his own mother" (154). But the mask of wifely respectability she assumes according to his wishes hardens as it obscures her individuality. Finally, she has become a type rather than a person, as Weldon's narrator sarcastically notes:

> What we have here, ladies and gentlemen, is no woman, but a housewife. And what a housewife! Note her rigid, mousy curls, kept stiff by spray; her quick eyes, which search for dust and burning toast, and not the appraisal or enquiry of the opposite sex; the sharp voice, growing sharper, louder, year by year: at home in a bus queue or ordering groceries or rebuking the garbage, but hardly in the bed. Does that suit you, Victor?
> No.
> (154–155)

Bored by his own creation, Victor turns to Elsa, but he returns to Janice once she is rejuvenated by an affair with a Polish carpenter and her own daughter's involvement with an American student. The carpenter's wife laments the separation of women required by male fantasies—"I only wish women would stick together a bit" (160)—and Gemma echoes the same sentiment when she says, "If only . . . we women could learn from one another" (183).

Gemma's statement is both plaintive and ironic, reminding us that women in Weldon's fiction *do* learn from each other—sometimes the wrong things, such as Gwyneth's old wives' tales and Mary Fisher's romances, and sometimes the right things, the "words of advice" that cut through the bonds of myths and fairy tales. Weldon's critique of the power of the tale is by no means completely negative. To believe you are a princess when you are actually a beggar girl may be dangerous, to be sure, and some frogs, when kissed, remain frogs. But Weldon's use of fairy-tale plots and motifs is also a way of honoring that tradition, of honoring women as tellers of tales, and ultimately a way of recognizing the human desire for magic and transformation that created those tales in the first place.

Angela Carter has traced her own disruption of the fairy-tale tradition to the feminist movement of the late 1960s, when "it felt like Year One," and she felt encouraged to investigate "the social fictions that regulate our lives" (*On Gender and Writing*, 70). Carter rejects any authority that mythologies may derive from a sense that they exist timelessly outside of human agency. "I believe that all myths are products of the human mind and reflect only aspects of material human practice." If myths are created out of direct human experience, then they are subject to revision by human hands, and Carter continues by explaining what she means by asserting that she is "in the demythologising business":

> *I'm interested in myths—though I'm much more interested in folklore—just because they are extraordinary lies designed to make people unfree. (Whereas, in fact, folklore is a much more straightforward set of devices for making real life more exciting and is much easier to infiltrate with different kinds of consciousness.)*
> (70 – 71)

Carter distinguishes between myth and folklore in two senses. She sees myths as negative and confining, whereas folklore has the potential to

enliven ordinary existence. Further, she finds folklore (in which she includes fairy tales) easier to infuse with revisionist thinking. Myths, such
as the Garden of Eden story she addresses in *The Passion of New Eve*
(1977), tend to have a single shape, whereas fairy tales, as part of an oral
tradition, have "shifting structures" (71) that make them more perme-
able. Hence she speaks of *The Passion of New Eve* as an "anti-mythic
novel," and of having "relaxed into" the fairy tales she refashions in her
1979 collection, *The Bloody Chamber* (71). She suggests that myths are to
be resisted, whereas fairy tales may be manipulated; in *The Passion of New
Eve* she actually addresses both, but in *The Bloody Chamber* she is
squarely in the world of the traditional tales, particularly those collected
in France by Charles Perrault, which she translated for publication in
English in 1977. Writing particularly about Carter's "The Tiger's Bride,"
Sylvia Bryant comments on Carter's perception that such stories needed
to be "translated" in a different way as well:

> To tell a different story, to imagine and construct oth-
> erness as positive not negative difference, and to offer
> positive positionalities for identification within that
> otherness, to disrupt the ideological status quo enough
> to disturb the heretofore complacent acceptance it has
> met among readers and viewers; such is precisely the
> work of Carter's fairy-tale narratives.
> (452)

In her essay "Through the Looking Glass," Ellen Cronan Rose contrasts
the pessimism of Sexton's *Transformations* to the optimism of Carter's
The Bloody Chamber, noting that Carter's revisions of fairy tales show her
"sense of the possibilities for a woman's growth toward healthy adult
identity" (222). But the difference is more complex than optimism or
pessimism, having as it does to do with the way the two authors view
the tales and their susceptibility to revision. For Sexton the tales are fixed
as they were written down by the Brothers Grimm, as implacable as the
doll-like figures she makes of some of their heroines; her purpose in
Transformations is to expose this rigidity and its pernicious effect. Carter,
however, not only feels free to alter the plots of the tales, but also takes
the reader inside them, frequently by giving the narrative point of view
to the heroine rather than retaining the flat, distanced perspective of the
traditional versions. The women who are thus given storytelling agency

take on a complexity and a reality they lack as the stereotyped figures of parable. The result is to heighten both the humor and the horror inherent in the tales and to bring to the foreground the sexual elements that are latent in the versions passed down to us. In "Re-imagining the Fairy Tales: Angela Carter's Bloody Chambers," Patricia Duncker points out that "the sexual symbolism of the fairy tales may now appear to us ludicrous, transparent, but, to the child their meanings remain mysterious. Carter's rewriting of the tales is an exercise in making the mystery sexually explicit."[10]

The two tales that Carter gives the greatest prominence in *The Bloody Chamber* are "Beauty and the Beast" and "Little Red Riding Hood," both of which feature intimate encounters between human females and animals. The original tales convey messages about the efficacy of female nurturance and the vulnerability of female innocence, respectively; in Carter's revised versions, however, such tender qualities are eclipsed by mature self-realization. Her method of granting her heroines their own perspectives on the situations they find themselves in rather than merely being seen externally is both metaphorically and substantively a measure of this difference. The narrator-heroine of "The Tiger's Bride," for example, articulates her consciousness of the patriarchal constitution of women:

> *I was just a young girl, a virgin, and therefore men denied me rationality just as they denied it to all those who were not exactly like themselves, in all their unreason. . . . I could not see one single soul in that wilderness of desolation all around me . . . since all the best religions in the world state categorically that not beasts nor women were equipped with the flimsy, insubstantial things when the good Lord opened the gates of Eden and let Eve and her familiars tumble out.*
> (63)

The girl *in* the fairy tale thus speaks with knowledge that has heretofore been *outside* the tale.

"The Tiger's Bride" is the second version of "Beauty and the Beast" in *The Bloody Chamber*. In the first, "The Courtship of Mr. Lyon," the plot resembles that of the traditional version; the girl is obedient to her father and loyal to the Beast, whom she marries when he assumes human form. But Carter sets her tale in modern times, and her alternation between the high-blown language of traditional tales and the informality of everyday discourse undercuts the authority of the former. On first encountering the Beast, Beauty's father addresses him as would any London men's-club member—"My good fellow"—to which the Beast responds as if to remind him they are characters in a fairy tale, "I am no good fellow! I am the Beast" (44). Nor is Beauty a thoroughly passive young woman. As she prepares to acquiesce to paying her father's debt to the Beast, the narrator comments, "Do not think she had no will of her own" (45). Carter also distances Beauty from the world of the tale even as she spends her first night in the Beast's house. Left alone to eat the dinner that has mysteriously appeared, Beauty leafs through "a collection of courtly and elegant French fairy tales about white cats who were transformed princesses and fairies who were birds," but the book does not hold her attention: she "found herself yawning; she discovered she was bored" (46).

Such alterations are subtle and do not preclude the traditional ending of "The Courtship of Mr. Lyon"; Beauty marries the Beast-turned-man. "The Tiger's Bride," however, presents Beauty as a potential victim not of the Beast, but of the social construction of the female that dictates docility. Carter's story has affinities with Weldon's *The Rules of Life*, in that Beauty's father is an unsuccessful gambler who loses her to the Beast, and like Gabriella Sumpter, Beauty discovers sensual pleasure without marriage. As the Beast caresses Beauty at the end of the story, "each stroke of his tongue ripped off skin after successive skin, all the skins of a life in the world," and she returns to her natural animal state as, symbolically, her "earrings turned back to water" (67). As Ellen Cronan Rose points out, "Beauty has nothing to lose and everything to gain by stripping herself of her clothes and her socialized identity" (224). "The Tiger's Bride" also makes reference to other fairy tales, especially "Little Red Riding Hood." Just as that tale, in its Perrault version, was intended to frighten young girls into obedience, so Beauty's nurse has threatened her with tales of a tiger-man who, if she is not good, will "GOBBLE YOU UP!" (56).

The Red Riding Hood story receives three treatments in *The Bloody Chamber*, each of which asserts woman's sensual animal nature over a socially constructed femininity. Two of these stories, "The Werewolf" and "The Company of Wolves," are variants on the traditional tale;

the third, "Wolf-Alice," incorporates elements of "Snow White" and "Beauty and the Beast" as it presents a young girl raised by wolves who retains the instinctual nature of her foster family. In "The Werewolf" Carter suggests that, rather than merely wearing the grandmother's clothes, the wolf *is* the grandmother. After courageously confronting the wolf in the forest and cutting off its right paw, the young girl finds her grandmother in bed with her right hand severed. After the villagers stoned the wolf/woman, the girl settled into her grandmother's house and "prospered" (110). Precisely how she prospers is not told, but because the villagers have suspected the grandmother of being a witch, Carter suggests that her Red Riding Hood figure joins the company of myriad women who survived by practicing ancient arts.

For "The Company of Wolves," Carter reaches back beyond the Grimm and Perrault stories to model her tale on earlier versions that included elements of a seduction scene. In these versions, the girl is instructed to remove one article of clothing after another before the wolf eats her. Carter follows this plot to the point of the girl's nakedness, but then changes it to make her a partner in seduction. The girl unbuttons the collar of the wolf's shirt and "freely gave the kiss she owed him" from their wager in the woods. When her comment on his teeth elicits the standard response, "all the better to eat you with," she takes command of the situation: "The girl burst out laughing; she knew she was nobody's meat." The seduction, now mutual, proceeds, and at the end the girl is asleep "between the tender paws of the wolf" (118).

The Bloody Chamber concludes with "Wolf-Alice," which is based on no single tale but incorporates elements of several. Here the conflation of wolf and girl is nearly complete. Though she lives almost as a pet in the castle of an old duke, she has not abandoned the feral habits of her upbringing—"nothing about her is human except that she is *not* a wolf" (119). She enters puberty, menstruating with the full moon, but remains innocent of the snares of civilized life. Lacking Snow White's consciousness of feminine beauty, she does not recognize herself in the mirror, but thinks her reflection is a playmate. Even when she poses before the mirror in the Duke's grandmother's ball gowns, her pleasure has to do not with her appearance, but with the textures and smells of the garments. This animal unselfconsciousness also informs her relationship with the beast-duke. A werewolf, the Duke has no reflection in the mirror; he sleeps by day and hunts his prey by night, no longer human. When Wolf-Alice senses that the Duke has been wounded, she is drawn to his pain, and her ministrations restore him to human form, a process reflected in the mirror, where, "as if brought into being by her soft, moist, gentle tongue, finally [appeared] the face of the Duke" (126).

Wolf-Alice, in restoring the Duke's humanity, models her behavior on that of her "gaunt grey mother" (126); even across barriers of species, the mother-daughter bond remains strong. Carter emphasizes this bond also in the title story of *The Bloody Chamber*, which revises the Bluebeard tale. In traditional versions of this tale, the girl who disobediently unlocks the "bloody chamber" and discovers the mutilated bodies of other women is saved from a similar fate by her brothers. In Carter's version the heroine's mother, sensing her plight, arrives in time to shoot Bluebeard in the head. "You never saw such a wild thing as my mother," the narrator tells us, "her hat seized by the winds and blown out to sea so that her hair was her white mane" (39). Robin Ann Sheets, who is generally skeptical of Carter's success in reformulating the basic power relations of the tales, sees her creation of this mother figure an exception:

> *This is the mother who invests in her daughter's career rather than her price on the marriage market; and it is the mother's spirit, the courage incidentally of the Gothic heroines who pass unraped, unharmed down into the dungeons of the castle, which accompanies the daughter to learn the truth of the bloody chamber.*
> (355)

Nor is this the mother's first act of such bravery; in a passage that may remind us of the narrator's mother's youthful heroism in Maxine Hong Kingston's *The Woman Warrior*, the narrator of "The Bloody Chamber" tells us that "on her eighteenth birthday, my mother had disposed of a man-eating tiger that had ravaged the villages in the hills north of Hanoi" (40).

"The Bloody Chamber" does not conclude with the mother's heroic intervention; having revised the tale itself, Carter also exposes the dangerous romanticism of those who tell such tales to children as a means of instructing them. In an epilogue, the narrator tells us that her old nurse, who "had taken so much secret pleasure in the fact that her little girl had become a Marquise," has "passed away in a sorry state of disillusion" and that the young widow is "scarcely a penny richer," living with a piano tuner on the outskirts of Paris (40–41). Such a conclusion is not the

happily-ever-after of the fairy tale or of the stories in society magazines
that the nurse had read avidly.

4

Myth is a made thing, not a found thing.
ANGELA CARTER, *THE PASSION OF NEW EVE*

If, as Zipes and others have noted, fairy tales originally emerged not only
from the socioeconomic circumstances of the "folk" but simultaneously
from their "wish fulfilment and utopian projections" (*Breaking the Magic
Spell*, 6), it follows that in seeking to resist the tales' limiting formulations for women, female writers would in turn use the utopian form to
address the traditional stories. Conscious, in other words, of the tales'
continued power in the present, they imagine the future as the site of
alteration. That a change in a culture's relation to its mythologies might
not necessarily be positive, moreover, is reflected in the distinctively *dystopian* elements of such fictions as Atwood's *The Handmaid's Tale*, Weldon's *The Rules of Life*, and Carter's *The Passion of New Eve*.

Carter has described *The Passion of New Eve* as an "anti-mythic
novel . . . a feminist tract about the social creation of femininity, amongst
other things" (*On Gender and Writing*, 71). Her use of the term "tract" is
perhaps an unfortunate choice of words, because it seems to have led such
critics as Paulina Palmer to see the novel solely in terms of its ideological
thrust. Of the intertextuality of the novel, for example, Palmer accurately notes that it "advertise[s] the fictionality of the text," but she goes
on to state that *The Passion of New Eve* is "first and foremost a vehicle
for ideas" (19)—ideas that Palmer proceeds to analyze for their feminist
"correctness." Such an approach fails to take into account the richness
and complexity of Carter's plundering of the Western literary and mythic
tradition in order finally to suggest the extent to which modern human
beings live by fictions, façades, and tales.

Like *The Handmaid's Tale*, *The Passion of New Eve* is set in an indeter-
minate future in a United States torn apart by social decay and interne-
cine warfare, and the biblical allusions of both titles point to the fact that
religious ideology is at the heart of the conflict. Implicit in Carter's novel
is the concept of America as the "New Eden," a concept corrupted from
the beginning by a religious fanaticism that substituted usurpation and

near-genocide for the peace and harmony of the Garden. Her narrator
and central character, Evelyn, comes to America from England as previous generations of immigrants had, full of optimistic dreams that
are based on illusions. The novel's epigraph is a quotation from John
Locke—"In the beginning all the world was *America*"—and Evelyn has
derived his image of America from Hollywood films; "all manner of old
movies ran through my head when I first heard I'd got the job [in New
York]." He imagines "a clean, hard, bright city" peopled by "loquacious
cab-drivers, black but beaming chambermaids and a special kind of crisp-
edged girl with apple-crunching incisors" (10). Evelyn finds instead a
city filled with racial and gender conflict, and a country breaking apart
into warring factions.

Evelyn's adolescent fantasy has been a Hollywood actress named Tristessa de St. Ange, and it is around this figure that much of the fairy-tale
and Edenic imagery is clustered. Tristessa is both Sleeping Beauty and
Snow White. Preparing to leave London for New York, Evelyn, having
heard that Tristessa lives in secluded retirement in California, muses that
he "never imagined I might find her there, waiting for revivification, for
the kiss of a lover who would remove her from her perpetual reverie"
(8–9). When he does find Tristessa, she feigns death on a glass bier at the
top of a glass tower, recapitulating the role of the dying heroine she had
so often played on film. Lying amid wax effigies of film stars such as
James Dean, Jean Harlow, and Marilyn Monroe, Tristessa cheats death
by pretending death: "She had cheated the clock in her castle of purity,
her ice palace, her glass shrine. She was a sleeping beauty who could
never die since she had never lived" (119).

Tristessa has "never lived" in the sense that she has always played roles
under an assumed name. Carter inverts completely the image of the
fairy-tale virgin princess in the tower, for Tristessa is a female imper-
sonator, whose "ineradicable . . . maleness" had caused a plastic surgeon
to refuse to perform a sex-change operation, and who ultimately im-
pregnates Evelyn—now Eve—whose own forced sex-change has been a
success. Radical transformations, as in Weldon's *The Life and Loves of
a She-Devil*, are accomplished by technology rather than by magic, but
nothing is what it appears to be—or, put another way, everything *is*
appearance, façade, illusion.

It should not be surprising, then, that one of the most consistent images in *The Passion of New Eve* is the mirror. Like the Queen in "Snow
White," Carter's female characters peer into mirrors to see how they
appear to others—to judge how they will be judged by a world that

has set the standards for the "fairest of them all." But Carter's use of mirrors extends the fairy-tale image into a world of artifice and deception. Snow White's stepmother inquires of the mirror how *she* looks, whereas Carter's characters consult mirrors to assess how they have *created* themselves—by means of makeup, costumes, or plastic surgery. It is not themselves at which they gaze, but instead a version or mask of themselves. Further, several of these mirrors are cracked, so that the image they return is distorted, making the goal of self-assessment itself illusory.[11]

The first of the mirror-gazing women is Leilah, the black prostitute with whom Evelyn (not yet Eve) lives in New York. In preparing herself for her customers, Leilah transforms herself into a different person; the process is patently not natural, but artifice:

> *Unlike a flower, she did not grow beautiful by a simple process of becoming. Her beauty was an accession. She arrived at it by conscious effort. She became absorbed in the contemplation of the figure in the mirror but she did not seem to me to apprehend the person in the mirror as, in any degree, herself. The reflected Leilah had a concrete form and, although this form was perfectly tangible, we all knew, all three of us in the room, it was another Leilah. Leilah invoked this formal other with a gravity and ritual that recalled witchcraft; she brought into being a Leilah who lived only in the not-world of the mirror and then became her own reflection.*
> (28)

The Leilah who has the magic power to create an alternate self and then to become that self ironically erases herself, becoming a nonbeing in the "not-world" of the mirror. Yet in a further ironic meditation on "Snow White," Carter allows Leilah a triumph not available to the Queen in the tale. The Queen is passive, the victim of time, which robs her of her beauty while enhancing that of Snow White. In Shuli Barzilai's persuasive reading of the traditional tale, the Queen's abortive attempts to kill Snow White constitute an unsuccessful attempt to "recapture the sense of totality, albeit of an imaginary order, which the birth of her daughter had extended and enriched" (529–530). But by growing up, becoming her own person, Snow White ceases to be an extension of her mother, so that, Barzilai posits, "something is taken from [the Queen], a vital part of her is cut off. . . . The mirror reflects disintegration without any possibility of regeneration" (530). But Carter's Leilah regenerates her alternate self again and again: "Regular as clockwork, once a night she witched me, night after night" (29). Moreover, in the Edenic plot of the novel, Leilah is revealed to be Lilith, Adam's first wife, who says of herself, "I am ageless, I will outlive the rocks" (174).

Tristessa, whose onscreen role-playing has obscured his/her far more fundamental masking of man as woman, testifies to the power of mirrors to create images when, late in the novel, he tells Evelyn (now Eve) of being possessed by the image of the woman he would pretend to be:

> *Tristessa is a lost soul who lodges in me; she's lived*
> *in me so long I can't remember a time she was not*
> *there, she came and took possession of my mirror one*
> *day when I was looking at myself. She invaded the*
> *mirror like an army with banners; she entered me*
> *through my eyes.*
> (151)

Tristessa's possession by his female persona is thus made to seem as much outside his own agency as is the Queen's aging. Evelyn/Eve's transformation from male to female is similarly beyond his control and results, finally, in a loss of identity rendered symbolically by an inability to see his/her mirror image. The group of women, led by the imposing "Mother," who have subjected Evelyn to sex-change surgery have created Eve's physical form from a distillation of reflected images: "a team of women had worked on my new shape according to a blueprint taken from a concensus [sic] agreement on the physical nature of an ideal woman drawn up from a protracted study of the media" (78). The physical appearance of "the fairest of them all," drawn from the "media," is the mirror reflection of cultural desires. Eve's behavior as a woman is as much an artifice as her appearance; she must constantly guard against any gesture that would be regarded as masculine. But Carter suggests that appropriately "feminine" behavior is merely an act that many women strive to perfect, as Eve muses, "although I was a woman, I was now also passing for a woman, but, then, many women born spend their lives in just such imitations" (101). The combination of physical and behavioral artifice finally removes from Eve any recognition by the mirror. Groping through a cave in search of the Mother who has created her, the naked Eve encounters her nonexistence: "There was a mirror propped against the rugged wall, a fine mirror in a curly, gilt frame; but the glass was broken, cracked right across many times so it reflected nothing, was a bewilderment of splinters and I could not see myself nor any portion of myself in it" (181). Eve's mirror disintegration signals the end of Edenic possibilities, and Eve leaves America in a flimsy boat, doomed to dream of Tristessa and tell her tale.

Near the end of "Feminism and Fairy Tales," Karen E. Rowe asks, "do we have the courageous vision and energy to cultivate a newly fertile ground of psychic and cultural experience from which will grow fairy tales for human beings of the future?" (253–254). The first step in answering that question is to engage, as Carter, Weldon, Sexton, and others have done, the fairy tales of the tradition we have inherited, and to understand the sources of their power. One result of such engagement is the creation of stories that simultaneously expose the fictive nature of all such tales and refuse to obey their authority by revising and appropriating them. In Gilbert and Gubar's reading of "Snow White," it is the unruly Queen who claims the ability to "plot" Snow White's story; in the work of modern feminist writers, however, the mirror of the tale must be both examined and broken.

PART
TWO

*Reaching past
the "New Eden"*

Three

RESISTING AMERICAN MYTHOLOGIES: INDIVIDUALISM & SENTIMENT

1

Let it not be for a moment supposed that we are about to attempt a crusade in defence of the bluestockings! Better undertake, single-handed, to lay a Trail to the Pacific, tunneling the Rocky Mountains. Whether the prejudice entertained against this class—is it numerous enough to claim the title of a class?—be just or not, it is most potent; and, like the deaf adder, it stoppeth its ears. We hardly know of one more obstinate, unless it be that against old maids,—or that other, perhaps worse one, against stepmothers.

CAROLINE KIRKLAND, "LITERARY WOMEN"

Charming woman! feminine from her shoe-lacings to the tips of her eyebrows; no bluestockings peeping from under the graceful folds of her silken robe. What a charmed life a man might lead with her! Her fingers never dabbled with ink, thank Heaven!

FANNY FERN, *FERN LEAVES*

The speaker in Fanny Fern's sketch "A Chapter on Literary Women," published in her 1853 collection *Fern Leaves from Fanny's Port-Folio*, is one Colonel Van Zandt, who has a "perfect horror" of literary women, or "bluestockings," as they were called. The colonel discovers only after his marriage that his wife is a writer, but by this point she has proven to have priorities that allow him to be reconciled to this fact, and he is moved to declare that "a woman may be literary, and yet feminine and lovable; content to find her greatest happiness in the charmed circle of Home" (179).

The fact that both Caroline Kirkland and Fanny Fern (pseudonym of Sara Willis Parton) made satiric use of the prejudice against the "bluestocking" reveals both their irritation at negative images of "literary women" and a certain security in their roles as women writers. By the early 1850s, both women enjoyed considerable success as authors—and not, like most of their female contemporaries, primarily as novelists, but as journalists and social commentators. Kirkland, born in 1801, had first come to public attention with her 1839 book *A New Home, Who'll Follow? Or, Glimpses of Western Life*, an account of settlement in frontier Michigan based on her experiences as a settler there earlier in the decade. By 1850, when she wrote "Literary Women," she had written two more books on life in what was then the American West and had become editor of *Sartain's* magazine and a contributor of articles to this periodical and to *Putnam's*.

Fanny Fern, born in 1811, was in 1853 at the beginning of an illustrious career as a newspaper columnist and novelist. The next year she published her highly controversial novel *Ruth Hall*, and in 1855 she signed a contract to write a weekly column for the *New York Ledger* that made her the highest-paid columnist in the country. During the decade of the 1850s, each author had three volumes of columns and articles published and enthusiastically received by readers.

Despite such success, the appellation "bluestocking" could—and did—sting. Its use began a hundred years earlier in England to refer to groups of upper-class women who conducted literary salons in their homes to encourage each other in intellectual pursuits—including writing. The term linked women with the life of the mind, but, because they were careful to conduct themselves as "ladies," the term was not necessarily pejorative. Indeed, according to Janet Todd, in *The Sign of Angelica*, "accepting much of the ideology of womanhood and impeccably chaste in their private lives, these ladies could encourage considerable intellectual activity in women without disturbing the hierarchies of gender and class" (123–124).[1]

By the middle of the nineteenth century, however, the intellectual or "literary" woman—especially one who wrote for publication—was viewed in many quarters as disturbing, unnatural, and a usurper of male prerogative. Literary involvement was popularly believed to adversely affect a woman's appearance and manner, as is illustrated in the image that Kirkland presents in order to debunk it: "inky fingers—corrugated brows—unkempt locks—unrighteous stockings—towering talk—disdain of dinner—aspirations after garments symbolic of authority" (195). And that the bluestocking was perceived as a threat to the male ego is articulated by Fern's Colonel Van Zandt, who expresses his desire for a wife with "the capacity to appreciate me, but not brilliancy enough to outshine me" (*Fern Leaves*, 176).[2]

Although there is no evidence that Caroline Kirkland and Fanny Fern (who was primarily known by her pseudonym to her friends and even to her third husband, James Parton) ever met,[3] there are remarkable parallels between their lives and careers. Both became widows while they still had children to support. Sara Willis's first husband, Charles Eldredge, died of typhoid fever in 1846, leaving her with two young daughters; in the same year, William Kirkland drowned, leaving Caroline with five children, the oldest of whom was eighteen. Although Caroline Kirkland had been a published author for several years prior to her husband's death, economic necessity caused her to regard her writing and her various editorial posts as a profession rather than a pastime. Similarly, the death of Charles Eldredge gave birth to Fanny Fern, as Sara settled on writing as the means of support for her family. As writers, both women faced adverse reactions to their first book-length works, and for somewhat similar reasons. Sara Willis hoped that her pseudonym "Fanny Fern" would conceal her identity as the author of *Ruth Hall*, but when a spurious "biography" identified her as the novel's author, reviewers castigated her for portraying satirically her father and brother; to thus depict members of her own family was considered a serious breach of feminine behavior. Kirkland's *A New Home* was warmly praised by reviewers, but her former Michigan neighbors quickly penetrated her authorial disguise of "Mrs. Mary Clavers" and were outraged by her less-than-flattering depictions of them. Public reaction seems to have had an effect on the two authors' subsequent careers. In her next books about frontier life—*Forest Life* (1842) and *Western Clearings* (1845)—Kirkland muted her social criticism, and Fanny Fern's second novel, *Rose Clark* (1856), lacks much of the biting commentary on social institutions that characterizes *Ruth Hall*.[4]

Neither Kirkland nor Fern, however, ceased to write with conviction about issues that concerned her, and their concerns are strikingly similar. Both responded to an increasingly materialistic and status-conscious culture by denouncing avarice and pretension. One of Kirkland's central concerns in *A New Home* is the greed of land speculators, who seemed to feel no compunction about defrauding the unsuspecting investor or settler into purchasing a piece of worthless property; Fanny Fern again and again took to task those she termed the "fashionables," who were more interested in their finery than in the proper upbringing of their children. Both writers visited prisons and wrote about the deplorable conditions they found there, and both advocated clothing reform for women, accurately perceiving tightly laced corsets as a threat to women's health—though neither went so far as to wear the famous "bloomers" advocated by some reformers. In addition, both women were staunchly in favor of the abolition of slavery, although Kirkland was more directly and frequently outspoken on this issue. Fern and Kirkland were, of course, not unique in espousing such causes and opinions at the time, but as women speaking publicly on issues of public rather than domestic concern, they risked being considered "unwomanly" by some.

And yet the "separate spheres" ideology that so infused nineteenth-century discourse about education, politics, and social reform must be seen for what it is—an ideology rather than a description of reality, a rhetorical strategy instead of a map of social behavior. Even as the disheveled, somewhat masculinized figure of the "bluestocking" joined (as Kirkland noted) other negative female stereotypes such as the old maid and the stepmother, women were firmly part of nineteenth-century literary culture, despite frequently articulated assumptions about their lack of intellectual capacity and their supposed affinity for the intuitive and spiritual rather than the rational. Indeed, from the perspective of the late twentieth century, it is possible to perceive a double overlay that has obscured the role of women as writers during this period. One overlay is the public rhetoric that denigrated women's intellectual ability and marked out for their agency the arenas of the maternal and the moral, as a way of preserving a power structure that endorsed white male dominance. The very frequency of such pronouncements and prescriptions—in sermons and book reviews, in conduct books and popular iconography—in fact suggests that the values and behaviors they advocated were far from a uniform status quo. A continued reiteration, in other words, of the parameters of woman's "proper role" suggests strongly that this ideal was under constant threat of disobedience of various kinds.

The second overlay is the tendency of twentieth-century literary criticism and literary history to behave as though the ideology had been, in fact, reality. That is, by adopting and promulgating the notion that women and people of color played only a minor and insignificant role in the creation of literature and the molding of public taste and opinion, scholars have constructed a tradition that relegates women to the position of sentimental scribblers. According to this version of literary history, Lydia Maria Child, for example, could be admitted as the author of manuals on housekeeping and the care of the sick, but not of novels dealing with interracial marriage, such as *Hobomok*, and Harriet Beecher Stowe could be commended for taking the moral high ground in *Uncle Tom's Cabin* while at the same time excluded from the literary canon for having employed the "subliterary" devices of melodrama.

In *Canons and Contexts*, Paul Lauter traces the origin of such a version of literary tradition to the 1920s, when a generation of scholars who had been receptive to the contributions of women and, to a lesser degree, of African Americans, was supplanted by a generation who found the supposed "gentility" of women's texts and the folk traditions of black Americans antithetical to their aesthetic standards. The reasons for the change in evaluation of literary texts were, according to Lauter, "the professionalization of the teaching of literature, the development of an aesthetic theory that privileged certain texts, and the historiographic organization of the body of literature into conventional 'periods' and 'themes'" (27). Judith Fetterley, in her introduction to *Provisions: A Reader from 19th-Century American Women*, pushes the timing of the shift from an inclusive to an exclusive roster of America's "great" writers back into the late nineteenth century, noting that an 1891 anthology of "Masterpieces of American Literature" included no women writers (19–20). In fact, Fetterley notes that she finds it "difficult to imagine a time in the history of American literature when the phrase 'the man of letters' did not mean just that" (19), even though earlier lists of American "greats" had included writers such as Fanny Fern, Lydia Sigourney, Caroline Kirkland, and Margaret Fuller.

But even if the phrase "woman of letters" has an odd ring to those schooled in nineteenth-century American literature as seen by twentieth-century literary history, the fact remains that the "bluestocking" epithet was a response to the success, not the failure, of women writers, and to the threat which that success posed, as revealed in Kirkland's reference to their "aspirations after garments symbolic of authority." Authors such as Kirkland and Fern can be seen as doubly disobedient, then: once by claiming the authority to resist the ideologies of (male) frontier individualism and (female) submission and sentiment; and a second time by disrupting the scholarly formulations that for more than a century denied their significance to literary history.

2

*I little thought of becoming an author before I lived in
the wilderness—there, the strange things I saw and
heard every day prompted me to description, for they
always presented themselves to me under a humorous
aspect.*

CAROLINE KIRKLAND, *A NEW HOME*

A dozen years after the publication of *A New Home, Who'll Follow?*,
Caroline Kirkland identified amusement as the impetus for her first
book. Like many other women who accompanied their husbands to the
American frontier during the nineteenth century, Kirkland wrote long
letters to her friends and family in the East, and when, with their encouragement, she decided to set down her experiences in book form, it
seems doubtful that she did so with any particular trepidation about en-
croaching on male turf in writing about frontier life. She had been un-
usually well educated for a woman of her era, and by the time of the
move to Michigan in 1837 she had worked as a schoolteacher and, with
her husband, had headed the Detroit Female Seminary for two years.
The Kirklands' marriage seems to have been a remarkably egalitarian one
for the period; following the couple's move back to New York in 1843,
Caroline—who by this time had five children—wrote for the New York
Mirror, of which her husband was an editor.

A New Home, written "under the assured belief that the author would
never be discovered" (Kirkland, *A New Home*, xvii), has a tone of confidence and witty self-assurance. Kirkland displays her "bluestocking"
credentials, adorning her chapters with epigraphs and other quotations
from Shakespeare, Pope, Milton, Spenser, La Rochefoucauld, and a host
of other writers whose world of letters she did not hesitate to enter, albeit
as "Mary Clavers"—a pseudonym that seems to have been more a device
to protect her identity from her Michigan neighbors (as she, in turn,
changed *their* names) than an attempt at self-effacement. In fact, she announces early on her intention to provide a revised version of life on the
frontier, a version that will be in several ways a corrective to the various
narratives that presented the West as a land of rich, easy opportunity, as
a rugged testing ground for individual assertion, and above all as a place
for men: as entrepreneurs, as artisans, as city builders, and as Indian
fighters. Kirkland's amusement springs primarily from her perception—
as a woman and as a realist—of the disparity between the picture of the

frontier presented by the glowing advertisements of land speculators, the accounts of male travelers such as Charles Fenno Hoffman and James Hall (whom she names in her text), and the emerging frontier fiction whose most notable exponent was James Fenimore Cooper, and her own experience. A close reading of the text, however, reveals that Kirkland was acutely conscious of writing as a woman who could not lay full claim to the status of historian.

The epigraphs that begin *A New Home*—quotations from Shakespeare's *A Midsummer Night's Dream* and Sidney's *Arcadia*—signal the fact that Kirkland will be dealing with utopian visions, of which America, and especially the American West, was a powerful one. Against this visionary backdrop, as Kirkland announces in her preface, she wishes to set her realistic account of frontier life, an account that she claims is "very nearly—a veritable history; an unimpeachable transcript of reality; a rough picture, in detached parts, but pentagraphed from the life" (1). Although her record is not a journal "entire and unaltered," she nonetheless asks that her readers have faith in the accuracy of depictions that might strike them as fanciful creations:

> *I would desire the courteous reader to bear in mind . . .*
> *that whatever is quite unnatural, or absolutely incred-*
> *ible, in the few incidents which diversify the follow-*
> *ing pages, is to be received as literally true. It is only*
> *in the most commonplace parts (if there be compari-*
> *sons) that I have any leasing-making to answer for.*
> (1)

Just how Kirkland would have distinguished between the "unnatural" and the "incredible," on the one hand, and the "commonplace," on the other, is not clear, but two things *are* clear early on in her narrative. One is that hers will be no tale of heroic exploits or individualistic survival; she announces in a rather tongue-in-cheek manner on the first page that she has at her disposal "but meagre materials for anything which might be called a story. I have never seen a cougar—nor been bitten by a rattlesnake" (3).[5] Kirkland thus differentiates her story from those that emphasize the dangers to be confronted on the frontier. But she is even more eager to distinguish her account of frontier settlement from those that tout the idyllic nature of western life, for it is those that have set up expectations that her own experience has exposed as dangerously misleading:

> *When I first "penetrated the interior" (to use an in-*
> *digenous phrase), all I knew of the wilds was from*
> *Hoffman's tour or Captain Hall's "graphic" delinea-*
> *tions: I had some floating idea of "driving a barouche-*
> *and-four anywhere through the oak-openings"—and*
> *seeing "the murdered Banquos of the forest" haunting*
> *the scenes of their departed strength and beauty. But I*
> *confess, these pictures, touched by the glowing pencil*
> *of fancy, gave me but incorrect notions of a real jour-*
> *ney through Michigan.*
> (6)

A "real" journey through Michigan, Kirkland discovers, involves having her carriage stuck in a marsh and enduring cramped, uncomfortable lodgings along the way—the very opposite of the welcoming vistas that previous writers had led her to expect.

The second characteristic of *A New Home* that becomes obvious early in the narrative is that Kirkland is dealing specifically with *women's* experience of the frontier. On the first night of their sixty-mile journey from Detroit to the fledgling town of Pinckney (renamed "Montacute" in *A New Home*), she and her husband stay at a "wretched inn" in the woods that is presided over by a drunken, abusive man "whose wife and children were in constant fear of their lives from his insane fury." Kirkland's narrator feels deep sympathy for the man's wife, who tells of "her change of lot—from a well-stored and comfortable home in Connecticut to this wretched den in the wilderness" (7). Nor does the woman's story have a happy ending: Mary Clavers learns later that the husband has been put in jail for stabbing a neighbor. He dies there of alcoholism, leaving his family with no means of support. Like many other women writers of her day, Kirkland saw the abuse of alcohol as a common cause of the poverty of women and children, and the nameless woman at the inn is just one of several victims of such abuse that she describes in *A New Home*. "So much," she writes sarcastically at this point, "for turning our fields of golden grain into 'fire water'—a branch of business in which Michigan is fast improving" (7).

Kirkland's attention to the physical details of the environment in which the Michigan settlers live is part of her domestic reformulation of the frontier saga, and, as Lori Merish suggests, it also contributed to an ideal of "pious consumption," which gained force in the antebellum period. According to this viewpoint, "refined domestic artifacts would civilize and socialize persons and awaken higher sentiments" (487). The "wretched inn" is devoid of such uplifting adornments, which many believed could have positively affected the moral and spiritual lives of its inhabitants. In a manner that seems paradoxical today, in the wake of more than a hundred years of rampant materialism, domestic consumption was linked with progress toward religious piety. Merish argues convincingly that *A New Home*, in its concern with the interior spaces of Montacute and environs, participates in furthering this ideology: "As a self-consciously feminine alternative to previous traditions of frontier literature, Kirkland's text registers in detailed form the role of women and material refinement in the civilizing process and illuminates the ideological underpinnings of American consumer culture" (491–492).

In turning from the private form of letters to family and friends to the public form of a published account of her frontier experience, Kirkland was acutely conscious of addressing her readers *as a woman*. At numerous points in the text, she calls attention to the fact that her perspective is different from the one that readers have come to expect. Reflecting on the time that she and her family spent living in a small log home, she comments that her "floating visions of a home in the woods were full of important omissions" (49). Annette Kolodny, in *The Land before Her*, refers to Kirkland's "abiding perception that the 'important omissions' weighed most heavily on women" (133). Rectifying such omissions is no small part of Kirkland's intention in *A New Home*, and she accomplishes this intention both through her authorial voice and in the content of her narrative.

Kirkland repeatedly has her narrator, Mary Clavers, issue mock apologies for the nonlinear, "feminine" quality of her narrative. At the end of chapter 19, she accuses herself of "sermonizing" and "beg[s] pardon [to] resume my broken thread" (78). Just two pages later she informs us, "I certainly can make long digressions, if nothing else. Here I am wandering like another Eve from my dearly beloved garden" (80), and at the beginning of the next chapter she equates her style to the supposedly female penchant for gossip and wordiness:

> *I know this rambling gossiping style, this going back*
> *to take up dropped stitches, is not the orthodox way*
> *of telling one's story; and if I thought I could do any*
> *better, I would certainly go back and begin at the very*

> *beginning; but I feel conscious that the truly feminine*
> *sin of talking "about it and about it," the unconquer-*
> *able partiality for wandering wordiness would cleave*
> *to me still; so I proceed in despair of improvement.*
> (82)

Near the end of *A New Home*, Kirkland's narrator speaks of her "attempt to write one long coherent letter about Montacute," but declares that "history is not my forte," and thus she will "lower [her] ambition to the collection of scattered materials for the use of the future compiler of Montacutian annals" (177).

Yet rather than an admission of failure, Kirkland's comments should be read as an invitation to discern her revisionary method, as a passage a few pages later makes clear. Pretending to lament the fact that Montacute is a rather ordinary village, in which "not a single event has occurred which would have been deemed worthy of record by any one but a midge-fancier like myself," she proceeds to quote the language of promotional tracts and political rhetoric that glorified the frontier in particularly masculine terms: "'prodigious undertaking!' 'brilliant success!' 'splendid fortune!' 'race of enterprise!' 'march of improvement!'" (187). What Kirkland's "apologies" point to is that she is writing a radically different kind of frontier narrative: one that brings women's experience to the center rather than continuing to leave it as an "omission," and that reveals the reality behind these lofty phrases.

Kirkland's observations of women in frontier Michigan led her to some acute perceptions of why the pioneering enterprise was more eagerly embraced by men than by women. In chapter 36 of *A New Home* she explains why the accommodation to a more primitive and rugged way of life weighed unequally on the sexes. For men, she observes, very little may actually have changed with the move west:

> *The husband goes to his work with the same axe or*
> *hoe which fitted his hand in his old woods and fields,*
> *he tills the same soil, or perhaps a far richer and more*
> *hopeful one—he gazes on the same book of nature*
> *which he has read from his infancy, and sees only a*
> *fresher and more glowing page; and he returns to his*
> *home with the sun, strong in heart and full of self-*
> *gratulation on the favourable change in his lot. . . .*

> *What does he want with the great old cushioned rock-*
> *ing chair? When he is tired, he goes to bed, for he is*
> *never tired until bed-time.*
> (146)

But when this representative man returns home, he finds "the homebird drooping and disconsolate":

> She *has been looking in vain for the reflection of any*
> *of the cherished features of her own dear fire-side. She*
> *has found a thousand deficiencies which her rougher*
> *mate can scarce be taught to feel as evils. . . . Women*
> *are the grumblers in Michigan, and they have some*
> *apology. Many of them have made sacrifices for*
> *which they were not at all prepared, and which de-*
> *tract largely from their every day stores of comfort.*
> (146 – 147)

What may have been considered necessities back East, such as the "cush-ioned rocking chair" and certain cooking utensils, have been sacrificed to the exigencies of the journey and the cramped conditions of the log cabin, so that cooking, cleaning, child rearing, and the care of the sick must be accomplished without the accoutrements of a more settled way of life. Mary Clavers is sensitive to this transition, having experienced it herself. As she remarks early in her narrative, "My ideas of comfort were by this time narrowed down to a well-swept room with a bed in one corner, and cooking-apparatus in another—and this in some fourteen days from the city!" (44).

Another gender difference that Kirkland notes in life in the developing West goes directly to the heart of her critique of frontier individualism: the ways in which men and women regard new settlers. Recalling her first meeting with the newly arrived Mrs. Rivers, Mary Clavers com-ments, "In this newly-formed world, the earlier settler has a feeling of hostess-ship toward the new comer." But she continues abruptly, "I speak only of women—men look upon each one, newly arrived, merely as an additional business-automaton—a somebody more with whom to try the race of enterprize, i.e. money-making" (64). For women, then, new settlers promise companionship; for men, they are potential custom-ers or competitors. The value of Mrs. Rivers for Mary Clavers lies partly in shared intellectual interests—she is "fond of novels and poetry"—but mainly in the prospect of having someone to ease the isolation of rural life. As Mary Clavers remarks with pleasure, "I had a neighbor" (64).

Indeed, in contrast to most of the men in Kirkland's account, who scramble for status through land acquisition, political power, or the "race of enterprize," the women depend on one another in a communitarian bond that works against class differences. As Sandra Zagarell points out in her introduction to the 1990 edition of *A New Home*, one of the distinguishing features of Kirkland's book is its delineation of the process of community formation. The area of Michigan where the town of Pinckney was emerging was already home to "highly individualistic farmers and woodsmen who, with little formal education but considerable determination, formed the backbone of Jacksonian democracy" (xxviii), whereas the settlers who arrived from the East in the 1830s brought middle-class educations and tastes with them. "For Kirkland," Zagarell writes, "the 'West' is a site where a culture must be created from these heterogeneous and often conflicting groups, and *A New Home* traces the process of their slow and usually testy mutual accommodation" (Kirkland, *A New Home*, xxix). For the women in particular, such "accommodation" was necessary for survival, as Mary Clavers discovers early on when her family succumbs to the "ague": "My neighbors showed but little sympathy on the occasion. They had imbibed the idea that we held ourselves above them, and chose to take it for granted that we did not need their aid" (61).

In Kirkland's often comic chapter on the frontier custom of perpetual borrowing of household objects and farm animals (chapter 18), her narrator is somewhat exasperated by the fact that "not only are all kitchen utensils as much your neighbours as your own, but bedsteads, beds, blankets, sheets, travel from house to house" (67); however, she understands the necessity of such sharing on a practical level. Moreover, she understands that to refuse such cooperation on the grounds of class difference can have dire consequences:

> *What can be more absurd than a feeling of proud distinction, where a stray spark of fire, a sudden illness, or a day's contre-temps, may throw you entirely upon the kindness of your humblest neighbor? If I treat Mrs. Timson with neglect to-day can I with any face borrow her broom to-morrow? and what would be-*

> *come of me, if in revenge for my declining her invita-*
> *tion to tea this afternoon, she should decline coming to*
> *do my washing on Monday?*
> (65)

It is in the everyday, domestic, gendered experience of homemaking that
Kirkland challenges the narrative of frontier individualism. As Maureen
St. Laurent writes:

> *In this radical condition of equality, Kirkland discov-*
> *ers a damaging myth at the heart of the American*
> *ideologies of freedom and equality. Real equality,*
> *Kirkland learns, does not result in a situation and*
> *celebration of radical individualism. Rather, the*
> *equality of Montacute society yields a radical interde-*
> *pendence of all members of the community. Far from*
> *being the space of frontier fantasies of individual mas-*
> *culine heroism and endeavor, Kirkland perceives the*
> *frontier as a condition where isolated individualism is*
> *destructive of both the person and the community.*
> (160)

When individualism becomes translated into unfettered freedom and
even lawlessness, its effects are pernicious, leading to behavior ranging
from alcohol abuse (and the consequent destitution of women and children) to fraud. Like others in *A New Home*, Mary Clavers and her husband are the victims of a dishonest land speculator, Mr. Mazard, and
the husband of Mrs. Clavers's friend Mrs. Rivers is ultimately caught
running the bank in nearby Tinkerville with bogus capital. Such fraudu-
lent schemes not only injure individuals, they also threaten the egalitarian tendencies of frontier communities. Kirkland's narrator imagines
the natural reaction of settlers trying to buy flour with unsecured, worthless paper money: "Can we blame them if they cursed in their agony,
the soul-less wretches who had thus drained their best blood for the
furtherance of their own schemes of low ambition? Can we wonder
that the poor, feeling such wrongs as this, learn to hate the rich, and to
fancy them natural enemies?" (126). Domestic consumption, in the form
of decent furniture, eating utensils, and decorative objects, could have
moral and even spiritual benefits, but the "business" of settling the fron-

tier demonstrated humankind at its worst. As Joanne Dobson notes, "This wilderness is not so much being conquered as it is being contaminated and exploited by an unbridled and unscrupulous commercialism" (173).

The myth that the American frontier offers limitless personal freedom not only misleads those who move from the eastern United States, but crosses the Atlantic in a particularly distorted form, Kirkland believes. True democracy consists, she contends, in cooperation and mutual respect rather than in individual enterprise—a concept not understood by some of the English emigrants she observes in Michigan:

> *The better classes of English settlers seem to have left their own country with high-wrought notions of the unbounded freedom to be enjoyed in this; and it is with feelings of angry surprise that they learn after a short residence here, that this very universal freedom abridges their own liberty to do as they please in their individual capacity; that the absolute democracy which prevails in country places, imposes as heavy restraints upon one's free-will in some particulars, as do the over-bearing pride and haughty distinctions of the old world in others; and after one has changed one's whole plan of life, and crossed the wide ocean to find a Utopia, the waking to reality is attended with feelings of no slight bitterness.*
> (139 – 140)

Utopian notions of "unbounded freedom" must perish, Kirkland perceives, in a wilderness culture in which absolute self-sufficiency is a myth, and in which rights entail responsibilities to the rights of others. One of Kirkland's chief correctives to the myth of the frontier is her depiction of those whom it disappoints either because the supposed "freedom" is illusory or because some have interpreted freedom as the right to dispense with moral scruples and make others their victims. The latter primarily take the form of land speculators who entice settlers with "advertisements, choicely worded and carefully vague, never setting forth any thing which might not come true at some time or other; yet leaving the buyer without excuse if he chose to be taken in" (31). Freedom from the restraints present in more settled areas may permit the fruition of individual aspirations, but it also permits fraud and dashed hopes for the "poor artizan, the journeyman mechanic, the stranger who had brought his little all to buy government land to bring up his young family on"—all of whom may discover that the land they seek is "at that moment a foot under water" (31).

Such sympathy for the underdog, and Kirkland's insistence on egalitarian give-and-take in the process of community formation are, however, perspectives that Mary Clavers—and, one assumes, Caroline Kirkland herself—must learn as time goes on, not perspectives she brings with her from New York or even the newer Detroit. In other words, it is her own process of accommodation to the necessities of "western life" that gives rise to both her analysis of community building and her admonitions to those who would follow her. As Zagarell puts it, "the formation of Montacute thus occurs within Clavers as well as around her: her developing capacity to accommodate westerners as well as easterners constitutes one dimension of the community's development" (Kirkland, *A New Home*, xxix). The very fact that Mary Clavers must remind herself to be cordial to "Mrs. Timson" lest she be unable to rely on her services suggests that Mrs. Timson is not a social equal whom she would readily seek out, and her initial reaction to Montacute is clearly that of the educated easterner for whom the habits, speech, and living conditions of the "indigenous" people are the object of amusement, discomfort, or scorn. The log houses are tiny and rough, the female schoolteacher smokes a pipe, and much of Mary Clavers's furniture proves useless in frontier conditions. But because Kirkland composes her narrative after she has become more or less acculturated to life in Michigan, she takes a mocking view of her own snobbishness and naïveté; recalling her reaction to a tavern where she and her husband spend the night on the way from Detroit to Montacute, for example, she remarks, "I was then new in Michigan" (8).

About a third of the way into *A New Home*, Mary Clavers begins to speak as a resident rather than a visitor, using the pronoun "we" in reference to the inhabitants of Montacute, and when Mrs. Rivers arrives, Mrs. Clavers has learned enough about negotiating her surroundings to give the newcomer advice. "I assumed the part of Mentor on this and many similar occasions," writes Kirkland, "considering myself by this time quite an old resident, and of right entitled to speak for the natives" (66). Not long after this point, in chapter 20, she writes of gardening in the fertile Michigan soil in a manner that suggests she is literally putting down roots.[6]

The chapter on gardening, in which Kirkland rhapsodizes about the flowers and vegetables she is able to raise, uses Edenic references. The land, though slow to be cleared of the roots of trees and shrubs, is an "incipient Eden," and Mary Clavers places herself as Eve amidst this promise of abundance. In fact, Kirkland's particular use of the Eden story is to underscore that hers is a woman's story, for there is no Adam in this Eden, and the Eve figure is the agent of fruition rather than disgrace. It seems no accident that in this Eden chapter Kirkland places Mary Clavers in the most direct contact with Native Americans. Neither threatening nor "noble" savages, these "Indians" engage in peaceful trading with the settlers, bringing strawberries, cranberries, venison, and horses to exchange for prices established by hand signals. Nowhere in *A New Home* is the figure of the Native American presented as menacing, but Kirkland shows that she is aware of the easterner's presumption that they are dangerous when, on a horseback ride through the woods with Mrs. Rivers, the latter turns "ashy pale" at her first sight of an Indian. Mary Clavers remarks, "It had never occurred to me that the Indians would naturally be objects of terror to a young lady who had scarcely ever seen one" (85). For Kirkland, the *truly* indigenous people of Michigan are simply another element of the community rather than the occasion for heroic posturing.

Both masculine heroism and feminine sentimentality receive satiric treatment in *A New Home*. The men in Montacute and Tinkerville are as likely to be alcoholics and swindlers as they are to approach the nobility of Natty Bumppo, and even Kirkland's own husband is prey to delusions about the easy mastery of western lands. While Mr. and Mrs. Clavers are still in Detroit awaiting "the arrival of our chattels from the east," Mr. Clavers accepts an invitation to accompany several men on "a tour with a view to the purchase of one or two cities." In mock-heroic tones, Kirkland describes the accumulation of provisions for the "expedition," including bottles of brandy to "defy the ague" (25). The only advice Mrs. Clavers gives to her part of this group of eager empire builders is to "keep out of the water, and to take care of his spectacles" (26), but such cautions do not begin to address the problems encountered by "gentlemen who have been for many years accustomed to pavements and gaslamps" (27), and who are "a little rheumatic" (26). The expedition gets lost in the dark, partly because the self-styled deer hunter of the group spends time trying to "ascertain whether that white moving thing he had seen in the woods was a deer's tail or not" (26), and the party gratefully accepts the meager hospitality of a family of settlers before returning, chastened, to Detroit:

> *The party were absent just four days; and a more dismal sight than they presented on their return cannot well be imagined. Tired and dirty, cross and hungry, were they all. No word of adventures, no boasting of achievements, not even a breath of the talismanic word "land," more interesting to the speculator of 1835–6 than it ever was to the shipwrecked mariner.*
> (26)

In the account of both the trip and the unheroic homecoming, Kirkland has Mary Clavers tell an inverted tall tale, a tale not of mastery but of defeat. Whereas in the tall tale, the deer not only would have been shot, but would have been the largest ever seen in Michigan, here the erstwhile hunter is not even sure he has seen it; and rather than camping out, these city-bred men "accustomed to pavements and gas-lamps" take refuge in a crude log house instead of what they had "manfully" planned (27).

Kirkland's tone in writing about this failed expedition is one of amused sympathy, and the tone of amusement that permeates *A New Home* counters an image of the "literary woman" that was different from, but coexisted with, the more masculinized "bluestocking": the identification of the female writer—especially the female poet—with sentimentality, passivity, and weakness of mind and body. It was this figure that Mark Twain was to both satirize and perpetuate in his portrait of Emmeline Grangerford later in the century in *Huck Finn*. Both Caroline Kirkland and Fanny Fern also satirized this figure, but they could do what Twain could not, which was to place beside it, as counterweight and more congenial model, their own narrators as strong-minded, unsentimental authors.[7] The cultural narrative that linked women with sentiment rather than with intellect, and that assumed that one precluded the other, insisted on a construction of the feminine that could produce only a literature that, though popular with readers, could not rank as "major," especially by the standards of modern literary criticism. Further, this female author was, like the bluestocking, commonly depicted as an unmarried woman, although unlike the bluestocking, her overwhelming desire was to marry, which led her to emphasize her own dependence— the "clinging vine" in search of a sturdy tree.

The character that Kirkland causes to carry the burden of this stereotype in *A New Home* is Miss Eloise Fidler, who comes to Montacute to visit her younger sister, Mrs. Rivers. The fact that some of Kirkland's heaviest sarcasm is directed at Miss Fidler suggests the extent of the distance she wishes to put in this, her first book, between this image of the woman writer and herself. Kirkland's mockingly elevated style echoes the pretensions of Miss Fidler, who talks about everything except her age and has allowed books to substitute for reality in her understanding of life:

> *Her age was at a stand; but I could never discover*
> *exactly where, for this point proved an exception to*
> *the general communicativeness of her disposition. I*
> *guessed it at eight-and-twenty; but perhaps she would*
> *have judged this uncharitable, so I will not insist.*
> *Certain it is that it must have taken a good while to*
> *read as many novels and commit to memory as much*
> *poetry, as lined the head and exalted the sensibilities*
> *of our fair visitant.*
> (99)

Eloise Fidler's literary tastes may be judged in part by the album she brings with her—for, Kirkland notes acidly, "she was just the person to have an album" (99)—in which she collects favorite poems contributed by her friends. Mary Clavers confesses that she has been in possession of this album for three months, waiting, "I blush to say, for a contribution which has yet to be pumped up from my unwilling brains" (100). With heavy irony, she then announces that she will reproduce for her readers "a few specimens" from the album "for the benefit of the distressed, who may, like myself, be at their wits' end for something to put in just such a book" (100). The five poems she proceeds to quote are characterized by archaisms, flowery language, and sentimentality, and it is clear that Kirkland's narrator is at her "wit's end" for such a contribution precisely because her "unwilling brains" refuse to replicate such language and sentiment. Suggesting that Miss Fidler's intellect has not kept pace with her chronological age, Kirkland remarks that her tastes were "peculiarly young-lady-like" (103).

The second insight into Eloise Fidler's literary sensibilities is afforded by her response to the fiction writers of the period:

> *She praised [William Harrison] Ainsworth and*
> *[George Payne Rainsford] James, but thought Bul-*
> *wer's [Bulwer-Lytton] works "very immoral,"*
> *though I never could discover that she had more than*
> *skimmed the story from any of them. [James Feni-*
> *more] Cooper she found "pretty"; Miss [Catharine]*
> *Sedgwick, "pretty well, only her characters are such*
> *common sort of people."*
> (103)

Kirkland offers no further comment on Miss Fidler's critical assessments, but for contemporary readers of *A New Home* they would have consti-tuted a quite telling characterization. Ainsworth and James were British writers of historical fiction in the tradition of Sir Walter Scott.[8] Catharine Sedgwick's 1827 novel *Hope Leslie* opposed the European subjugation of the Native Americans ("such common sort of people") and proposed a communitarian as opposed to an individualistic model of society that Kirkland would have approved.

For a twentieth-century reader, James Fenimore Cooper is the most familiar name in this list, and Miss Fidler's response to his novels as "pretty" goes to the heart of Kirkland's revisionary intent. In contrast to Cooper's stylized frontier, with clear demarcations of morality and of social classes, Kirkland's Montacute is a place of constant accommoda-tion to bad roads and uncertain weather, where class distinctions inevi-tably bow to practical considerations of survival. Eloise Fidler, come to spend several months in what she calls "this peaceful retreat," is obvi-ously not prepared for the reality of the experience. Her clothing is "in the height of fashion," including a "highly-useful apron of blue silk" (99), and although she is a poet who would like to benefit from the in-spiration of nature, she has no sensible shoes, and so is "obliged to make out with diluted inspiration" (103), sitting on the woodpile instead of walking in the woods. In a developing settlement that demands constant work on the part of its inhabitants, Miss Fidler is singularly useless, in part because "no guest at morning or night ever found the fair Eloise ungloved": "Think of it!" Kirkland expostulates. "In the very wilds to be always like a cat in nutshells, alone useless where all are so busy! I do not wonder our good neighbors thought the damsel a little touched" (103). To some extent, of course, Eloise Fidler's naïveté about the frontier parallels that which Kirkland had initially brought to Michigan, but whereas Kirkland's Mary Clavers is able to revise her ideas—as Kirkland attempts to revise previous presentations of frontier experience—Miss Fidler seems intractably set in her own romance.

In "From Enlightenment to Victorian: Toward a Narrative of American Women Writers Writing History," Nina Baym argues convincingly that the tendency of literary historians to assign all nineteenth-century women writers to a category of "domestic" writing fails to take into account the differences between the Enlightenment ideology that held sway in the early decades of the century and the Victorian ideology that became pervasive by mid-century. Enlightenment thinking differentiated mind and body in a way that Victorian thought did not, so that biological difference did not mandate distinctions in intellectual capacity between male and female nearly as much as was true later in the century. An "Enlightenment republicanism," Baym points out, "guaranteed women intellectual parity with men and offered them the chance to serve their nation if they developed their minds" (107).

As one result, the women writers of the first two generations in the new nation tended to write history rather than fiction—to take on, in other words, the "public" function of recording and defining the American experience rather than identifying themselves with domestic fiction. Similarly, Zagarell notes that in the 1820s "women turned a sharply analytic eye on public matters, and while they wrote from a consciously female viewpoint and drew on values of antebellum women's culture, their writing was quite directly concerned with the foundations and organization of public life" ("Expanding 'America,' " 225).

Writing *A New Home* in 1839, Caroline Kirkland was part of a transitional era. Her realistic account of frontier settlement resisted and revised both fictional and nonfictional accounts that glorified individual, masculine achievement; at the same time, as the figure of Eloise Fidler suggests, she felt the encroachment of Victorian ideals of femininity, about which her text shows her to be deeply equivocal. While she scorns Miss Fidler's sentimentality and ornamented uselessness, she nonetheless refuses for herself the role of official historian of Montacute, claiming only to have collected "scattered materials" for such a person. And at the end of *A New Home* she metaphorically adopts the stance of one who has entered where she perhaps does not belong, comparing her narrative self to a guest who overstays her welcome. With Montacute still in the process of development, her closing chapter is necessarily "a conclusion wherein nothing is concluded," but she ends with an image of feminine self-effacement:

> *But such simple and sauntering stories are like Scotch*
> *reels, which have no natural ending, save the fatigue*
> *of those engaged. So I may as well cut short my mazy*
> *dance and resume at once my proper position as a*
> *"wall-flower," with an unceremonious adieu to the*
> *kind and courteous reader.*
>
> (189)

Yet despite Kirkland's demure farewell to the reader, she seems never to have abandoned the role of historian and revisionist. Her last major book, *Personal Memoirs of Washington* (1856), was a foray into history and biography intended to revise some of the standard public perceptions of the first president created by previous biographers.[9] By the early 1850s, when Fanny Fern wrote her autobiographical novel *Ruth Hall*, Victorian ideology proposed a distinctly feminine intellect whose bent was intuitive rather than rational and analytical, so that the realism and satire of her novel could be regarded as disobediently "unwomanly."

3

> *Thank heaven! there are women writers who do not*
> *disturb our complacency or serenity; whose books lull*
> *one to sleep like a strain of gentle music; who excite*
> *no antagonism, or angry feeling. . . . it gives us great*
> *pleasure, when we can do so conscientiously, to pat*
> *lady writers on the head.*
>
> FANNY FERN, *NEW YORK LEDGER*
> (10 OCTOBER 1857)

In her mock review of her own work, in which she declares, "We have never seen Fanny Fern, nor do we desire to do so," Sara Willis Parton captured perfectly the language and tone of critics and reviewers who wished to prescribe a narrow range for women's literary efforts. By the 1850s, such pronouncements constituted part of a backlash against an increasing number of women writers and the outspoken feminism of some of their work. Such authors as Sarah Josepha Hale, Hannah Gardner Creamer, and Laura Curtis Bullard openly advocated greater freedom and equality for women as the women's rights movement gained momentum, and were viewed by traditionalists as nearly as much of a threat to the status quo as women who took to the lecture platform to advocate female suffrage. Three years after numerous critics had castigated her for *Ruth Hall*, Fanny Fern was continuing in her newspaper column to point out hypocrisy, inequality, and the special concerns of women, having if anything benefited professionally from the controversy attending the publication of her first novel.

Although *Ruth Hall* has begun to regain its place in American literary history since its republication in 1986, some scholars still practice the critical equivalent of patting Fanny Fern on the head. David Reynolds, for example, in *Beneath the American Renaissance*, claims that she is worthy of critical attention not for her work, but because "she had direct connections with several major authors of the American Renaissance" (402); that is, Hawthorne admired her work, she knew Whitman and publicly praised *Leaves of Grass*, and Emily Dickinson is known to have enjoyed her "Fern Leaves" sketches. Reynolds also characterizes Fern's work as having a "preliterary complexity" (403) and sounds remarkably like his nineteenth-century counterparts when he states that she was "shifty and manipulative by nature," and that *Ruth Hall* was the product of her "combined manipulativeness and her vindictiveness against family members" (404). Such remarks are both condescending and inaccurate, and Reynolds seems unable to decide on his own critical evaluation of *Ruth Hall*, calling it both "innovative" (404) and "preliterary"; similarly, in a single sentence he claims that the novel is based "loosely" on the author's life and also that it is a "*record* of woman's suffering and of woman's triumph" (404; emphasis added).[10]

In fact, as Fanny Fern's biographer, Joyce W. Warren, ably demonstrates, not only *Ruth Hall*, but also parts of her second novel, *Rose Clark*, and many of her Fern Leaves sketches are highly autobiographical, so that both her life and her writing stand as counters to the prevailing ideology of the sentimental, intuitive, and, above all, domesticated woman. Her disobedience to this ideology consists in her character Ruth Hall, who embodies, as did Fanny Fern, the rags-to-riches success story reserved in the popular imagination for men—and which it is part of Caroline Kirkland's project to debunk—and in the irreverence of many of her newspaper columns.[11] Though capable of writing in the sentimental style for which reviewers were most apt to reward women writers, her true talent was for realism and satire, and her popularity with mid-nineteenth-century readers would suggest that her attitudes toward marriage, religion, social pretension, and social injustices were widely shared.

Before examining the ways in which *Ruth Hall* revises the cultural mythology of sentimentality and domesticity, we should explore briefly Fanny Fern's literary relationships with two of the nineteenth century's most notable iconoclasts: Emily Dickinson and Walt Whitman. While there is little evidence to suggest that Fern directly influenced Dickinson, despite the fact that Dickinson was familiar with some of Fern's work (most likely her 1853 best-seller, *Fern Leaves from Fanny's Port-Folio*), Reynolds is accurate in pointing out that certain formulations of woman's emotional nature shared by the two writers were common to what Dickinson family friend Samuel Bowles termed in 1860 the "literature of misery," in which the wrongs suffered by women create in them a volcano-like anger that threatened to erupt in revenge, and that did erupt verbally in the "stabbing phrase and the ingenious, taunting ellipsis" (Reynolds, 395). In her brief sketches and at times in her novels, Fanny Fern employed what Reynolds terms "pre-Dickinsonian" dashes to create pauses suggestive of barely controlled emotion (415). Although the term "literature of misery" is both misleading and limiting when applied to the work of either Dickinson or Fern, it is true that they share a penchant for wearing a variety of masks, which take the form of shifting, alternating tones of voice. The donning of multiple masks suggests a consciousness of role-playing in life as well as art, and Sara Willis's adoption of the pseudonym Fanny Fern is a complex instance of such masking: while the selection of an alliterative pen name drawn from the natural world represented her mocking acquiescence to a fad among women writers, it so firmly became a mark of her professional identity that it is the only name engraved on her tombstone.

Fanny Fern's relationship with Whitman was far more direct and personal, although it ended acrimoniously over James Parton's insistence that Whitman repay money that Parton had lent him. In her account of the relationship in Shirley Marchalonis's collection *Patrons and Protégées*, Joyce Warren points out that Fern and Whitman's professional association reverses the normal expectation of the male patron and the female protégée. At the time they met, in 1856, Fern, by then a widely known columnist for the *New York Ledger*, was in a position to help Whitman, rather than the reverse. Her enthusiastic review in the *Ledger* of *Leaves of Grass*, which Whitman had published in 1855 at his own expense, was one of the few positive public reactions to his work, and the first one by a woman. Warren suggests that Whitman may have borrowed the organic metaphor of leaves and the cover design of the first edition of *Leaves of Grass* from Fern's 1853 collection, *Fern Leaves*. Beyond this, the two authors had little direct influence on each other's work, but they shared some fundamental views: both preferred the natural over the artificial, the ordinary individual over the social climber, a direct writing style over literary artifice and ornateness. Though their work is different in style and genre, the points on which Fern praised *Leaves of Grass* have strong parallels in her own work: the naturalness of Whitman's language, his strength of mind, his belief in true democracy, his candid approach to sexuality, his inclusion of women in the democratic ideal, and his individualism (Warren, "Subversion versus Celebration," 73–75).

Like Caroline Kirkland, Fanny Fern, in *Ruth Hall*, resists and revises not a single text or set of texts, but a cultural story that assumed the proportions of myth. This story allocated the sentimental, the spiritual, and the moral spheres to women, and individualism, self-reliance, and material achievement (measured in land, money, or authority) to men. To be sure, this cultural story found its way into fiction, and reviewers were quick to praise female characters who took their appointed roles in the plot. The language of the following description of an approved fictional heroine is fairly typical of reviews of the 1850s. The woman is

> the cheerer of her husband in despondency, the kind
> and wise guide of her children in the right way, with
> modesty prompting the wish to shrink from publicity,
> but high principle curbing the indulgence of that
> wish, she appears the true pastor's wife, ready when
> occasion calls to be the friend and counselor of those
> around her, but finding her peculiar sphere of duty in
> her own home.[12]

The goal of the cultural plot for women was marriage, and this was as true in Sara Willis's life as it was in the popular novel. In fact, one of the major departures from her own autobiography in *Ruth Hall* is the omission of her second marriage. Following the death of her first husband, Sara Willis was pressured by her family into a disastrous and short-lived second marriage, but in her novel Fanny Fern revises her own story to allow Ruth greater independence.

In a sense, Kirkland and Fern revise the same mythology but in different ways. Setting *A New Home* in rural, frontier Michigan, Kirkland reveals rugged individualism to be an unworkable ideal and emphasizes the necessity of community; the setting of *Ruth Hall* is largely urban, so the forms of community are already in place, but Fern shows that when community—in the form of family, friends, and religion—fails, a woman may build a life apart from that which is supposed to be the center of her being. In Kirkland's Montacute, the potentially ennobling quality of new land and new beginnings is marred by greed and class consciousness, while in the settled Northeast of *Ruth Hall*, the inequalities of capitalism have created crowded tenements for the unfortunate and fostered an effete pretentiousness in the wealthy. Further, both Mary Clavers and Ruth Hall undertake similar journeys from the known to the unfamiliar. Kirkland's persona, in moving from city to frontier, must shed her sense of superiority and her romantic notions of western settlement. Ruth Hall loses the protection of husband and money and develops self-reliance based on her talent and perseverance.

In writing *Ruth Hall*, Fanny Fern both used and resisted the conventions of the women's novel of her period. The typical plot of the mid-nineteenth-century novel with a female central character, as Baym points out in *Woman's Fiction*, subjects the heroine to some early hardship—frequently she is orphaned—that forces her to make her own way in the world, developing strengths and resources that allow her a sense of self-respect. But far from being an end in itself, this self-development occurs so that it can be put to the service of an eventual husband and children. As Baym puts it, "the happy marriages with which most . . . of this fiction concludes are symbols of successful accomplishment of the required task and resolutions of the basic problems raised in the story" (12)—problems that include poverty, loneliness, and various threats posed by the public world. When Ruth is widowed early in the novel, and when, in addition, both her parents and her husband's parents refuse to provide more than minimal financial assistance to her and her children, it seems that Fern is setting her on the difficult but inevitable road to remarriage—rescue by a prince of whom she is finally worthy. Instead, after working at a series of menial jobs, Ruth discovers her talent for writing and is soon rewarded not with a husband, but with professional success and financial security that she has won for herself. Instead, in other words, of developing a positive self-concept so that she can cheer and nurture a family, "finding her peculiar sphere of duty in her own home," she is, at the end of the novel, preparing to move to another city to further her career, just as Fanny Fern moved from Boston to New York to write for the *New York Ledger*.

Omitting her own second marriage from this otherwise highly autobiographical account is just one of the strategies that the author employs
in order to avoid the closure of the marriage plot and to emphasize instead her heroine's autonomy. Marriage as an institution is portrayed
throughout the novel not as a haven for women, but rather as a relationship filled with difficulties and even dangers. Although Ruth's marriage
to Harry is happy until the moment of his death, Ruth enters into it not
with naïve romanticism but with a clear sense of the potential for abuse
or abandonment. On the eve of her wedding, her joy is tempered with
trepidation:

> *Had that craving heart of her's* [sic] *at length found
> its ark of refuge? Would clouds or sunshine, joy or
> sorrow, tears or smiles, predominate in her future?
> Who could tell? The silent stars returned her no an-
> swer. Would a harsh word ever fall from lips which
> now breathed only love? Would the step whose light-
> est footfall now made her heart leap, ever sound in
> her ear like a death-knell? As time, with its ceaseless
> changes, rolled on, would love flee affrighted from the
> bent form, and silver locks, and faltering footsteps?
> Was there no talisman to keep him?*
> (13)

Ruth has good reason to be apprehensive about marriage, for her chief
memory of her now-deceased mother concerns her fear of her husband's
anger. She remembers that her mother "always looked uneasy about the
time her father was expected home," and on his arrival the children were
admonished to be quiet to avoid incurring his wrath (14). Ruth's in-laws
scarcely provide a more encouraging model. Their marriage is characterized by "conjugal collisions," and whatever measure of peace they manage is imposed only by their "Calvinistic church obligations" (22).

Later in the novel, Fanny Fern reinforces the dangers of marriage by
introducing two vignettes that are otherwise extraneous to the plot. The
story of Mr. and Mrs. Skiddy has a comic tone because of Mrs. Skiddy's
level-headed triumph over her husband, who abandons the family to
seek his fortune in the California gold rush. Rather than becoming des-
titute, Mrs. Skiddy skillfully increases the income of their rooming house
and refuses to send her husband money for the passage home when he
fails to strike it rich. Drawing on her own experience, Mrs. Skiddy ad-

vises Ruth, "When a woman is married, Mrs. Hall, she must make up her mind either to manage, or to be managed; *I* prefer to manage" (106–107).

A different kind of abandonment is involved in the tragic story of Mary Leon, whom Ruth meets at a resort hotel. Mr. Leon is a wealthy but heartless man who commits his wife to a lunatic asylum, where her protestations of sanity fall on deaf ears, and she eventually dies. Fanny Fern uses Ruth's visit to the asylum following Mary's death to introduce a theme she develops more fully in her second novel, *Rose Clark*: women's lack of legal protection against such abuse. The matron tells Ruth about another inmate of the asylum, a woman whose husband left her and took their child. "She went to the law about the child," the matron says matter-of-factly, "and the law, you see, as it generally is, was on the man's side" (111). Grief and anger at such legal injustice have driven this woman truly insane.

Ruth's own experience with a husband is far more positive than any of these, but after Harry's death she never considers remarriage. Two of the male characters in the novel have some of the attributes of suitors, but Fern is careful not to allow either to develop into a real romantic interest. One of these is Johnnie Galt, who performs two actions traditionally associated with aspiring lovers: he sends Ruth flowers, and later, in his role as a fireman, he saves Ruth and her children from a burning building. But Ruth interprets neither gesture as a romantic overture. She regards the flowers as a token of regard not for her, but for her late husband, by whom Johnnie was once employed; and his act of rescue is part of his professional duty, for which she plans to reward him, but not—as in a fairy tale—with the gift of herself. John Walter, who plays a major role in Ruth's success as a writer, is safely and apparently happily married, and Fern stresses his "brotherly interest" in Ruth (144), which blossoms into "*true* friendship" (210). In a pivotal chapter, titled "Offers of marriage and offers to publish," Ruth turns decisively away from the former and embraces the latter. After reading a letter from a stranger who offers her "a box at the opera, a carriage, and servants in livery," she opens the "more interesting" letter from a publisher offering to bring out a collection of her newspaper columns. Not only does Ruth make no comment on the marriage proposal, but she demonstrates confidence in her own abilities by choosing a percentage royalty on the book instead of selling her copyright for a flat fee.

At the same time that Fanny Fern subverts the marriage plot in *Ruth Hall*, she takes narrative steps to make her heroine acceptable to contemporary readers. Susan K. Harris argues convincingly that nineteenth-century women writers, including Fanny Fern, used certain stylistic codes to identify their characters with appropriate feminine virtues and thus to mask their subversive intentions. By associating a female character with flowers, birds, sunlight, and other images drawn from the natural world, an author signaled her proper femininity. As Harris says of *Ruth Hall*, "By associating Ruth with flowers and piety Fern creates a protagonist her readers will recognize as deeply feminine, a woman who feels as a woman should feel, and who therefore qualifies as a heroine the general culture can accept."[13] Thus, in the first paragraph of the novel, Ruth is listening to the chiming of a church clock, and at the end she is serenaded by a bird who "trilled forth a song as sweet and clear as the lark's at heaven's own blessed gate" (211). The idea that Fanny Fern seeks in this way to suggest a conventional association between Ruth and piety is reinforced by the fact that in the two hundred pages that come between these references, the author has little positive to say about organized religion.

The one test that Ruth cannot fail—the major emblem of her proper femininity—is her identification with motherhood. In contrast to the many instances of bad parenting in *Ruth Hall*, Ruth is a devoted and fiercely protective mother. When Ruth's first child is born, Fern describes childbirth as "that most blessed of all hours," thus linking motherhood with religious piety. Motherhood is "God-commissioned"; the child "another outlet for [her] womanly heart" (24). The death of this first-born child is a severe blow, and following Harry's death, Ruth's central concern is to provide for her remaining two daughters. Yet, as sincere as her other writings show Fanny Fern to have been about the importance of motherly care and affection, there is evidence that, like Ruth's identification with church bells and birds, her devotion to her children is to some extent a device borrowed from sentimental culture to serve other purposes—in this instance, to underscore the failure of the familial support system that sets Ruth on the road to professional independence.

Ruth's first-born daughter's fatal illness, for example, though drawn from Fanny Fern's own experience in losing a child, is also a mechanism for pointing up the selfishness of her father-in-law, a doctor, who cannot be persuaded to come in the middle of the night to care for his own grandchild. After Harry's death, the doctor and his wife scheme to get custody of Ruth's children, not to assist the young widow, but to take revenge on her for "stealing" their son in marriage. Ruth's own father's heartlessness reemerges in this situation as well, for he tries to persuade Ruth to give her daughters to her husband's parents, calling it "perfect madness" that she does not wish to do so (68). Ruth's mother-in-law unwittingly enunciates Fanny Fern's plans for her heroine when she says to her husband, "I never supposed a useless, fine lady, like Ruth, would rather work to support her children than to give them up" (69–70), for it is toward self-sufficiency that the trajectory of the story is heading. When Harry's parents, in the guise of having the child visit them, in effect kidnap one of Ruth's daughters, she becomes more determined than ever to find suitable employment and discovers her talent as a "literary woman."

It seems no accident that Ruth Hall makes her professional mark in journalism; Sara Willis's father edited several newspapers before launching *The Youth's Companion* in 1827, and her brother, N. P. Willis, was editor of the New York *Home Journal*, so the transformation of Sara Willis into Fanny Fern/Ruth Hall is a logical one. Before her first marriage, Sara Willis helped her father edit *The Youth's Companion*; the world of publishing was familiar and congenial to her, although even she did not expect at this point any life's work other than marriage and motherhood. When circumstances propelled Sara Willis toward earning money by writing, as is the case with Ruth in the novel, it was natural that she would turn for advice and assistance to her brother, who had numerous publishing contacts and who had assisted the careers of other women writers. But here again, the family fails to provide help, leaving Sara/Ruth to make her way on her own. N. P. Willis's response to his sister's writing samples and request for professional counsel, quoted in Warren's biography, is dismissive and condescending. He professes not to like her writing, stating, "you overstrain the pathetic, and your humor runs into dreadful vulgarity sometimes." He finds her a potential embarrassment: "I am sorry that any editor knows that a sister of mine wrote some of these which you sent me" (Warren, *Fanny Fern*, 93). In using this distressing rejection in *Ruth Hall*, Fanny Fern both takes revenge on her brother and underscores her heroine's ability to succeed on her own, without a boost from a well-placed relative. Ruth's brother, named Hyacinth in the novel, is described as a selfish social-climber with an extravagant lifestyle even as his sister struggles to buy bread and milk. Hyacinth's rejection is critical to strengthening Ruth's resolve. Immediately after receiving his letter she declares, "I *can* do it, I *feel* it, I *will* do it,"

and says to her daughter Katy, "when you are a woman you shall remem-
ber this day" (116)—the day on which her career as the writer named
"Floy" begins.

Other relatives, as well as Ruth's friends, also unwittingly push Ruth
into autonomous action by their neglect. When Ruth's mother-in-law
says of her that "she's so independent that she never would complain if
she had to eat paving stones" (117), she is not paying Ruth a compliment,
but rather is expressing her disgust at Ruth's refusal to give up her children. Mrs. Hall echoes a cultural ideology that sees independence in a
woman as perverse and dangerous, but, ironically, it is her actions and
those of others that strengthen just this quality in Ruth. Ruth's wealthy
cousin grudgingly allows her to wash clothes at her house, providing she
brings her own soap, and her former friends cannot bring themselves to
visit her in her cheap boardinghouse. But isolation never makes Ruth
yearn for the protection and support of a man; as much as she wants
financial security, she assumes that it is her responsibility to provide it
for herself and her children.

Once Fanny Fern has taken Ruth to the point of self-sufficiency, most
of the language of sentiment falls away, and the confident, mocking, satiric tone prevails, as though the author is escaping symbolically from the
bonds of the traditional "woman's novel." The last quarter of *Ruth Hall*
abounds with good humor that mirrors Ruth's sense of well-being. Ruth
shares with the reader her often-comic fan mail, she reacts with amused
skepticism to the findings of a phrenologist, and both Hyacinth and
Mrs. Hall are forced to confront Ruth's success. In the penultimate chapter, Ruth is presented with a certificate for one hundred shares of bank
stock, which completes the rags-to-riches cycle of the novel; no mere
wage earner, she is a solid citizen with investments. In addition, rather
than being the rescued princess, she rescues her daughter Katy from her
mother-in-law, thus reuniting her family. The "harmony" that John Walter predicts for Ruth at the end of the novel (211) is compounded of those
factors that increasingly, as the nineteenth century progressed, characterized the male success story: self-sufficiency, perseverance, pride in accomplishment, and public recognition.

Neither Caroline Kirkland nor Fanny Fern succeeded, of course, in
stemming the growth of the cultural myths they addressed. The ideologies of rugged frontier masculinity and feminine domestic nurturance
were—and are—too deeply ingrained in the mythology of America to
be seriously challenged by even these widely read authors. But their

work is significant for reasons that have brought both authors renewed attention in recent years.

First, it is important to recognize that such ideologies were not accepted uncritically by those they most affected. Whereas the body of American literature that has been accepted as canonical since the early twentieth century—including such popular works as the Horatio Alger stories—endorses and perpetuates the dualities of public and private, individual achievement and familial nurturance, the quest and the hearth, it is clear in such works as *A New Home* and *Ruth Hall* that these categories were perceived as fluid rather than fixed. Kirkland demonstrates that frontier settlement required the interdependence of community and rested more on domestic arrangements than on individual encounters with the wilderness. Fanny Fern presents individual success and financial security as reasonable goals for women and posits that marriage may be more a trap than a reward. Further, by basing their accounts so closely on their own lives, these writers present those lives as exemplary instead of peripheral: women's experience is at the center rather than on the edges of the narrative.

PART
THREE

*Telling
Tales*

Four ONE'S
OWN
STORY

1

*As we write ourselves into existence, the class, race
and sexual political structures of society inevitably
change. The notion of who has rights, whose voice
can be heard, whose individuality is worthy, comes
under revision.*
JILL JOHNSTON, "FICTIONS OF THE SELF
IN THE MAKING"

It is my privilege to do myself justice.
RACHEL MADDUX, *COMMUNICATION:
THE AUTOBIOGRAPHY OF RACHEL MADDUX*

The concept of writing oneself into existence suggests an emergence from a private into a public self. Pushed further, it also suggests that existence within a written narrative has a different reality from existence in space and time. It is this difference that gives the eternal quality to Ruth's voice in Marilynne Robinson's *Housekeeping*: presumed to be locked in death beneath the waters of Fingerbone Lake, Ruth instead claims a life in narrative that permits her, as Robinson notes, "completeness in a way that is not compatible with the existence of time" (*Belles Lettres*, 38). The autobiographical form of the first-person narrative is a reminder that if, like Chopin's Elizabeth Stock, one feels shut out of the themes and forms of what is regarded as "literature," there always remains one's own story to tell.

Yet Elizabeth Stock put her story in a desk drawer, an action symbolic of the problematic relationship between women and the presentation of an autobiographical self that has been the focus of a great deal of recent autobiographical theory. Put simply, if autobiography as traditionally conceived is the record of an exemplary life, in the manner of Benjamin Franklin's *Autobiography*—a narrative of public achievement—then it constitutes a form to which few women have had full access. Further, even without the postmodern skepticism about the possibility of a stable "self," women have typically taken a route to self-definition that is relational rather than isolated—referential to one or more "others" or to a defining cultural narrative. In this sense, women's autobiographical writing has much in common, as Margo Culley has pointed out, with Puritan "conversion narratives"—accounts of the individual's relation to God and to the tenets of religious faith that are aimed at conformity to the spiritual expectations of the community. Culley makes this similarity explicit in terms of the relationship between the woman autobiographer and her audience:

> *Just as the Puritan self-absorption stands in paradoxical relationship to their belief in self-denial, so too the act of writing for a public audience stands in some tension with the prevailing idea of woman. In defying the traditional injunction to silence for women, the autobiographical act itself contests WOMAN, something of which many autobiographers are aware as they await the judgment of their community of readers.*
> (11)

It was such a judgment that provoked strongly negative responses to Fanny Fern's *Ruth Hall*: reviewers, thanks to the revelation of Fanny Fern's identity as Sara Willis, reacted to the novel's autobiographical elements—specifically to the portraits of Sara/Ruth's father and brother—rather than to the work's merits as literature. That is, the novelist as autobiographer contested "WOMAN" in two senses: first by daring to make public her version of her own life, and second by refusing obedience to her male relatives and the reader's expectations of female propriety.

Ruth Hall provides just one of many examples of the fact that the line between fiction and autobiography is often blurred—that what purports to be fiction may represent to a greater or lesser degree the author's own personal history. Much recent autobiographical theory, however, has emphasized the opposite side of this proposition, pointing to the fictive qualities of autobiography. Whether by accident—faulty memory, inadvertent self-censorship—or by design, autobiography has come to be seen as narrative shaped and determined by many of the same considerations that guide the writer of fiction: the selection and arrangement of material, the creation of memorable characters, and the imposition of order on otherwise disorderly existence. Even though, as Timothy Dow Adams puts it, "a promise to tell the truth is one of autobiography's earliest premises," constituting an article of faith between writer and reader, that promise cannot be fulfilled. Adams continues by pointing out why this is so:

> As fundamental as truth is to autobiography, modern readers have increasingly come to realize that telling the truth about oneself on paper is virtually impossible. Even if writers could isolate "the truth" of their past, how could they know it would remain true as they wrote, much less in the future? How would readers know if they were reading the truth, and how could writers separate poetic truth from factual truth, psychological truth from family truth?
> (9)

Long before autobiographical theorists began debating the contingent nature of "truth," Virginia Woolf explored these same issues in "A Sketch of the Past." This brief memoir has elements of metanarrative, as Woolf constantly interrogates the process of writing autobiography while in the act of recounting memories from her childhood. Acknowledging the vagaries of memory, for example, Woolf writes, "Unfortunately, one only remembers what is exceptional. And there seems to be no reason why one thing is exceptional and another not" (11). One "exceptional" experience that Woolf struggles to render accurately is the incident of sexual abuse by her half-brother when she was a small child. Woolf makes a causal link between this incident and her feeling of shame when looking into a mirror, but then casts doubt on the accuracy of her recollection: "I do not suppose that I have got at the truth; yet this is a simple incident; and it happened to me personally; and I have no motive for lying about it" (10).

Although Woolf claims to have no motive for lying about this child-hood experience (and readers have generally believed that she is telling the "truth" about it), one can easily imagine reasons why a woman might, if not lie, then at least suppress the incident—or parts of it, such as the name of the half-brother who sexually molested her: family em-barrassment, personal reprisals, even accusations of libel. In fact, "A Sketch of the Past" was not published until after Woolf's death, and the fact that she intended it only as an exercise in memoir writing may well have dictated her decisions about what to include and to omit. For even in the midst of her effort to get at a kind of autobiographical "truth," Woolf is conscious that she is deliberately presenting a self, even without a specific potential reader in mind; the failure of most memoirs, she writes, is that "they leave out the person to whom things happen" (5), and so she takes pains to represent the sensibility of the young Virginia Stephen.

In her 1993 essay "Fictions of the Self in the Making," from which one of my chapter epigraphs is taken, Jill Johnston is far more overt about the autobiography as a deliberate creation of self. "Of course when we write the life," Johnston writes, "we are making it up (not the facts but the ways of seeing and organizing them), and this is a political act of self-recognition" (29). By "political" Johnston means that because autobiog-raphy posits the worth of the individual who speaks, the existence of increasing numbers of autobiographies by women and minorities has the potential to revise our notion of "who has rights, whose voice can be heard." As a young woman, Johnston had learned that "women them-selves did not have stories, or were not supposed to have them. That minorities and outsiders in general lacked stories" (29). The emergence of stories—created selves inserted in the cultural narrative—constitutes what Johnston terms "plebeian autobiography" (29), the stories not of those with power, but of the heretofore powerless. Such self-creation, for Johnston, has particular meaning for women:

> For a woman, a conscious autobiography means fac-ing not only her past as a "female impersonator"— the realization that every accouterment of her self has been culturally determined—but the ways in which she has been and continues to be victimized in that role, even when she no longer looks or acts or dresses or for that matter feels the part.
> (29)

Just as Evelyn, in Carter's *The Passion of New Eve*, comes to understand that to be a woman is to accommodate oneself to prescribed behavior, so Johnston, as autobiographer, perceives that for a woman to write her life means that she must balance between two narratives: the cultural mythology that tells her what to be and what to expect, and her own perception of her negotiations with this story. As a result, women's autobiographical writing typically reveals the tension between these two forces.

In *A Poetics of Women's Autobiography*, Sidonie Smith speaks of the female autobiographer's uniquely gendered relationship to her audience:

> *Attuned to the ways women have been dressed up for public exposure, attuned also to the price women pay for public self-disclosure, the autobiographer reveals in her speaking posture and narrative structures her understanding of the possible readings she will receive from a public that has the power of her reputation in their hands.*
> (49)

What Smith suggests is that, whereas any author of an autobiography to some extent fashions a self for public display, the pressure to take care in the construction of a self-image is felt with more intensity by women. Culley makes much the same point, using the familiar metaphor of a mirror:

> *No woman, as we know, truly sees herself in a mirror; she sees herself through the imagined (or real) gaze of another. And to the extent that the autobiographical text can be thought of as a mirror, it is a mirror gazed at in public. Any woman can tell you of the difference (in degree, at least) between viewing her image in the privacy of a bathroom or bedroom mirror and catching a glimpse of herself in a mirror in public, a store window or mirror placed strategically in a department store. For women, all mirrors in public are two-way mirrors behind which invisible security guards convict her of her failures or her crimes.*
> (9)

It seems no accident that Virginia Woolf's sense of guilt is what she calls her "looking-glass shame" ("A Sketch of the Past," 9); after being

fondled by Gerald Duckworth, she takes on the guilt that should properly have been his and is thereafter "ashamed or afraid of [her] own
body" to the extent that she "cannot now powder [her] nose in public"
(9). The image that Snow White's aging mother sees in her mirror is not
a true and unmediated one, but rather the gaze of cultural standards according to which only the young are beautiful.

The two autobiographies with which the rest of this chapter is concerned demonstrate dramatically different responses to the act of female
autobiography. Both Margaret Halsey and Rachel Maddux, in their presentations of self, are acutely conscious of the gaze of the audience for
which they write, a consciousness that seems intensified by each author's
convictions about the power of the written word. Yet in form and emphasis, Halsey's *No Laughing Matter: The Autobiography of a WASP* (1977)
and Maddux's *Communication: The Autobiography of Rachel Maddux* (written in 1941) represent the extremes of a continuum in negotiating public
and private, emotion and intellect, self and other. Halsey writes as a public figure, a person of accomplishment, who nonetheless sees herself as a
representative of the failure of the "American Dream." Maddux, in contrast, addresses her autobiography to a single reader, in the form of a
letter, yet she writes as one certain of her individual agency, in control of
herself and of the version of that self she chooses to present.

2

> *An effort has been made in the following pages to be*
> *as truthful as human fallibility permits, but for the*
> *sake of various people's privacy, some of the names*
> *of still-living individuals have been altered.*
> MARGARET HALSEY, *NO LAUGHING MATTER*

When Margaret Halsey published her autobiography in 1977, she was
sixty-seven years old, the author of six books and numerous articles;
she had been twice married and twice divorced, had raised an adopted
daughter, and was living in England. The "Author's Note" that precedes
the text of *No Laughing Matter* is a fairly standard disclaimer. Halsey
claims to have written a true story, though she has changed the names of
a few people to protect them from injury or embarrassment. Such a note
presupposes that readers are concerned about the difference between fact

and fiction and that they share with Halsey a belief that the "truth" may sometimes be distorted by "human fallibility."

In fact, the central message of Halsey's autobiography is human failure, on both a personal and a national scale, and not least her own failure: as wife, mother, and social critic crusading against racial prejudice, materialism, and moral decay. Although Halsey alludes to Abraham Lincoln and Franklin Delano Roosevelt as her heroes and moral exemplars, it is the figure of Benjamin Franklin that stands most closely behind the pages of Halsey's autobiography, as she revises the values and attitudes that inform Franklin's own *Autobiography*. In doing so, she implicitly claims the same freedom to propose hers as an exemplary life, but whereas Franklin focuses almost exclusively on his life as public figure, Halsey, like many women autobiographers, reflects the tensions between public and private that create a deep ambivalence in her account of her life. The result is a mixture of confession and self-defense, of rigorous self-assessment and defense against the gaze of the "other."

Halsey was born in Yonkers, New York, in 1910, and grew up in a middle-class family with "pretensions to culture" (20) and the sense of social superiority that afflicts those who are insecure about their position in the world. "One very happy part of my childhood," Halsey writes, "was the comfortable awareness that there were people in the world who were not as good as I" (23). Her parents' prejudice against Italians, Jews, and the poor, combined with her father's stern anger and her mother's devotion to propriety, caused Halsey to emerge from childhood as, to use her term, a "prig." The unquestioned dominance of white Anglo-Saxon Protestant culture that was an article of faith in her family, and that is an unspoken assumption in Franklin's autobiography, produced in Halsey an egotism that was only increased by her publication, at the age of twenty-eight, of a best-selling satire on British life titled *With Malice toward Some* (1938). As both praise and money began to roll in, Halsey comments, "the ego massage was voluptuous beyond description," and she found herself living in a "narcissist's paradise" (84).

Yet even while early success as an author was confirming Halsey's sense of personal and group superiority, other experiences began to develop in her the social consciousness that would cause her to devote most of her career to crusades against intolerance and greed. As a student at Skidmore in the late 1920s, she came under the influence of several liberal professors, although she confesses that the "Sealed Mind of the Halseys" (67) prevented her from adopting their views on more than an intellectual level. After graduation, she worked briefly for Max Eastman, former editor of *The Masses*, and later she married a Jew, Henry Simon—brother of one of the founders of the Simon and Schuster publishing company—much to the horror of her mother. While at the time Halsey reports that she was far too self-absorbed for these experiences to have any dramatic impact on her thinking or behavior—instead, she recalls them as part of her rebellion against her family—they nevertheless laid the groundwork for her later conviction that the sense of WASP superiority with which she had been raised was responsible for most of the major social ills of twentieth-century America.

Halsey's truly transformative experience was her work at the Stage Door Canteen during World War II. Separated from Henry Simon and still living on the proceeds of *With Malice toward Some*, she had begun dating another Jew, Joseph Bloch, and when a member of the Canteen's board of directors announced one day that "as soon as [she had] time, [she was] going to clean up this place and get rid of the Jews" (112), Halsey was inspired to write *Some of My Best Friends Are Soldiers* (1944), which combined witty observations of life on the home front during wartime with warnings against anti-Semitism and racism in general. Her work at the Canteen, which was one of the few recreation centers for servicemen in the country to be racially integrated at that time, also inspired her next book, *Color Blind* (1946). With this book, Halsey remarks, she had "completed a seemingly eccentric trajectory from entertainer to reformer" (131), and she remained a reformer, addressing rampant consumerism in *The Folks at Home* (1952) and political ethics in *The Pseudo-Ethic: A Speculation on American Politics and Morals* (1963).

By the time she wrote her autobiography in 1977, after Watergate and Vietnam had borne out her earlier warnings about the country's lack of moral leadership and dangerous hegemonic assumptions, Halsey was convinced that the era of WASP dominance of America had come to an end—not merely the dominance of the group of people to whom the acronym referred (and to which she herself belonged), but the values that group adhered to and promulgated. Her stated reason for writing the autobiography is to offer herself as a case study of a deservedly endangered species. As Benjamin Franklin wrote his autobiography to document a rise, not only in his own fortune and influence but also in those of the country whose framework he was involved in establishing, Halsey writes to document a fall: "The cutting down to size of the WASPs being a matter of historical necessity, it seemed as if an examination of WASP conditioning and WASP consciousness (so far as the latter goes) might be of interest and significance" (12). Franklin poses himself as an example to be emulated—"my Posterity may like to know . . . the conducing Means I made use of . . . as they may find some of them suitable to their own Situations, & therefore fit to be imitated" (27)—whereas Halsey presents her story as a cautionary tale: "Whatever happens to the WASPs, they have deserved it; but it might be a mere matter of common sense to sift out of their streaky legacy whatever it contains of proven usefulness" (15).

The most clearly gendered differences between the two texts involve the manner of self-presentation and the negotiation of public and private spheres. Franklin is candid about, even proud of, the fact that one of his motives for writing his autobiography is vanity:

> *Most People dislike Vanity in others whatever Share*
> *they have of it themselves, but I give it fair Quarter*
> *wherever I meet with it, being persuaded that it is of-*
> *ten productive of Good to the Possessor & to others*
> *that are within his Sphere of Action: and therefore*
> *in many Cases it would not be quite absurd if a Man*
> *were to thank God for his Vanity among the other*
> *Comforts of Life.*
> (28)

For Halsey, on the other hand, vanity—both national and personal—is part of the sense of superiority that has created the evils of racism and moral vacuity; it is to be confessed rather than celebrated. Even before the success of *With Malice toward Some*, Halsey reports that she "had two legs on the trophy for Most Self-Absorbed Girl on the Eastern Seaboard" (73) and was blissfully unaware that she was using people for her own purposes. A similar unexamined smugness permitted, she believes, the canteen director's remark about the Jews and, later, the Communist witch-hunts of Senator Joseph McCarthy's House Un-American Activities Committee. On both the personal and the national levels, it required a substantial shock to create awareness of the effects of such a sense of smug superiority. In Halsey's case, the turning point was her second husband's demand for a divorce; the national wake-up call, she believes, was the Watergate scandal, which "killed once and for all the idea that a white Anglo-Saxon Protestant is physically better looking and morally more reliable than a person who is not a white Anglo-Saxon Protestant" (11). If Franklin could see himself as representative of what was positive about America, Halsey sees herself as an example of what is wrong with

it: "When I finally understood the extent to which I was a personal im-
perialist, I perforce had to climb down, so that in an odd way my tiny
personal history has seemed to parallel the recent history of my country" (14).

For Franklin, influenced by the Puritan habit of self-scrutiny and
the Enlightenment belief in progress and perfectibility, the individual
self was a product of conscious formation. As Louis P. Masur comments,
"self-education, self-improvement, self-discipline—here were the con-
stituent parts of the self-made man. Selfhood was the key. Success
hinged on public identity, and Franklin's *Autobiography* aimed to teach
how to present an impeccable image to others" (Franklin, *Autobiography*,
15–16). In other words, not only does the *Autobiography* present a "carefully constructed persona" (17), but it constitutes a record of conscious
self-presentation in life. Halsey is similarly concerned with the creation
of a public image, but *No Laughing Matter* details the destructive split
between public image and private self. Whereas Franklin maintains the
façade of successful public figure, Halsey demonstrates that the very necessity of maintaining the façade may lead to personal failure—especially
for a woman.

Lessons in the importance of keeping up appearances began early in
Halsey's life, as did mixed messages about self-worth. During family
arguments, her mother closed the windows to conceal the conflict from
neighbors; she wanted them to think that "our household was one of
unimpeachable dignity, where all human passion was completely under
control" (19). Given this atmosphere, it is not surprising that Halsey was
kept ignorant about sexuality, or that her father tried to prevent her from
dating when she was a teenager and, when she did go out, waited up
with a nightstick until she came home. The son of German immigrants,
her father quit school after the eighth grade. He worked his way up to
the level of respectability, but even though he pushed his two daughters
to excel academically, he resented the fact that they had opportunities he
had lacked. These paradoxical attitudes lie behind his denunciation of
Margaret when she failed to win the D.A.R. essay prize on graduation
from grade school in Yonkers: "You're rotten, Margaret Halsey, you're
rotten to the core!" (44).

Although Halsey, from the vantage point of her sixties, does not make
the causal link, it seems reasonable that such gratuitous outbursts made
all the more urgent her subsequent need for approval—a need fueled as
well by the success of her first book. When *Some of My Best Friends Are*

Soldiers was published, she comments, "an emotionally well-balanced person . . . would have been satisfied with its reception" (118), but she was neither well-balanced nor satisfied. "I thought I had written a Deathless Message which would eventually take its place in people's minds and hearts a little below the Gettysburg Address" (118). Although the book was praised by no less than Walter Winchell and Eleanor Roosevelt, Halsey's self-esteem needed the uniform enthusiasm generated by her first book, and when this did not materialize, she reacted with the shock and anger that was to characterize her response each time one of her works of social criticism was published:

> *I expected universal applause for the goodness of my intentions, and naively supposed that my virtuous stance would make me immune from all but the most swallowable criticisms. In addition, I had always had a consuming need to get people to agree with me, and if they stubbornly adhered to what I considered their dangerously wrong opinions, I seethed with rage and despair. Thin-skinned was hardly the word for me, when the second book came out. I made Saint Sebastian with all those arrows in him look like a holidaymaker on a Caribbean cruise.*
> (119)

It is Halsey's feeling of moral superiority—part of what she has been taught is her WASP inheritance—rather than her talent as a writer that is supposed to ensure her success.

Thus, while Halsey may have seemed to the public to be a successful woman, a writer who had mined two of the richest traditions in American literature, humor and social critique, privately she felt herself to be a failure. And, though she would not realize it for a long time, she was a failure in the domestic as well as the public arena. In her marriages to Henry Simon and Joseph Bloch, she describes herself as tyrannical and manipulative, subjecting them to her rages (and Simon to her infidelities), and at the same time manifesting a helplessness that demanded their care. When Bloch was sent overseas during World War II, for example, she was bereft of both emotional and practical support. He (and Simon before him) had provided "the instant encouragement, praise and reassurance without which [she] seemed unable to function." Further, she had cultivated a "spacious" ignorance of matters of everyday living: "I did not know how to return things to department stores, how to read a contract, whom to call when things broke down or how to put new batteries in a flashlight. And I hugged my ignorance" (117). Such carefully nurtured ignorance of practical skills is not only the opposite of Franklinesque ingenuity, it is also a curiously feminine ineptitude that requires masculine expertise for survival in both the public and the private worlds.

Whereas Franklin chooses to write in his autobiography almost exclusively of his life as a public figure, Halsey's autobiography testifies to the fact that for a woman, the two spheres are inseparable. The sense of moral outrage that prompted her to write *Color Blind, The Folks at Home*, and *The Pseudo-Ethic* turned to anger and frustration at her inability to change the course of American culture, and she vented these feelings in her domestic life. When uncertainty about her writing reached the point of "tight, hard, unassuageable apprehension," she became "arbitrary, demanding and a snapper-out of commands; and when I was not being dictatorial, I was being dejected" (165). As she began to depend more heavily on alcohol, her rages increased:

> *Periodically and completely unpredictably, [alcohol]*
> *had the effect of releasing the bottled-up rage beneath*
> *the surface, and on those nights I kept Joseph up until*
> *three in the morning while I ranged like a tigress over*
> *the vast landscape of my grievances. They were infi-*
> *nitely repetitious, those jeremiads. Even when I was*
> *scuppers awash with Johnny Walker, I still had*
> *enough vestigial sense of style to be aware that this*
> *endless chewing over of the same thing in the same*
> *phrases was as boring to the listener as seeing a B pic-*
> *ture for the twentieth time.*
> (171)

In retrospect, Halsey is aware that she was having a nervous breakdown, but the damage to her second marriage was irreparable, even though she and Joseph Bloch were not divorced until their daughter was nearly grown.

Further linking Halsey's professional and domestic lives is her awareness that she is being judged in both spheres—that the gaze in the mirror assesses both her work as a writer and her performance as a wife, mother, and homemaker. Late in *No Laughing Matter*, she remarks on her realization that "I had all my life been a slave to what people might think of me" (228). In this autobiographical text, she devotes most of her attention to the public response to her books and her articles in *The New Republic* and *The Progressive*, but in her earlier foray into autobiography, *This Demi-Paradise: A Westchester Diary* (1960), she reveals (as did Jean Kerr and Shirley Jackson) that the expectations in the domestic arena for middle-class women during the postwar decades were equally stringent whether or not a woman had a career outside the home. *This Demi-Paradise* is part of the subgenre of "domestic humor" of the postwar period that also includes Kerr's *Please Don't Eat the Daisies* and Jackson's *Life among the Savages*; ostensibly lighthearted accounts of the daily lives of suburban housewives, such works are extremely revealing depictions of women's failures to live up to the glossy standards promulgated by the media of the 1940s and the 1950s. According to these standards, female perfectibility was both possible and mandatory, and its achievement was measured in its effects on others: well-behaved, academically talented children and well-fed, contented husbands living in clean, well-ordered households.

Two excerpts from *This Demi-Paradise* demonstrate most forcefully the fact that, for Halsey, the readers and reviewers who judged her public presentations of self had more amorphous but equally rigorous counterparts in her private life. One of these she terms, tellingly, the "Invisible Critic":

> *This Invisible Critic inhabited a corner of the room, up near the ceiling, and I unconsciously expected, whenever I had completed a task, to hear a loud, clear voice saying from the corner of the ceiling, "Margaret Halsey, that's the best goddamned mayonnaise that any women has ever made." Of course, no such voice ever made itself heard, but I never gave up hope, and what chronic, unassuageable tension that unrecognized hope generated!*
> (141)

The "Invisible Critic" is the embodiment of accumulated cultural judgments, what Culley calls the "invisible security guards" (9) that lurks behind the real or imagined mirrors in which women regard themselves.

While the Invisible Critic seems to be male, another of Halsey's judges is specifically female: the Girl Scout leaders who stand ready to discipline her if she fails as cookie chairwoman of her daughter's Brownie troop:

> *I could see myself being short of the required sum*
> *when the cookie drive was over. I could see the drum-*
> *head court-martial and the stern-faced women in field*
> *green. I could see the little back room where they left*
> *me with a revolver and a bottle of brandy. I could see*
> *the Girl Scout Council tapping their riding crops on*
> *the table and waiting to hear the shot which would*
> *heal the wounded honor of Troop 50, Neighbor-*
> *hood 6.*
> (57)

Despite Halsey's witty style and the humor of hyperbole, she conveys a clear sense of being watched and evaluated in her private life as in her public one.

The persona that Halsey presents in *No Laughing Matter* and *This Demi-Paradise* is disarmingly self-mocking, even self-deprecatory, and seemingly candid; her public and private failures are laid out for the reader's inspection. The fictive quality of Halsey's narrative—especially *No Laughing Matter*—comes not, as in Franklin's autobiography, from the conscious presentation of a public self at the erasure of the private, but instead from a paradoxical relationship between her stated intention and her textual performance. Both rhetorically and structurally, *No Laughing Matter* belies Halsey's insistence that WASP dominance—including her own—has come to an end. For as much as this autobiography is a confessional text, it is equally an attempt at self-justification. Each time that Halsey recounts the failure of one of her "Deathless Messages" to stem the tide of whatever evil she addressed, she explains again why she was right and others were wrong, establishing, in other words, her own morally superior position. If the WASPs, including Halsey herself, are supposed to, in her words, "climb down" from their positions of political and cultural dominance, her tone shows her to be clinging to a place near the top of the ladder. And the book ends, not with a personal summing-up, but with an indictment of the political climate of the 1970s. In effect, by ending her autobiography, as does Franklin, with issues of national rather than personal concern, Halsey refuses to remain in the private sphere to which the traditions of her culture would consign her.

3

So now, without need for haste, why should I make a straight line? Why should I not meander? Why should I not take pleasure in the telling?

RACHEL MADDUX, *COMMUNICATION*

In *Writing a Woman's Life*, Carolyn Heilbrun comments on the tendency of women autobiographers to practice a conscious or unconscious self-censorship in order to comply with cultural expectations of docility and piety in their presentations of self. In what she terms the "old genre" (that written before the 1970s) of female autobiography, the author "tends to find beauty even in pain and to transform rage into spiritual acceptance. . . . Above all other prohibitions, what has been forbidden to women is anger, together with the open admission of the desire for power and control over one's life (which necessarily means accepting some degree of power and control over other lives)" (12–13). Margaret Halsey's *No Laughing Matter* obviously does not belong to the "old genre" as Heilbrun describes it; Halsey's anger at both self and others is clearly expressed, and one of the central themes of the book is her desire to have power over self and others, sometimes with destructive results.

Long before the 1970s, novelist Rachel Maddux wrote an autobiography that, had it been published at the time it was written instead of fifty years later, would have disrupted Heilbrun's formulations about the "old genre." Maddux, like Halsey, expresses anger, and her sense of control over her own life and the telling of it is one of the central features of *Communication* (originally subtitled *Being the Mental Autobiography of a Sturdy Quest)*, written in 1941 and published in 1991. *Communication* is the unsparing, but often lyrical, account of the childhood and young womanhood of a gifted woman's search for recognition of her uniqueness, for a means of expressing herself that could convey her singularity to another human being. Maddux's autobiography is as private as Halsey's is public: not intended for publication, it was written in the form of a letter to a single individual and did not become a public document until eight years after her death. Halsey wrote her autobiography toward the end of her career, as a public figure whose previous work was familiar to at least some of her readers. Maddux was not quite twenty-nine when she wrote *Communication*; she had published three short stories and had begun work on her first novel, *The Green Kingdom*, which would not be published until 1957.

Despite these differences, Maddux and Halsey have a great deal in common, including coincidences of timing. They were nearly precise contemporaries, Halsey born in 1910 and Maddux in 1912. Halsey was twenty-eight when her first book was published, and at twenty-eight Maddux wrote her autobiography. Both women adopted daughters and wrote lovingly of raising them. Each was affected by the repressions and accusations of McCarthyism in the 1950s: Halsey was accused of having Communist ties when she gave a speech on civil liberties in Westchester County, New York, in 1954, and Maddux's husband had difficulty obtaining security clearance to work for an electronics company because of alleged Communist sympathies. (Halsey would have found as ironic as did Maddux the fact that it was then-senator Richard Nixon, the arch-villain of *No Laughing Matter*, who finally arranged for the clearance to be granted.) Both writers were lifelong political liberals. Maddux's *Abel's Daughter* (1960), like Halsey's *Color Blind*, is an indictment of racism, and in *The Orchard Children* (1977) she addresses the plight of unwanted children and an unfeeling legal system. Of most significance to a consideration of their autobiographical narratives, however, is the fact that both women wrote in large part out of a sense that their voices were not otherwise being heard.

In the case of *Communication*, this is true on a quite literal level. When, in her mid-twenties, Rachel Maddux finally met a person she felt was capable of listening to and understanding her accounting of herself, he refused to listen to her story and suggested that she write it down instead. In the early fall of 1941, she did so, sending him one copy and keeping a carbon for herself. The preface to *Communication* begins on a note of frustration and rebuke: "It seems strange to think that I have waited a year to tell you these things, and then traveled two-thousand miles, allowing myself six days to accomplish the telling, and, in the end, to have returned without speaking because you would not allow yourself to hear" (55). Maddux suggests that his refusal springs from both a fear of emotional commitment and a rather condescending desire to protect her from the resultant disappointment. She characterizes it as "a refusal to accept what you thought would be a greater responsibility than you dared carry" and writes of his "need to restrain me from a potential regret" (55), thus simultaneously evoking and rejecting the relational

nature of women's self-creation. By the end of the brief preface, Maddux has deftly turned his rejection of her spoken words into her freedom
in the written narrative. Whereas she had, in person, formulated her
thoughts so that "they needed about fifteen minutes to make a straight
line," on paper she plans to "meander" and to "take pleasure in the telling" (56). Further, she claims the right to decide what is included in and
omitted from her story as part of doing herself "justice":

> *I am not compelled to tell you about the time I was*
> *so stupid as to try to steal a handful of sugar while*
> *standing in front of a mirror, or about the time I hit*
> *Eloise Haycraft over the head with a doll buggy, or*
> *about my first infatuation at thirteen with a Swedish*
> *'cello player named Ivan.*
>   *So I won't.*
> (56)

The "long and discouraging search" that *Communication* describes is,
Maddux writes, for "the recognition of someone else who was *attentive
to the same things in the same way*, for another mind that could not fool
itself" (55). That this is a "mental autobiography" is thus clear from the
outset—an intellectual rather than an emotional "quest," although emotional issues are important in Maddux's narrative. Indeed, the attempt to
separate the intellectual from the emotional proves dangerous, and just
as public and private worlds constantly resonate with each other in Halsey's autobiography, so thought and feeling—culturally represented as
masculine and feminine qualities—must finally be reconciled for Maddux. What begins as the rigorous intellectual journey of a precocious
child, marked by pain and isolation, ends with the realization that intellectual achievement and emotional involvement need not be mutually
exclusive in a woman's life.

The first chapters of *Communication* describe Maddux's search for the
secret to adult knowledge and authority. She begins, at the age of three
or four, by asking questions about her surroundings, only to be given
indirect, dishonest answers. When she asks why a chair is called a chair,
she is told, "because you sit in it"; knowing this answer to be false, she
writes, "once I called it a flower and sat in it to see if it would hold me
up" (61). When questioning fails, she decides that books hold the secret,
and so teaches herself to read, avoiding fairy tales and fantasy—"I was
sure that wouldn't get me anywhere" (63)—and when books in turn fail

to supply her with the mastery she seeks, she decides that it is a matter of time, and that when she turns twenty-one "the world [will] open to me":

> *I would look at an oak tree then and it would slowly*
> *change from being a member of a group of trees to be-*
> *ing this tree. It would shimmer all over and come to*
> *life, the way trees do in Walt Disney's cartoons, and*
> *it would show me its oakness and I would show it my*
> *rachelness. Also the grocery man would no longer be*
> *a list filler. I would look directly at him and he would*
> *not say anything silly.*
>
> *He would say, I am Mr. Whitlock. There is a*
> *whitlockness about me that keeps me from being*
> *Mr. Moore. No doubt you see it.*
>
> *And I would see it.*
> (63)

Without such a revelation of essences, Maddux feels cut off, isolated: "People . . . remained behind the glass wall; they had a film over their eyes" (63). Nor is she isolated only from adults. Though younger than most of her grade-school classmates, she is regarded as somehow "old" by her peers. "I wore about me," she writes, "some invisible kind of hoop which kept off the children" (71).

But if a lack of understanding creates isolation, so certain kinds of understanding may, paradoxically, only increase such isolation. On her seventh birthday, Maddux realizes that she exists in time as well as in space, and that this means that she, along with the rest of humanity, is mortal. Believing that she alone knows this, she feels frustrated and help-less: "I wept for the millions of people on the earth, for their smallness, for their fragility. I wept that they were all, all going to die and they could DO NOTHING ABOUT IT" (69). Compounding Maddux's childhood isolation was the fact that the two people she loved most pas-sionately, her father and her older sister, Erma, showed her little affec-tion. Erma was eight years older—too old to be a playmate—and her father alternated silence with "horrible, blind, incoherent rages" (75). From the perspective of adulthood, Maddux knows that "children do not like comfort. They worship whatever demands the most of them" (76). As a child, her efforts to claim her father's attention were themselves intellectual ones; she "memorized pages of a book on civil engineering in order to ask him questions" about his work (76).

Maddux's descriptions of her parents' personalities and attitudes is strikingly similar to Halsey's account. Both fathers are stern figures given to angry outbursts; both mothers are deeply concerned with propriety and appearances, rushing to close windows when their husbands raise their voices. Halsey eventually severed all ties with her mother, and at the time of writing *No Laughing Matter* had not seen her for twenty years, although she concedes that she has taken on many of her mother's characteristics. Maddux rejects certain of her parents' values and behavior, but becomes reconciled with each of them as individuals by understanding the sources of their insecurities, just as she undergoes a rigorous investigation of her own fears. While in grade school, she one day realizes that her father's instruction to bluff when she doesn't know the right answer is wrong, and later, trying to come to terms with her fear of him, she realizes that his rages stem from his own fears: "He was afraid that someone would think he was ignorant. He was afraid my mother would laugh at him. He was afraid to die" (85). Later, as a young woman, Maddux rejects her mother's pattern of "little subterfuges and hypocrisies and glossings of the truth" (124), but still later comes to understand that in a household full of people with manic-depressive tendencies she had felt required to provide stability. "There had to be somebody, she said, in the house who could stay calm and the same every day in order to hold it together" (142). Her mother's behavior, too, arises from insecurity; having grown up on a farm, she felt inferior in the city, and so had been "living year after year by her pride and what she called dignity, a continual compensation for the fact that she had not been born in a city—living in silence" (143).

By the age of ten, Maddux writes, periods of intense depression, such as the one she experienced on her seventh birthday, became more frequent, and she began a deliberate project of ridding herself of all emotions in what she terms "an extraordinary struggle for self-preservation" (78). As she reconstructs the moment of this decision in her autobiography, Maddux creates a dialogue between her rational and emotional selves, with the former quizzing the latter about the causes of the depressions and their accompanying headaches. When finally she has arrived at a list of things she is afraid of—including trains and her father's swearing—she overcomes each one in turn by forcing herself to experience it repeatedly. The process of developing what she calls "self-sufficiency" took six years; at the end of it, she writes, "I saw a puppy run over and it did not touch me at all and I was proud" (87). From the ages of seventeen to nineteen, then, Maddux operated as pure intellect:

> *Everything looked absolutely clear to me, as though it*
> *were made out of glass, and it was all perfectly static.*
> *It never moved . . . I insisted that everything must*
> *be submitted to my mind, that I should consciously*
> *control everything that had to do with me. . . . I*
> *could do wonderful mental feats that I cannot do now,*
> *can never do again. I could memorize anything I*
> *chose to. . . . I could get along without anything or*
> *anybody.*
> (88 – 89)

In short, Maddux had become a female intellectual parody of the extreme individualism that Caroline Kirkland had addressed a hundred years before in *A New Home.*

Maddux's posture of calm rationality during her teenage years led to an isolation as absolute as that of her childhood, and it proved to be dangerous. Her cool demeanor made her seem older than she was, and it attracted men who were determined to get past what they perceived as a façade. "Each one would come up against that coldness and be delighted because he was absolutely sure that he was just the very guy to break it down. Then he would come up against it again and again and finally in frustration, he would want to force me to feel something—even anger" (107). The male response to the emotionless female began in disbelief and often ended in physical violence:

> *I was kidnapped three times and I had my head hit*
> *with the butt of a gun and I had it banged on a car*
> *door handle and once I was strangled on a road and*
> *thrown into a ditch which, fortunately, was full of*
> *cold water, and several times I was beaten up. One*
> *very fine and brilliant man became so utterly confused*
> *that he tried to kill us both in a car and later tried to*
> *kill himself. And I was always completely relaxed*
> *and silent and never frightened and each time I*
> *thought I would be killed and I did not really mind.*
> (107)

In *No Laughing Matter* Margaret Halsey describes herself at about the same age as "The Girl in the Glacier," and remarks that she did not at that time drink, "fearing above all things loss of control" (67). Both women—one instinctively and one deliberately—fended off the chaos of adolescence by suppressing that part of themselves traditionally constructed as feminine. But whereas the cool, rational intellectual became Halsey's public persona, Maddux realized that "self-sufficiency is not a great, free, sunlit meadow as I had thought. It is a deep well with a high wall around it and I wanted . . . OUT" (104–105).

Learning to feel again after years of denying her emotions was not easy, but Maddux's transition was eased by the development of a warm relationship with the older sister she had formerly worshiped from afar. In adulthood, the age difference ceased to matter, and Erma became one of the first people to take Maddux seriously on her own terms. In particular, she did not ridicule Maddux's ambitions, which at the time included going to medical school. "She did NOT remind me that I was a girl. She did NOT remind me of my health. She did not tell me that as soon as I got married I would get over all that" (112). By assuming that Maddux had authority over her own life, Erma in effect granted her that authority rather than assuming that she could achieve identity only in relation to another person, and *Communication* thus becomes a testament of selfhood.

By the end of *Communication*, Maddux has recaptured the emotional side of her nature and has fallen in love with a man many years her senior. When he declares his love for her, she must release "all the threads which had held me for so long so tightly bound together" and let loose the pent-up feelings "roaring and sweeping and taking possession" (129). Learning to feel again also makes possible a reconciliation with her mother. Whereas in Maxine Hong Kingston's *The Woman Warrior,* the mother's stories empower the daughter to become a storyteller, in *Communication* the daughter empowers the mother by finally convincing her that she wants to hear the stories her mother has to tell about life on the farm. "And they simply rolled out of her, these simple beautiful stories, and each one pure art without sentimentality or interpretation—the real thing" (143). In the process of telling the stories about her childhood, Maddux's mother also talks about her life as a wife and mother, and Maddux begins to see the strength of this woman she has misunderstood for so long—including the mother's one defiant act of taking long walks by herself. As her mother ages, Maddux takes on the maternal role, especially after her mother writes to say, "You be the mother now and let me be the child. I am tired" (145).

But it is not as a daughter, mother, or lover that Maddux ends her autobiography. She ends it as a writer, certain of her gifts and her potential. She had long been convinced of the power of the written word, even though she had discovered that books did not instantly unlock the secrets of the universe. She reports that as a child, she had written to the governor of Kansas to seek a pardon for a man sentenced to a long jail term for stealing chickens in order to feed his children. When the man was in fact pardoned, she felt both relief and responsibility: "This writing, I thought, is a serious thing, not to be fooled around with" (79). At twenty-eight, having published her first stories, she defines herself as a writer who aspires to be one of the great ones:

> *Here I am, a writer, a writer who is absolutely con-*
> *fident that she will some day write a great book, a*
> *writer who will attempt no compromise, who will try*
> *for no small safe goals, a writer who, in the privacy*
> *of her own boudoir, is sometimes not ashamed to say*
> *that she is trying to be with Milton and with Joseph*
> *Conrad and with Thomas and part of Carlyle.*
> (117)

Writing her autobiography—attempting truly to be in command of "communicating" herself—is preparation for this future work, as she notes in the concluding chapter: "By writing this to the only person in the world who could understand ALL of it *the way it is said*, I think I have learned how to write so that later things can be understood by any human being who has breathed the air in and breathed it out and learned to read and asked himself one question" (156). What Maddux suggests in this passage is that to write one's own life may be the most difficult task of all—that composing a self to present to even a single reader both develops the skills of a writer and establishes a perspective from which future stories can be told.

Jill Johnston makes a similar point in "Fictions of the Self in the Making." In response to the view that "the life can't be *written*, it must be lived first, then written *about*—provided it meets certain standards of achievement and propriety," Johnston argues that autobiographical writing early in one's life alters the concept of privilege and authority:

> *As we remake the past, we alter the way we see our-*
> *selves in the present and the way we cast ourselves*
> *into the future. This is not the concept of the tradi-*
> *tional autobiography, usually the prerogative of the*
> *famous or powerful, who look back at a life of accom-*
> *plishment and tell a straight chronological and "fac-*
> *tual" story.*
> (29)

For those not "famous or powerful," then, the autobiographical act performs a different function. Rather than serving as a record of an exemplary life, it is an act of self-creation with at least as much value to the
writer as to the reader. That such an act may take place even without the
production of a text is suggested by one of the ways in which Carolyn
Heilbrun suggests that a woman's life may be written: "in advance of
living it, unconsciously, and without recognizing or naming the process"
(11). Rachel Maddux both recognized and named the process, but the
purpose of *Communication* is strikingly similar: to announce herself *to*
herself, and in the process to claim her own worth.

Both *No Laughing Matter* and *Communication* challenge and resist traditional conceptions of the form and purpose of autobiography. Each
writer both writes *about* herself and writes as a process of bringing herself
into being. Each is concerned with examining the effect of family and
the larger culture in determining the shape and limitations of a woman's
life, and with detailing her own resistance to such determination. For
both Halsey and Maddux, such resistance involved dramatic and even
dangerous realignment of the self in relation to the intellect. In her desire
to be heard, Halsey sacrificed domestic harmony and suffered panic at-
tacks and alcoholism. Maddux, writing in advance of her public career,
examines the dangers for the woman who denies herself emotion, and in
the process dramatizes woman's capacity for self-determination. Both
writers are conscious that there are two gazes in the mirror—her own
and that of the "other"—but each claims the freedom to "do herself
justice."

Five   # OF HESTER
                 # AND OFFRED

1

What Hawthorne will need is what every potential
past needs in order to survive—for the living present
to continue to make it the image of its living concerns
and needs.
RICHARD BRODHEAD,
THE SCHOOL OF HAWTHORNE

This is a reconstruction.
MARGARET ATWOOD, *THE HANDMAID'S TALE*

Richard Brodhead's *The School of Hawthorne* is a study of the formation
of American literary tradition and canonicity that uses Nathaniel Hawthorne as its chief exemplar. Brodhead's purpose is to demonstrate that
variations over time in the relative prominence of American authors are
the result of both their influence on subsequent readers and writers and
the demands of particular cultural moments. Thus, according to Brodhead, "literary tradition has a genuinely and distinctly intraliterary dimension to its actions. . . . But this intraliterary drama never ceases to
operate within the cultural dimension of literature's life" (13). What
Brodhead terms the "conditions of possibility" (12) of a work of literature include generic predecessors, assumptions about audience, the author's understanding of his or her function as a writer, and the cultural
weight accorded certain forms and styles at a given time. As these "conditions of possibility" change over time, so do the needs, tastes, and val-

ues of the—increasingly academic—critical establishment. Brodhead traces the high and low points of Hawthorne's critical valuation, showing that a reaction against the separation of "high" and "low" culture in the early twentieth century prompted a diminished status for Hawthorne's work following his canonization in the late nineteenth century, but that by mid-century his reputation was ascendant again, thanks to scholars such as F. O. Matthiessen and writers—most notably Faulkner—who made Hawthorne's work integral to their own. The chapter epigraph is the last sentence of *The School of Hawthorne*—an almost wistful, though no doubt accurate, statement of the fact that a continued high regard for Hawthorne, as for any author, would depend on the "living concerns and needs" of future generations.

In the same year that *The School of Hawthorne* was published, two of North America's most prominent contemporary authors published novels that testified to Hawthorne's continuing vitality in the "living present" of the 1980s. John Updike's *Roger's Version* is the second of his three novels inspired by the central characters of *The Scarlet Letter. A Month of Sundays* (1975) recalls Arthur Dimmesdale in its account of an adulterous minister; *Roger's Version* turns Roger Chillingworth into the modern-day Roger Lambert, a professor of theology who ponders the existence of God while one of his students has an affair with his wife; and in *S.* (1988), Sarah Worth is Updike's version of Hester, who leaves her New England home, her doctor-husband, and her daughter, Pearl, to go to a Hindu commune in Arizona in search of spiritual and sexual fulfillment. Not a trilogy in the usual sense, the three novels constitute a series of meditations on what Updike has called Hawthorne's "strange little fable" from the perspective of the late twentieth century. Updike's enduring interest in both religion and adultery in a twentieth-century context perhaps made Hawthorne's tale especially compelling as a point of departure for these three novels, but as Cushing Strout points out in *Making American Tradition*, Updike was by no means the first to find inspiration in *The Scarlet Letter* for their own work. William Dean Howells's *A Modern Instance* (1882), Henry Adams's *Esther* (1884), and Harold Frederic's *The Damnation of Theron Ware* (1896) all, as Strout says, bear "the shadow of Hawthorne's triangle" (23).

While these authors and Updike refer in their plots, themes, and language (including names) to *The Scarlet Letter*, Margaret Atwood's *The Handmaid's Tale* works by far the most complex revision of Hawthorne's text. In revising, inverting, and extending *The Scarlet Letter*, Atwood does more than bring the elements of Hawthorne's story into her own time, as her predecessors had done. She also interrogates the relationship of the past to the present, as had Hawthorne himself, but, unlike Hawthorne, she questions our ability to *know* the past—including our own personal histories. Thus, while on one level Atwood retells Hawthorne's story, granting to Offred/Hester the agency of storyteller, she simultaneously casts doubt on the possibility of any telling of a "true" story; as her tale is a "reconstruction" of *The Scarlet Letter*, Offred's/Hester's autobiographical text is both a *self*-construction and a *re*-construction that questions the very concept of the self.

But before exploring Atwood's revisionary use of *The Scarlet Letter*, it is worth considering the use she makes in *The Handmaid's Tale* of the motifs of the traditional fairy tales, for one of the ways in which Atwood questions Hawthorne's narrative is to set it as one story among many possible stories in her own text: historical narrative, biblical narrative, personal memoir—all contingent. Atwood has written that she sees herself as "part of a community, the community of writers, the community of storytellers that stretches back through time to the beginning of human society" ("Nine Beginnings," 154) and in calling her narrative a "tale" she signals her connection with the oral tradition of the folk tale. And, indeed, *The Handmaid's Tale*, as the reader learns in the "Historical Notes" section at the end, originated as an *oral* tale, recorded on cassette tapes following Offred's apparent escape from Gilead. Further, just as the precise original authorship of the folk tale or fairy tale cannot be established, so the scholars at the Twelfth Symposium on Gileadean Studies announce that they are unable to determine the identity of the "author" of the tapes. And as the tales themselves have undergone alterations in both oral transmission and written form, so Professor Pieixoto is careful to note that the version of the tale extant in the year 2195 is a "reconstruction," a "soi-disant manuscript" (381) transcribed by two scholars who may not have understood clearly the "accent, obscure referents, and archaisms" (383) of the narrator. Like the Brothers Grimm and Charles Perrault, Professors Pieixoto and Wade can claim only to present *a* version, not *the* version of the tale, and the Gileadean scholars regard it as partial, folkloric evidence of the values and practices of the Republic of Gilead in much the same way as we might regard the European fairy tales in their early written forms as informal indices of the cultures in which they were transcribed.

Within *The Handmaid's Tale* itself, Atwood recapitulates elements common to the traditional tales. The Aunts resemble evil fairies and antagonistic stepmothers as they indoctrinate the Handmaids into their new roles, reducing them to the level of children who sleep, closely guarded, on flannelette sheets in dormitories, and reciting quasi-biblical incantations. The relationship between Offred and her Commander's wife recalls that between Snow White and her stepmother, with the younger woman displacing the older one in a way that makes explicit the sexual jealousy of the stepmother in the fairy tale. During the ritual sexual "Ceremonies" between Offred and the Commander, Offred can feel his wife Serena Joy's hatred of her as the fertile woman that Serena Joy is no longer: "There is loathing in her voice, as if the touch of my flesh sickens and contaminates her" (123). Offred does, in fact, symbolically take on the role of the Commander's wife later in the novel. On the night that the Commander takes her to the brothel, Offred puts on her makeup while looking in Serena Joy's mirror and wears Serena's light blue cloak in order to deceive the security guards. Later the same night, as Serena Joy leads Offred to Nick's apartment, Offred sees the two of them reflected in the "brief glass eye of the mirror" and thinks, "Myself, my obverse" (336). (Although Serena Joy does not attempt to kill Offred in the manner of Snow White's stepmother, there are rumored stories of other Commanders' wives who have made such attempts: "Stabbed her with a knitting needle, right in the belly. Jealousy, it must have been, eating her up" [14].)

The mirror so central to the Snow White tale is also present in the numerous images (common in so much of Atwood's work) of the doubled self. Offred and Serena Joy lie together in identical postures in bed with the Commander; the Handmaids travel the streets in pairs; Offred imagines the previous occupant of her room as her "double"; and Moira and Offred represent different forms of prostitution—one traditional, illicit, and subterranean, the other a publicly sanctioned means of perpetuating Gilead's ruling class.

Elements of "Beauty and the Beast" and "Sleeping Beauty" are also present in the novel. Like Beauty, Offred has little choice but to occupy the house of the "beast"; the father to whom Beauty is obedient in the fairy tale is magnified in Atwood's tale into the patriarchal structures of Gilead. Offred's initial response to her Commander is compounded of fear and disgust, but as they continue their clandestine games of Scrabble, he gradually seems more "human" to her. During an early sexual "ceremony," which has the character of the emotionless, ritual mating of animals, Offred imagines the Commander's "white, tufted raw body" (123). Later, when after a Scrabble game he asks her to kiss him, Offred remarks that "he's like someone I've only just met" (181), and during their next sexual ritual she realizes that "he [is] no longer a thing to me" (207). In the tale of Beauty and the Beast, it is Beauty's love that ultimately tames and humanizes the beast; in Atwood's dystopia, however, love has been replaced by power ("*Love*," says Aunt Lydia, "is not the point" [285]), so that at the end of *The Handmaid's Tale* it is the threat posed to the Commander by Offred's capture (or escape) that allows her to feel sorry for him: "Possibly he will be a security risk, now. I am above him, looking down; he is shrinking" (377–378).

Sharon Rose Wilson, whose *Margaret Atwood's Fairy-Tale Sexual Politics* is the most thorough analysis of Atwood's use of fairy-tale and mythological motifs, argues convincingly that the tale most in evidence in *The Handmaid's Tale* is "Little Red Cap," the Grimm tale better known to modern readers as "Little Red Riding Hood." Offred's red cloak and the basket she carries while shopping are visual signals of reference to the tale (Atwood has commented, "What do you think of when you see someone in red carrying a basket?" [Wilson, 271]). On a more significant level, Offred, like the girl in the tale, is an innocent, fertile, and somewhat naïve young woman who is separated from her mother and undertakes a journey that leads to her encounter with the wolf (the Commander) and the grandmother (Serena Joy). As Wilson points out, Atwood makes some important changes in the traditional tale. By using the first-person narrative perspective, Atwood "privileges Red Cap's point of view" and restores her "inner resourcefulness and power" (278). In addition, by suggesting Offred's escape at the end of the story, Atwood suggests that "Offred may reach at least the 'safe house' of her sisters, a place where she can consume the sacramental cake and wine of healing once brought to the grandmother" (290).

Like the heroines of a number of fairy tales, the role of the Handmaids is passive in the extreme. Their lives are ordered and without choices; they wait to become pregnant and await whatever fate will befall them if they do not. Atwood reinforces this passivity in both the structure and the rhetoric of her novel, and in the process makes Offred an avatar of Sleeping Beauty. Of the fifteen chapters in *The Handmaid's Tale*, seven are titled "Night," one is titled "Nap," and another, "Waiting Room." In the second of the "Night" chapters, Offred thinks about her enforced inactivity: "The night is mine, my own time, to do with as I will, as long as I am quiet. As long as I don't move. As long as I lie still. The difference between *lie* and *lay*. Lay is always passive. . . . I lie, then, inside the room, under the plaster eye in the ceiling, behind the white curtains"

(49). Regular naps, in fact, are part of the Handmaids' training: "They were giving us a chance to get used to blank time" (91). For this Sleeping Beauty, Nick is an ambiguous Prince. When he appears at her room in the final chapter and calls her by her real name, he could be either savior or executioner, and Offred is aware of the extremes of possibility: "'Trust me,' he says; which in itself has never been a talisman, carries no guarantee" (376).

Even before she becomes a Handmaid, Offred has experienced the passivity and dependency of the fairy-tale heroine. When the Gileadean regime prepares for its takeover by stripping women of the means of independent action, Offred loses her job as a librarian and access to her bank account. Her consequent powerlessness affects dramatically her relationship with her husband, Luke:

> *Something had shifted, some balance. I felt shrunken,*
> *so that when he put his arms around me . . . I was*
> *small as a doll. I felt love going forward without me.*
>
> *He doesn't mind this, I thought. He doesn't mind*
> *it at all. Maybe he even likes it. We are not each oth-*
> *er's anymore. Instead, I am his. . . .*
>
> *We never talked about it. By the time I could*
> *have done that, I was afraid to. I couldn't afford to*
> *lose him.*
> (236)

The word "afford" has both emotional and economic meanings. The leaders of Gilead understand intuitively that if their regime is to be successful, women must be reduced to doll-like status.

Many critics have drawn attention to Atwood's use of the dystopian form, though most see it as an extension of her realist purpose: to dramatize the social tendencies of the 1980s, which, if taken to their logical extremes, could create a society like Gilead. Lorna Sage, however, sees such narrative strategies on the part of women writers as a way of resisting a realism that can imprison women:

> *Realistic representation confirms the separation of*
> *groups, genders, kinds; it reinforces the bad faith of*
> *role-playing; and reproduces a fossilized world, a*
> *realm of unfreedom. This has a relevance to their po-*

*sitions as women writers, for they clearly suspect that
the roles offered to women are peculiarly awful.*
(33)

The roles offered to women in Gilead *are* peculiarly awful, but the fairy-tale motifs and the dystopian mode are ways of resisting the fixed realistic narrative: both forms are predicated on change (including the magic transformations so commonly a part of the fairy tale). And by positing, in the Historical Notes as well as in the tale itself, that her text is merely an approximate "reconstruction," Atwood maintains an ironic distance that makes other versions of the story—including Hawthorne's—equally possible.

2

*the music lingered, a palimpsest of unheard sound,
style upon style . . .*
ATWOOD, *THE HANDMAID'S TALE*

In a taped interview with Tom Vitale of the American Audio Prose Library, Atwood discusses the inevitable comparison of *The Handmaid's Tale* with George Orwell's *1984*. Both *The Handmaid's Tale* and *1984* are dystopian novels that depict totalitarian societies set in a near future that the authors could envision emerging from the political and social realities surrounding them. One significant difference between these two novels, as Atwood points out in the interview, is that, whereas the central consciousness in *1984*, Winston Smith, is a member of the political elite, her own central character, Offred, occupies a position more analogous to that of the "proles" in Orwell's novel. Although Offred, as a Handmaid, is a relatively "privileged" member of the Republic of Gilead, Atwood says ironically, "as everyone keeps telling her," she is still a captive of the social system rather than one of its executives.[1] The perspective in *1984*, in other words, is that of a member of the ruling class, one of those who practices the deceptions by which the society operates, whereas the perspective in *The Handmaid's Tale* is that of one forced to occupy an uncomfortable niche in the new social order. Even though Winston Smith becomes a victim of the state at the end of *1984*, he does so because he has chosen to defy the rules. Offred, in Atwood's novel, has far less choice about which rules to abrogate; because she is a woman, she is trapped by her own biology in the intricate and highly stratified social structure of the Republic of Gilead.

Reading *The Handmaid's Tale* with *The Scarlet Letter* in mind, however, reveals how fundamentally Atwood understands the power of Hawthorne's text as both literary artifact and cultural icon.[2] The striking similarities between these two works illuminate the persistence of certain cultural realities: the use of fundamentalist religious doctrine as a justification for political repression, the distance between official rhetoric and the "truth" of actual life, and the use of women as cultural symbols. The differences between Hawthorne's and Atwood's works, on the other hand—primarily differences in narrative strategy and tone—point to the emergence of a feminist consciousness that recognizes in a different way than did Hawthorne the absurdity of repression. By controlling—even revising—her own ironically narrated story, Offred achieves a freedom of consciousness that is denied to both Winston Smith (because of his own brainwashing) and Hester Prynne (because of the omniscient narrator). Indeed, *The Handmaid's Tale* often reads as ironic commentary on the plot, themes, and characters of Hawthorne's often-ironic "romance," inverting both the narrative perspective and the function of the love triangle that Strout finds so compelling to Hawthorne's successors. By allowing Offred narrative centrality, Atwood grants to her the power of storyteller, allowing her to engage in a critique of the changing values of her culture.

Some of the parallels and inversions that Atwood's narrative performs are fairly obvious. Hester Prynne is branded as an adulteress because of her illicit relationship with Arthur Dimmesdale and the resultant birth of her daughter, Pearl; in contrast, Atwood's narrator, Offred, is forced into an adulterous relationship by a society that values *only* her fertility. In both cases, the woman is viewed by her community as a symbol (of sin and of status, respectively) rather than a person, and as an occasion for public rituals intended to cleanse the community's moral fiber. The scaffold scenes in *The Scarlet Letter* are replaced in Atwood's novel by "Birth Days" and "Salvagings." Hester's symbolic scarlet "A" and Offred's red cape set them apart from other categories of women and make them objects with particular functions: Hester is to serve as the community's warning against promiscuity, and Offred and the other Handmaids are to serve as incubators for the perpetuation of the ruling class. Further, despite the fact that Hawthorne's novel is set in colonial New England and Atwood's in a society of the future, both narratives describe cultures that, motivated by religious or quasi-religious zeal, create an order that seeks to deny individual agency to women and the free expression of both thought and passion.

In addition to such resonances (and there are many others) is the fact that Hawthorne as well as Atwood was writing a revisionary narrative in a number of senses. Not only did several historical texts inform his understanding of the seventeenth-century Puritan colonists and their moral and spiritual dilemmas—among them Caleb Snow's *History of Boston* and John Winthrop's *Journal*[3]—but he creates a decidedly nineteenth-century narrator who interprets the drama he recounts in light of the philosophical currents and social history of his own day.[4] Such projects of reinterpretation inevitably create ambiguities, as the lens of the author's present focuses on the past, and Hawthorne's narrator seems to exist in a particularly ambiguous relationship with both Hawthorne himself and Hester Prynne. In her growing dignity and self-sufficiency, Hester seems to escape the narrator's original intentions for her. In a "tale of human frailty and sorrow," from which readers are to derive a "moral blossom," Hester is particularly unchastened by the constant reminder of her sin. Even though, as Michael Davitt Bell argues, at the end of *The Scarlet Letter* "Hester returns to her obligations and subordinate position" (53), it is noteworthy that she *chooses* to do so. Even though Hawthorne seeks to encode Hester within the mid-nineteenth-century genteel plot of domesticity and so gain narrative control over her potential for rebellion, she is, as Judith Fryer notes, "a woman who acts, not a woman who is acted upon" (14). The more, then, the narrator intrudes to offer pronouncements on "woman," the more Hester belies such pronouncements, resembling not the nineteenth-century woman Hawthorne wants her to be, but her seventeenth-century predecessors Anne Hutchinson and Mary Webster.

In contrast to Fryer, Sacvan Bercovitch argues in *The Office of the Scarlet Letter* that Hester returns at the end to resume her A not because she has become an individual capable of exercising free will, but "as representative of the need for law and the limits of free will" (14). Bercovitch sees Hester not as a woman who frees herself from guilt, but as Hawthorne's representation of his nineteenth-century belief that social order and progress are not imposed by external authority, but arise from the individual's consent to the necessities of the community. In this view, Hester "re-forms herself, voluntarily, as the vehicle of social order" (15).

If Hester becomes, as Bercovitch argues, a symbol of order, Offred represents disruption on several levels. Her mother's active feminist rebellions have not inspired her to similar activism—indeed, the reverse is true—but they have taught her a skepticism about authority and a sense of personal rights. She defies the rules of Gilead in a number of ways: subversive conversations with Ofglen; clandestine sexual encounters with Nick; games of Scrabble, magazines, and books in her Commander's study. Most significant, she disrupts her own narrative—revising, interpolating, reconstructing. And in the end, she escapes not merely Gilead but efforts to identify her two hundred years later.

In contrast to Hawthorne's omniscient, morally certain narrator, the consciousness that guides us through *The Handmaid's Tale* is that of the central character, the bewildered but fully conscious Offred, who can only guess at the meaning her life has assumed. Instead of Puritanical demarcations between good and evil, the culture that Atwood depicts features reversals and subversions of the values depicted in *The Scarlet Letter*. The Handmaids' adulterous relationships with the Commanders are schooled for and mandated; fertility rather than virginity is a young woman's greatest prize; and religion has little to do with personal salvation, but is used solely to reinforce the dictates of the state. The first words of Atwood's novel signal the ambiguities of the culture in which Offred lives: "We slept in what had once been the gymnasium" (3). Not only do we not know who "we" are at this point, but one culture has been superimposed on several others, so that nothing is quite what it seems to be. Whereas Hawthorne locates *The Scarlet Letter* firmly in a time and place, beginning his narrative with the "Custom-House" section, which puts his romance in both historical and moral context, Atwood keeps us off balance, allowing us only gradually to discover that the Republic of Gilead is a projected incarnation of the northeastern United States in the late twentieth century, a totalitarian society in which rules have no reference to clearly understood and agreed-upon cultural values.

Despite these clear differences in narrative perspective, which are significant as they illuminate Atwood's feminist critique of American culture, both Hawthorne and Atwood compel the reader to question the values of a society ruled by a religious fundamentalism that forces its members to behave as hypocrites. Indeed, as the many correspondences between the two texts make clear, Atwood has used *The Scarlet Letter* as a means of increasing the resonances of her own text. Working within the emerging romance tradition of the mid–nineteenth century, Hawthorne uses its conventions to heighten his critique of Puritan morality; more than a century later, Atwood projects a return of fundamentalist hegemony, but adopts a first-person narrative that magnifies both the isolation and the centrality of her narrator and uses irony to call into question fixed meanings.

The romance, as Hawthorne used it, presupposes a stable moral order, in which "the truth of the human heart" is presumed to be a constant that can be understood and conveyed in a straightforward manner. Thus, Hawthorne's narrator tells us that "human nature . . . loves more readily than it hates" (155), and he defines for us woman's "character and person," proposing, in keeping with nineteenth-century belief, that women discern with their emotions rather than their intellect. Hester, like all women, the narrator says, has her "truest life" in the "ethereal essence"; the mind is, for her, a "dark labyrinth" in which she wanders "without a clew" (160). Offred, in Atwood's novel, is confused by the dramatic changes in her culture—changes that have removed her from her life as wife, mother, and daughter and placed her in a situation in which all relationships are forced and artificial. But it is precisely Offred's *mind*—her late-twentieth-century ironic intellect—that Atwood offers us: her first-person narrative is a record not primarily of events, but of the narrator's attempts to understand and accommodate herself to these changes—and her mental and emotional rebellions against them—and of her effort to reconcile past and present. Atwood's novel proceeds by means of the juxtapositions common to the ironic mode: past versus present, truth versus lie, reality versus fantasy.

As Lilian Furst has pointed out, the novel, more than other literary forms, is conscious of itself as a "fiction": "This recognition of the pretence inherent in all fictional narrative breeds a consciousness of art as art on the part of the writer and the reader alike" (45). Further, this inherent awareness of its own artifice opens the novel naturally to irony:

> *The narrator may tell, besides his story, of himself and the story he is telling. . . . And because the novel, more than any genre, has the freedom to enlarge its spaces, it has the greatest aptitude for irony. . . . It is indeed arguable that the novel is an intrinsically ironic gesture because its form tends to foster a radical scrutiny of its own fictive constructs.*
> (46)

The Scarlet Letter calls attention to itself as a "fictive construct" just as forcefully as does *The Handmaid's Tale*. Hawthorne's narrative presence is a constant reminder that what we are reading is a construction by that consciousness of a certain fictive reality. But Hawthorne's intention is in large part historical—to present Hester as a player in a specific socioreligious drama that is located in a particular time and place and has direct implications for his own century—whereas Atwood's intention is to make the reader question the stability of Offred's tale. The fact that Offred narrates her story *as* a story that she constantly reminds us is a "reconstruction" is an invitation to the reader to perform additional reconstructions.

In fact, the entire structure and meaning of *The Handmaid's Tale* depend on an ironic method that is much more profound than the obvious situational inversions. The narrator must construct an impossible social logic as she attempts to make sense of her transformation from the complex relations of daughter, wife, and mother to the single-purpose role of Handmaid. In doing so, she challenges the reality of both her current circumstances and the lives that we as readers lead in the years just prior to the establishment of the Republic of Gilead. As Wayne Booth posits in *A Rhetoric of Irony*, the ironist presents statements that the reader recognizes as being untrue, and the reader, rejecting these statements, must then determine what the author's real meaning is and mentally reconstruct a statement that more nearly conforms to this meaning (10–12). Such statements permeate *The Handmaid's Tale*. Offred refers to the Bible, which she and the other Handmaids are not allowed to read, as "an incendiary device" (112); of the uniforms that women are required to wear, she says to her Commander, "So now that we don't have different clothes, . . . you merely have different women" (308). Behind each of these statements is another statement about women's subjugation; behind the witty utterance is an awful truth.

3

we may prate of the circumstances that lie around us,
and even of ourself, but still keep the inmost Me be-
hind its veil.
NATHANIEL HAWTHORNE,
"THE CUSTOM-HOUSE"

By using Hawthorne's novel as a palimpsest for her own, Atwood superimposes the figure of Offred on the figure of Hester Prynne and extends Hawthorne's quarrel with narrow-minded zealotry into a dystopian vision that calls into question the very notion of social progress—especially for women—that Hawthorne assumes to be inevitable. The elements that the two narratives have in common demonstrate Atwood's perception that the values and structures of Puritan culture are enduring forces in American culture, while her decision to tell the story from Offred's perspective gives Offred narrative control at the same time that the conditions she describes in Gilead's postfeminist era are more bleak than the ostensible ostracism to which Hester is subject. Hawthorne's narrative paternalism distances Hester from the reader, leaving her bathed, ultimately, in a grudging admiration. Offred is alone, presenting her version of life in Gilead and deciding what we shall know and fail to know about it.

Hawthorne sets *The Scarlet Letter* two centuries before his own time, in a colonial Boston founded optimistically as "the city on the hill," to stand as the perfect embodiment of Puritan doctrine. Atwood's novel is set in the same geographical location—more precisely, in Cambridge, near Harvard University, founded in 1636 by the Massachusetts Bay Colony for the education of Puritan ministers. By placing her narrative on the site of such a venerable institution of learning, Atwood underscores the failure of enlightened reason to fend off the human greed for power and domination. The location also makes clear certain ways in which Atwood uses her narrative to conjure up figures in American literary history besides Hester Prynne. Hester's expertise at embroidery and Anne Bradstreet's comment about the needle and the pen, for example, are evoked when Offred, denied both, remarks, "If only I could embroider. Weave, knit, something to do with my hands" (89).

In her interview with Tom Vitale, Atwood indicates that she set *The Handmaid's Tale* in America rather than in her native Canada in part because of America's history of revolution and the American tradition of utopianism, a tradition that includes the Puritan colonists. She further reminds us that despite our mythology about the colonists' search for religious freedom, they sought it only for themselves and were intolerant of differing religious views. Indeed, as Hawthorne acknowledges on the first page of his romance, human perfection is impossible in such an experiment: "The founders of a new colony, whatever Utopia of human virtue and happiness they might originally project, have invariably recognized it among their earliest practical necessities to allot a portion of the virgin soil as a cemetery, and another portion as the site of a prison" (55).

Atwood's novel depicts a late-twentieth-century culture in which the

doctrines of the Old Testament and those of Marxism are used, inter-
changeably, to justify totalitarian rule. Yet, Atwood maintains, *The
Handmaid's Tale* is not about "the evils of religion," but rather a "speculation" about the most effective means of taking over the United States—
through religious indoctrination rather than through the imposition of a
different political system.[5] Religious rhetoric, in fact, is used to encode
that of political ideology, as when the Handmaids are taught Marxist
doctrine disguised as biblical injunction: "*From each*, says the slogan, *according to her ability; to each according to his needs.* We recited that, three
times, after dessert. It was from the Bible, or so they said. St. Paul again,
in Acts" (151). The Aunts have done their own revising here, changing Marx's pronouns to reinforce the subjugation of female to male in
Gilead.

Both *The Scarlet Letter* and *The Handmaid's Tale* are purported to be
"found" manuscripts. Hawthorne's narrator describes in "The Custom-
House" how "a large portion of the following pages came into my possession" (16). In the attic room of the Custom House, he finds "a small
package, carefully done up in a piece of ancient yellow parchment." The
package contains documents "of a private nature" (39) and the faded
scarlet "A," along with "several foolscap sheets, containing many partic-
ulars respecting the life and conversation of one Hester Prynne" (41).
Hawthorne thus lends his romance an aura of historical authenticity, even
though his readers were and are aware that the finding of a manuscript is
a conventional fictional device. But Atwood works a revision on even
this device: the reader does not know until the "Historical Notes" section
at the end that the story Offred tells has been recorded on cassette tapes
and sealed in an army surplus trunk that has been unearthed in Maine
two hundred years later. The air of mystery and romance that Hawthorne attributes to the faded scarlet letter and the yellowed manuscript
pages are, in Atwood's postscript, transformed into a mockery of the
tone of scientific inquiry, as the scholars at the Twelfth Symposium on
Gileadean Studies in the year 2195 discuss the authentication of Offred's
"manuscript." The academic conference, which Atwood satirizes for
its casual pomposity, has the effect of trivializing Offred's experiences,
as the scholars seem concerned only with the cleverness of their pro-
cedures, whereas Hawthorne's remarks in "The Custom-House" cause
Hester Prynne to take on mythic proportions even before the reader
knows her story in detail.

Hawthorne's use of the found-manuscript device, though patently a
time-honored technique, posits a belief in the possibility of history—that

is, in the existence of a time before the present that can be recovered, and its meaning understood. It is precisely this sense of historical recoverability that Atwood's narrative denies, both in Offred's "text," with all of its reconstructions, and in the Historical Notes section, where the scholars confess to being unable to identify Offred because they cannot determine the "Fred" to whom she was assigned as a Handmaid. Further, they fault Offred for having "written" the kind of narrative she did, leaving many "gaps" in the historical record. "Some of them could have been filled by our anonymous author, had she had a different turn of mind" (393). At the end of the Historical Notes, Professor Pieixoto muses on history, here cast as an elusive woman:

> *We may call Eurydice forth from the world of the dead, but we cannot make her answer; and when we turn to look at her we glimpse her only for a moment, before she slips from our grasp and flees. As all historians know, the past is a great darkness, and filled with echoes. Voices may reach us from it; but what they say to us is imbued with the obscurity of the matrix out of which they come; and, try as we may, we cannot always decipher them precisely in the clearer light of our own day.*
> (394 – 395)

Not surprisingly, Professor Pieixoto here revises the Greek myth of Orpheus and Eurydice, attributing Eurydice's disappearance to her own volition rather than to Orpheus's violation of his vow not to turn to look at her.

Part of Atwood's challenge to historical certainty is her use of and revision of Hawthorne's text, which she brings into her own present. And by giving Offred the role of storyteller, she asserts the primacy of the female intellect; were Offred to wear a scarlet "A," it would stand for "Author."[6] Both colonial Boston and the Republic of Gilead are organized as patriarchal cultures, with power emanating from the top of a male hierarchy, and with women expected to behave according to rules they have not made and do not fully understand. In both cultures, woman's biology is a trap. Hester Prynne's adultery might well have gone unnoticed had she not become pregnant, and the child Pearl is as constant a reminder of her sin as is the scarlet letter she wears. Hester dresses Pearl in red, like the red of the letter that stands for adultery, and Hawthorne notes that

> it was a remarkable attribute of this garb, and, in-
> deed, of the child's whole appearance, that it irresis-
> tibly and inevitably reminded the beholder of the to-
> ken which Hester Prynne was doomed to wear upon
> her bosom. It was the scarlet letter in another form;
> the scarlet letter endowed with life! . . . [Pearl is] the
> object of her affection and the emblem of her guilt and
> torture.
> (103) [7]

We are not told whether Hester is conscious of the ironic resemblance between her daughter's clothing and the letter she must wear, but Offred is well aware of the irony of her own situation. Clothed, like Hester and Pearl, in red, Offred (whose name most obviously derives from "of Fred," but which also suggests taking *off* the *red*) sees her own body only when she takes a bath. The body that had once worn bathing suits is now usually covered completely, and Offred dislikes seeing it: "*Shameful, immodest. I avoid looking down at my body, not so much because it's shameful or immodest but because I don't want to see it. I don't want to look at something that determines me so completely*" (82; second emphasis added). The fertility that reveals Hester's sin is Offred's only hope. In the bathtub, Offred notices the Handmaid's tattoo on her ankle and comments wryly, "It's supposed to guarantee that I will never be able to fade, finally, into another landscape. I am too important, too scarce, for that. I am a national resource" (84–85).

As Pearl is the manifestation of Hester's sin, Offred's inability to become pregnant as a result of her ritualized encounters with the Commander could symbolically remove her gender altogether and cast her into the company of "Unwomen"—the aged (including, she discovers, her own mother), the infertile, and the "incorrigible"—who are sent to the "Colonies" to do the dirtiest work of the society: burying or burning bodies after battles and cleaning up toxic wastes. In ironic contrast to Hester, who is branded and ostracized for her sexuality, the Handmaid in Atwood's novel who fails to conceive is linguistically denied gender identity and exiled to do work that will soon kill her.

The power of language to identify and limit people—especially women—is clear in both works. In *The Scarlet Letter*, a single letter is sufficient to mark Hester apart from her community. With the A on her breast, she is intended to become more symbol than person: "giving up her individuality, she would become the general symbol at which the preacher and moralist might point, and in which they might vivify and embody their images of woman's frailty and sinful passion" (83). As Hester continues to live a righteous and benevolent life among her towns-people, however, the scarlet letter takes on quite different associations: "Many people refused to interpret the scarlet 'A' by its original signifi-cance. They said that it meant 'Able'; so strong was Hester Prynne, with a woman's strength" (156). Finally, ironically, the letter becomes a badge of holiness: "the scarlet letter had the effect of the cross on a nun's bosom. It imparted to the wearer a kind of sacredness which enabled her to walk securely amid all peril" (157). Ultimately, Hawthorne says, "The scarlet letter had not done its office" (160); that is, although Hester remains in many ways apart from her community, she is more admired than hated, and her punishment loses its force.

In Atwood's Republic of Gilead, virtually *all* women are categorized and forced to wear clothing that indicates their function or role. The Wives of the Commanders, infertile or past childbearing age, wear blue; housework is done by Marthas, who wear green. Young women who cannot be Handmaids—or who refuse to be, like Offred's friend Moira—become Jezebels, working at the high-class brothel frequented by the Commanders. The Aunts, who prepare the Handmaids for their du-ties, are women past childbearing age who reinforce the philosophy of the Gileadean hierarchy. Not privileged to be Commanders' wives, the Aunts take a perverse pleasure in exercising their small compass of power. The presence and role of the Aunts is the most chilling manifestation of Gilead's repudiation of feminist principles, because, as Coral Ann Howells points out, their complicity with the power structure threatens a matriarchy little different from the systems of male authority that feminists have sought to dismantle: "What the Aunts' tyranny dem-onstrates is the danger that patriarchal authority may merely be dele-gated to become matriarchal authority if the psychology of power poli-tics with its traditional patterns of dominance and submission remains unchanged" (65). That Offred recognizes the distinction between the fe-male power that her mother's generation fought for and the power ex-erted by the Aunts is revealed when she addresses her mother in her imagination: "Mother, I think. Wherever you may be. Can you hear me? You wanted a women's culture. Well, now there is one. It isn't what you meant, but it exists. Be thankful for small mercies" (164). The ironic last line of this passage both mimics the cliché-ridden speech of the Aunts and serves as a form of apology to her mother, whose feminist activities Offred had earlier found annoying.

Relationships among these various groups of women are highly ritualized. The Handmaids go shopping in pairs, as a form of control; they speak in approved code, greeting each other with biblically inspired phrases that often relate to their own function as mothers: "Blessed be the fruit," "May the Lord open" (25). Just as the Boston townspeople in *The Scarlet Letter* go to witness the public humiliations of wrongdoers on the scaffold, so the Handmaids are confronted with the bodies of social offenders hanging on hooks on the "Wall." As Hester is supposed to stand as a warning to the people of Boston, so these bodies are intended to remind the people of Gilead of the punishment for certain "crimes": homosexuality, the practice of science, the performance of abortions: "It doesn't matter if we look. We're supposed to look: this is what they are there for, hanging on the Wall. Sometimes they'll be there for days, until there's a new batch, so as many people as possible will have the chance to see them" (42).

Terms such as "handmaid," "Martha," and "Jezebel" obviously have biblical origins, and their use as coercive categories is just one example of the perversion of religion in Gilead. In *The Scarlet Letter*, Hawthorne shows how human hypocrisy can undermine religious belief. Occasionally, Hester feels sympathy in the look of one of the other townspeople, and Hawthorne asks, "Had Hester sinned alone?" (89). The Reverend Dimmesdale, of course, is the clearest example of hypocrisy in Hawthorne's tale, continuing to serve as a spiritual leader while consumed by his own guilt. In *The Handmaid's Tale*, the rhetoric of Christianity is twisted to become part of the ironic texture of lies. Its language is used for totalitarian purposes, including the training of the Handmaids to be passive and accepting. Because women are forbidden to read, Offred is unable to check the accuracy of biblical texts that she believes have been distorted:

> For lunch it was the Beatitudes. *Blessed be this,
> blessed be that. They played it from a tape, so not
> even an Aunt would be guilty of the sin of read-
> ing. The voice was a man's.* Blessed be the poor
> in spirit, for theirs is the kingdom of heaven.
> Blessed are the merciful. Blessed be the meek.
> Blessed are the silent. *I knew they made that up,*

> *I knew they left things out, too, but there was no*
> *way of checking.* Blessed be those that mourn,
> for they shall be comforted.
>   *Nobody said when.*
> (I I 4 – I I 5)

As religious sanctions against adultery are one means of controlling
women's behavior in Hawthorne's colonial Boston, so the biblical ad-
monition to be fruitful and multiply is used to dictate the role of the
Handmaids. Hester Prynne wins a sort of victory by virtue of her pa-
tience and strength; though officially ostracized, in a sense an "Unwoman,"[8] she is ultimately respected for her good works. No such transformation seems possible for Offred, whose life has been reduced to
function, and whose very sense of reality is constantly challenged by the
pervasive ironies of her circumstance. Early in the novel, her isolation
within her own mind is complete, as she tells us:

> *I would like to believe this is a story I'm telling. I*
> *need to believe it. I must believe it. Those who can*
> *believe that such stories are only stories have a better*
> *chance.*
>   *If it's a story I'm telling, then I have control over*
> *the ending. Then there will be an ending, to the*
> *story, and real life will come after it. I can pick up*
> *where I left off.*
>   *It isn't a story I'm telling. . . .*
>   *I must be telling it to someone. You don't tell a*
> *story only to yourself. There's always someone else.*
>   *Even when there is no one. . . .*
>   *I'll pretend you can hear me.*
>   *But it's no good, because I know you can't.*
> (5 2 – 5 3)

Offred's sense of unreality here—the autobiographer's sense that there
can be no story, however private, that does not have a reader—is made
ironic by the fact that of course she *is* a character in a story. But Atwood's
narrative method makes her at the same time the author. Hawthorne's
Hester, by contrast, is powerless to write her own story because of the
narrator's omniscient viewpoint. Despite the fact that the people of Bos-

ton gradually come to see her as "Able" rather than "Adulterous," she is not able to be the bearer of the word, the "prophetess":

> *Earlier in life, Hester had vainly imagined that she*
> *herself might be the destined prophetess, but had long*
> *since realized the impossibility that any mission of*
> *divine and mysterious truth should be confided to a*
> *woman stained with sin, bowed down with shame,*
> *or even burdened with a lifelong sorrow.*
> (245)

In addition to the echoes of Hawthorne's romance that resonate throughout *The Handmaid's Tale* and that suggest Atwood's keen awareness of the heritage of and potential for fundamentalist repression in American culture, her novel also marks a particular stage in feminist literary consciousness, one that began in the late 1960s with such works as Margaret Drabble's *The Waterfall.* This consciousness entails the ability of the fictional *persona* to see herself with an ironic double perspective—to understand the extent to which she is enmeshed in a culture whose values denigrate her, and yet to stand apart intellectually and comment on her own situation with an emotional detachment expressed as wit. This double consciousness is the narrative analogue to the process of revision: the character is both within history and outside of it, feeling the force of the moment and at the same time exercising a rhetorical freedom from it.

Offred simultaneously inhabits past, present, and future. She is conscious of telling a story after its events have taken place—*reconstructing* a story—and so speaks from a time beyond the story to an unknown reader who exists in another future. "This is a reconstruction," Offred says, and "if I'm ever able to set this down, in any form, even in the form of one voice to another, it will be a reconstruction then too, at yet another remove" (173). The nature of "truth," in contrast to Hawthorne's "*the* truth," is in question here, as she realizes:

> *It's impossible to say a thing exactly the way it was,*
> *because what you say will never be exact, you al-*
> *ways have to leave something out, there are too many*
> *parts, sides, crosscurrents, nuances; too many ges-*
> *tures, which could mean this or that, too many shapes*

> *which can never be fully described, too many flavors,*
> *in the air or on the tongue, half-colors, too many.*
> (173 – 174)

Offred, as author of her story, juxtaposes the necessary selection process of the intellect to the supposed rigidity of the rules by which she lives. Even the power that the restrictive doctrines of Gilead seem to exert may be illusory, as she goes on to suggest:

> *But if you happen to be a man, sometime in the fu-*
> *ture, and you've made it this far, please remember:*
> *you will never be subject to the temptation of feeling*
> *you must forgive, a man, as a woman. It's difficult to*
> *resist, believe me. But remember that forgiveness too*
> *is a power. To beg for it is a power, and to withhold*
> *or bestow it is a power, perhaps the greatest.*
> (174)

Hester Prynne also understands the power of forgiveness. By assisting the townspeople in times of trouble, Hester implicitly forgives their harsh treatment of her. Indeed, she achieves a certain kind of freedom by virtue of her isolation—a freedom of, as Hawthorne puts it, "speculation":

> *The world's law was no law for her mind. It was an*
> *age in which the human intellect, newly emancipated,*
> *had taken a more active and a wider range than for*
> *many centuries before. . . . Hester Prynne imbibed*
> *this spirit. She assumed a freedom of speculation,*
> *then common enough on the other side of the Atlan-*
> *tic, but which our forefathers, had they known it,*
> *would have held to be a deadlier crime than that stig-*
> *matized by the scarlet letter.*
> (158 – 159)

Hester's mind cannot be imprisoned, yet the reader has no access to it. The nature of her "speculation" remains vague, and her very foray into the realm of thought is regarded as "unwomanly" by Hawthorne's narrator. "A woman never overcomes these problems by thought," but "if her heart chance to come uppermost, they vanish" (160). Having come close to allowing Hester the possibility of intellectual freedom, Hawthorne quickly withdraws it, emphasizing again her membership in a category called "woman," in which emotion is ascendant over intellect.

While Hester's ultimate superiority is moral, Offred's is intellectual, and much of her power derives from the ironic stance from which she narrates her tale. As Booth suggests, irony creates a particular bond between author (or narrator) and reader because of the reader's construction of meaning:

> All authors . . . invite us to construct some sort of
> picture of their views and to judge them as in some
> sense coherent or plausible or challenging. But ironic
> authors obviously offer that invitation more aggres-
> sively, and we must answer it more actively: since the
> reader has in a sense put the final position together for
> himself, he can scarcely resist moving immediately to
> the third judgment: "Not only do I see it for what it
> is, but it must be sound since it is my own."
> (41)

Hawthorne invites the reader to become complicit with his narrator, who in turn sees Hester Prynne as symbolic representation of "woman." Offred issues a direct invitation to fashion with her the meaning of her story, to participate in a critique of Gilead from the inside.

Frequently during the narrative Offred announces her role as ironist, and by doing so reinforces her own intellectual distance from the events of her life in Gilead. In the midst of describing one of her forced sexual encounters with the Commander, she comments, "One detaches oneself. One describes." And a paragraph later she remarks on the absurdity of the situation: "There is something hilarious about this, but I don't dare laugh" (123). Later, after she has begun to play Scrabble with the Commander in secret, she compares herself to men's mistresses in earlier times:

> The mistress used to be kept in a minor house or
> apartment of her own, and now they've amalga-
> mated things. But underneath it's the same. More or
> less. Outside woman, they used to be called, in
> some countries. I am the outside woman. It's my
> job to provide what is otherwise lacking. Even the

> *Scrabble. It's an absurd as well as an ignominious*
> *position.*
> (210)

The phrase "more or less" reminds us that Offred's situation is vastly different from that of the mistress: here there is no passion, no pleasure, certainly no love. Offred is merely a womb, a body to be impregnated during ritual intercourse. By articulating the similarity between her situation and that of a mistress, the narrator forces us to see the difference. A few lines later, she indicates her awareness of the games she is playing: "I laugh, from time to time with irony, at myself" (210).

Offred is also capable of laughing at others. Her depiction of the Aunts, with their cattle prods and their aphorisms, makes them appear ridiculous despite their ostensible power, and the Commander's wife, Serena Joy, who is neither serene nor joyful, is more to be pitied than feared. Ultimately Offred is able to make fun of the Commander himself, and thus by implication of the power structure of Gilead. When he takes her to the secret "club" where the Commanders spend time with the Jezebels, he justifies the continued existence of such places by invoking "natural law," as had his nineteenth-century ancestors who were opposed to women's rights: "Nature demands variety, for men. It stands to reason, it's part of the procreational strategy. It's Nature's plan. . . . Women know that instinctively. Why did they buy so many clothes, in the old days? To trick the men into thinking they were several different women. A new one each day" (308). Far from being convinced by this assessment of male and female "nature," Offred sees it for the justification of the double standard that it is and mocks the Commander:

> *"So now that we don't have different clothes," I say,*
> *"you merely have different women." This is irony,*
> *but he doesn't acknowledge it.*
>   *"It solves a lot of problems," he says, without a*
> *twitch.*
> (308)

Paradoxically, in a society in which women of Offred's station are denied both the needle and the pen, Offred is fascinated by language. Books, words, texts of all kinds have enormous metaphoric force in Atwood's novel, pointing to Offred's role as Author. The games of Scrabble with her Commander offer an opportunity to luxuriate in language:

> Larynx, *I spell.* Valance. Quince. Zygote. *I hold*
> *the glossy counters with their smooth edges, finger*
> *the letters. The feeling is voluptuous. This is free-*
> *dom, an eyeblink of it.* Limp, *I spell.* Gorge. *What*
> *a luxury. The counters are like candies, made of pep-*
> *permint, cool like that. Humbugs, those were called.*
> *I would like to put them into my mouth. They would*
> *taste also of lime. The letter C. Crisp, slightly acid*
> *on the tongue, delicious.*
> (180)

Such language, like the game of Scrabble itself and the old *Vogue* magazine the commander shows Offred, belongs to the time before Gilead, so
that Offred must struggle to keep it alive: "My tongue felt thick with the
effort of spelling. It was like using a language I'd once known but had
nearly forgotten, a language having to do with customs that had long
before passed out of the world" (199).

Appropriately enough, Offred's job in the time before Gilead had been
in a library, and even now she is a guardian of language. Her delight in
the multiple meanings and connotations of words is part of Atwood's
challenge to fixed meaning, her belief in the fictive character of hegemonic narrative. Although Offred recalls having teased her husband
about his interest in words, she shares that interest, especially now, when
language has been subverted to maintain the power structure of Gilead.[9]
Offred refers to her word-association musings as "litanies . . . to compose myself" (140); they begin with everyday words such as "household," "chair," and "job," each of which finally refers to the bleakness
of her own situation: "The hold of a ship. Hollow" (104); "a mode of
execution" (140); "The Book of Job" (224). Similarly, when she engages
in clandestine reading in the Commander's study, she reports reading
Charles Dickens's *Hard Times.* Yet despite such references to hardship,
Offred considers language to be as basic to her life as food or sex. She
reads "voraciously" on these occasions (238) and remarks that "if it were
eating it would be the gluttony of the famished; if it were sex it would
be a swift furtive stand-up in an alley somewhere" (239).

As compelling as her hunger for reading is Offred's need to tell her
story. Whereas early in her narrative she has little faith that her story will
reach a reader or listener ("I'll pretend you can hear me . . . But . . . I
know you can't" [53]), once she has begun to break the rules of the life
scripted for her by continuing her affair with Nick and visiting the Com-

mander's study, she is far more certain that she is communicating with someone:

> *I keep going on with this sad and hungry and sor-*
> *did, this limping and mutilated story, because after*
> *all I want you to hear it, as I will hear yours too if I*
> *ever get the chance, if I meet you or if you escape, in*
> *the future or in heaven or in prison or underground,*
> *some other place. What they have in common is that*
> *they're not here. By telling you anything at all I'm*
> *at least believing in you, I believe you're there, I*
> *believe you into being. Because I'm telling you this*
> *story I will your existence. I tell, therefore you are.*
> (344)

The act of narrative, that is, *creates* its own reader; it necessitates and demands a consciousness to receive it. Further, the reader that Offred brings into being—the "you" to whom she speaks here—is both victim and survivor: "After all you've been through, you deserve whatever I have left, which is not much but includes the truth" (344).

So suspicious is Offred of the official rhetoric of Gilead that she recites her own version of the Lord's Prayer, in which she acknowledges that it is man, not God, who creates such societies, who makes such a mess of things: "I don't believe for an instant that what's going on out there is what You meant" (252). A God might be necessary to create a Heaven: "We need You for that. Hell we can make for ourselves" (252). By acknowledging that it is man, not God, who creates such societies as Gilead, Offred calls into question all authority, all necessity. Her repression is arbitrary, not the result of woman's "nature" or divine order. Whereas Hawthorne could make sweeping statements about the characteristics of "woman," Atwood views the individual woman as inhabiting a context that she is free to consider, examine, alter—even if only intellectually. In *The Scarlet Letter*, Hawthorne considers for a moment that women might wish for a change to a more "fair and suitable position" in society. If this is to occur, he says, "the whole system of society is to be torn down and built up anew," and "the very nature of the opposite sex, or its long hereditary habit which has become like nature, is to be essentially modified" (160). Yet such a revolution would require that woman abandon "the ethereal essence, wherein she has her truest life" (160), a change that his narrator obviously does not approve. Such statements are a reminder that Hawthorne's romance was published just two years after the 1848 Seneca Falls Woman's Rights Convention, with its "Declaration of Sentiments," and Atwood's novel was published just after a wave of feminist activity had begun to inspire a concentrated backlash.

In the quite different "revolution" that Atwood posits in *The Handmaid's Tale*, the fundamentalist forces have ostensibly won, yet Offred's consciousness, if not her life, embodies a feminist critique of this culture's values. Before the creation of the Republic of Gilead, Offred was a member of what has been termed the "postfeminist" generation; embarrassed and somewhat annoyed by her mother's aggressive feminism, she has grown up to be more conservative, more traditional in her views, and she considers her mother an anachronism, a fighter for freedoms she takes for granted. Angered by this, her mother tells her, "you're just a backlash. Flash in the pan. History will absolve me" (156). The fact that history has *not* absolved her, but rather has negated the freedoms for which the feminists had fought, makes Offred realize, despite the attempted brainwashing by the Aunts, what has been lost.

Because of the repressions of Gilead, however, Offred must express these thoughts subversively, by means of irony. Remembering, for example, that she used to exercise a certain amount of control over her life merely by putting her own money into the machines at a laundromat, Offred follows this memory with a statement remembered from Aunt Lydia: "There is more than one kind of freedom. . . . Freedom to and freedom from. In the days of anarchy, it was freedom to. Now you are being given freedom from. Don't underrate it" (33). Shortly after this, Offred remembers movies with Lauren Bacall and Katharine Hepburn, "women on their own, making up their minds": "They wore blouses with buttons down the front that suggested the possibilities of the word *undone*. These women could be undone; or not. They seemed to be able to choose. We seemed to be able to choose, then. We were a society dying, said Aunt Lydia, of too much choice" (33–34).

The key to Atwood's method in *The Handmaid's Tale* is in the statement "Context is all" (187). Context determines both meaning and response. As long as Offred can tell her own story, she can control the context, and thus control our response to her as an individual. Whereas Hawthorne determines the context in which we see Hester Prynne, and thus is free to make her more symbol than person, Atwood chooses a mode in which the individual mind, with its ability to inhabit both present and past, reveals the arbitrary nature of human reality. This method is thrown into relief by the very different voices of the methodical historians in the Historical Notes at the end of the novel. As they search for the truth both of and in Offred's "manuscript," they see her, as Hawthorne sees Hester, as an artifact, a representation, even as the reality of her voice continues to ring in the reader's ear. To the final question of the novel, "Are there any questions?" (395), the only answer can be "Yes."

Margaret Atwood dedicates *The Handmaid's Tale* to Mary Webster and Perry Miller, a pairing that seems particularly apt in light of her project here. Miller, an eminent scholar of Puritan literature and culture, was Atwood's professor of American literature at Harvard; Webster, a colonial ancestor of Atwood's, was hanged as a witch but, the story goes, survived the noose and was therefore allowed to go free. Perry Miller thus stands before Atwood's text as a transmitter of cultural tradition, Mary Webster as a disrupter, disobedient to the norms of her culture. By using *The Scarlet Letter* as palimpsest for her own narrative, Atwood pays homage to both individuals; by revising many of its premises and narrative conventions, she escapes the noose of a literary tradition that could exclude her.

Epilogue

In *Rowing in Eden: Rereading Emily Dickinson*, Martha Nell Smith reminds us of Dickinson's habit of cutting up the texts of others in order to incorporate or append illustrations or groups of words to her own writing. Smith notes that such a practice demonstrates that Dickinson "did not regard works as untouchably sacred" (52). The interaction with literary tradition that Emily Dickinson accomplished in a physical sense parallels the imaginative appropriation of literary texts that many women writers have performed as a way of both reformulating the tradition and claiming their own spaces within it. Further, the fact that Dickinson understood, as Smith puts it, "the meaning-producing processes of give and take between author and text, text and reader, reader and author, inevitable in reading" (52), is illustrative of the intertextuality that much contemporary criticism posits as essential to the formation of literary traditions.

Yet as Smith also points out, Dickinson is unusual among writers in that her choice to "publish" her work in her own way—poems bound in fascicles, and sent in letters to friends—freed her from the constraints of both commercial printing, which would have altered her idiosyncratic punctuation and effaced her expressive handwriting, and critical reception, which would have assessed her unconventional work according to conventional expectations of women's art. Most women writers, however—whether for the sake of money or art—have sought a more public form of publication, and in doing so have entered consciously into negotiation with a cultural heritage in which artistic creation is largely defined as a white male prerogative. Even as a widely published professional author, Kate Chopin was aware of the forces that exclude women from this heritage, and in her 1898 story "Elizabeth Stock's One Story" she tells the deceptively simple story of an aspiring writer who leaves at her death an autobiographical fragment that constitutes the "one story" she is allowed to tell.

As the derogatory terms "bluestocking" and "scribbling women" used in the nineteenth century and the work of Tillie Olsen, Joanna Russ, and Dale Spender in the twentieth attest, a woman who writes is practicing a form of disobedience to the established order. Writing this epilogue a few months after Toni Morrison was awarded the 1993 Nobel Prize for Literature, I must remind myself that it was not so long ago that Caroline Gordon wrote to Katherine Anne Porter about John Crowe Ransom, "He can't bear for women to be serious about their art"[1]—one of countless such statements that women have shared with each other over the centuries.

My concern in this study has been with a second level of disobedience, a level on which the writer is first an astute reader of narratives—both literary and cultural—that tell persistent stories about her. The Judeo-Christian Bible, as translated and interpreted over centuries, tells some of the oldest and most pervasive of these stories, which bear the weight of belief as well as of tradition. To confront such texts is no small matter, as Alicia Ostriker recognizes:

> *What happens when women re-imagine culture?*
> *What is the relation of the female writer to the male*
> *text, the male story? How can we—how do we—*
> *deal with that ur-text of patriarchy, that particular*
> *set of canonized tales from which our theory and prac-*
> *tice of canonicity derives, that paradigmatic meta-*
> *narrative in which innumerable small narratives rest*
> *like many eggs in a very large basket—the Book of*
> *Books which we call the Bible?*
> (FEMINIST REVISION, 27)

The answers to Ostriker's questions are multiple and complex. For some writers, such as Gail Hamilton, the effort to make a garden flourish in competition with the condescending "Halicarnassus" replicates Eve's disgrace in Eden; the biblical trope has its early-nineteenth-century secular counterpart. More contemporary women writers tend to subvert the power of the Eden story, often, as is the case with Lynne Sharon Schwartz and Ursula Le Guin, using humor to do so. As Ostriker notes, "what is supposed to be sacred becomes a joke. . . . For laughter, the 'scourge of tyrants,' is the most revolutionary weapon in literature's arsenal" (*Feminist Revision, 29*).

The most thoroughgoing response to a traditional narrative such as the biblical account of Eden is the text that completely reformulates the story in order to overturn its basic premises. In Marilynne Robinson's *Housekeeping*, leaving the Garden (represented by the house in Fingerbone) is not expulsion, but rather a movement toward the identification of woman with nature that characterizes pre-Christian belief systems; instead of being trapped in fleshly degradation, Ruth and Sylvie are finally disembodied altogether, capable of movement outside time and space. In Atwood's *The Handmaid's Tale*, the Gileadean regime purports to base its social order on a literal interpretation of the Bible, but, ironically, its leaders pervert both the spirit and the letter of the "Book of Books." The Genesis story of Jacob and Rachel and Rachel's handmaid Bilhah loses its character as loving and generative and becomes a grim monthly ritual, which Kauffman describes as "an ugly perversion of the spirit of the biblical dictum" (227). Even the language of the Bible is altered to suit the repressive purposes of the state. Rather than performing her own revision of the Bible, then, Atwood shows how supposed reverence for its teachings may become a sham in the service of political goals.

Offred's enforced idleness, as she waits for her future to be determined by others, recalls the passive heroines of many traditional European fairy tales—women who await awakening or rescue in stories so pervasive and familiar that the mere mention of a glass slipper or a red cloak can evoke an entire complex of cultural assumptions and expectations. Always a fluid genre, beginning in an oral folk tradition and reinterpreted in print and then film versions over several centuries, the classic fairy tales have been the object of the revisionist and parodic impulses of both men and women for more than a century. Given the level of *obedience* women practice in the classic fairy tales—Beauty to her father, Red Riding Hood to mother, grandmother, and wolf—and the penalties for *dis*obedience—witness Bluebeard's young wife—it is little wonder that women writers who have engaged fairy tales have tended either to emphasize the price of obedience in loss of self or to posit disobedience as a means of breaking the frame. The doll-like heroines who appear at the conclusions of many of Anne Sexton's *Transformations* underscore the lifelessness and false promise of "happily ever after," while authors such as Fay Weldon and Angela Carter overturn the paradigms of the classic tales at the same time that their use of fairy-tale motifs testifies to their continuing force.

The messages embodied in traditional fairy tales at any given point in time reflect the ideologies of the cultures that produce them.[2] Both the violence and the sensuality that characterized some early versions of the tales, for example, were muted for the young readers of the Victorian period, and the passivity we now associate with Sleeping Beauty and Snow White was reinforced during the same era. In addition to shaping popular literature, cultural ideologies produce their own narratives— mythologies that are no less potent for arising from desire instead of reflecting actuality. Such narratives may also be read with disobedience and responded to with revision. Among many American mythologies, two of the most persistent ones are gendered in terms of the trajectories they propose for men's and women's lives: on the one hand, the isolated, self-sufficient male shaped by and shaping the frontier experience— whether the frontier is figured as Walden Pond, Huck Finn's "territories," or the racist white world of Ellison's "invisible man"; and, on the other, the woman as moral exemplar inhabiting domestic space, guided by sentiment to her "natural" state of marriage.

By the middle of the nineteenth century, those mythologies had already been called into question by women writers who reversed their assumptions in their own work. Caroline Kirkland's *A New Home, Who'll Follow?* posits the frontier experience as communal and cooperative rather than individualistic. In describing the settlement of a small town in Michigan in the 1830s, Kirkland uses her thinly disguised autobiographical narrative to present the woman's perspective on such experience and to refute the Edenic promises of ease and bounty promulgated by land speculators. Fifteen years later, Fanny Fern also used autobiography as the basis of a novel that depicted a woman's fulfillment through career rather than marriage. Yet because of the force of the narratives that Fern and Kirkland resisted, *Ruth Hall* and *A New Home* faded from public attention until the 1980s.

The use of autobiography as the basis for fictionalized narrative takes on particular significance in women's revisionary process. As the example of Chopin's Elizabeth Stock shows, when all other stories seem to have been told, there remains one's own story, which can be told by no one else in the same way. Similarly, as in the case of Fanny Fern and Caroline Kirkland, autobiographical elements become a sign of the fact that one's own experience and perception are at odds with accepted narratives. And just as Elizabeth Stock's account of her life serves in part as a rebuttal to the version understood by the townspeople of Stonelift, so the act of writing autobiography constitutes a re-visioning of the self for presentation to a public. For the woman writer, such an act involves the transformation of the self from object to subject—from player in someone else's narrative to center of her own.

It is not surprising, then, that Margaret Atwood chooses an autobiographical form in which to cast *The Handmaid's Tale*. In addition to giving voice to a woman who is barred from language, this method suggests Offred's efforts to take narrative control over a situation in which she is essentially a prisoner. The fact that such control is an illusion is part of Atwood's critique of Hawthorne's belief that history can be reliably recovered and understood, and the multiple paradoxes of Atwood's text challenge the omniscient authority of the narrator in *The Scarlet Letter*.

Above all else, a consideration of the revisionary impulse in women's writing demonstrates that the project is as much cultural as it is literary. Put another way, it shows that the literary artifact—the fairy tale, the frontier narrative, the novel—frames and reflects certain assumptions about the nature of truth and reality that the revision then challenges, whether explicitly or implicitly. In addition, this process serves to blur distinctions of genre and to conflate literary history. As Patrick O'Donnell and Robert Con Davis put it in their introduction to *Intertextuality and Contemporary American Fiction*, "intertextuality challenges those systems of signification which allow us to mark off the formal terrains of 'literary period,' 'genre,' 'author,' 'subject,' 'nation,' 'text' " (xiv). For women writers, the implications of intertextuality reach far beyond literature itself. Because the production and definition of a canon of literature is a political and social as well as an aesthetic process, and because women writers have commonly understood that their attempts to influence or contribute to that process have cultural as well as artistic consequences, their appropriation and revision of the narratives they have inherited constitutes disobedience not only to the traditional narratives themselves, but also to the ways women have themselves been "read" by those texts and their creators.

Notes

INTRODUCTION:
ACTS OF DISOBEDIENCE

1. For a witty and compelling analysis of the reasons why Brown rather than Rowson was elevated to his traditional position at the headwaters of American fiction, see Jane Tompkins, "Susanna Rowson, Father of the American Novel," in *The (Other) American Traditions: Nineteenth-Century Women Writers*, pp. 29–38.

1. IN THE BEGINNING:
REVISITING THE GARDEN

1. Although, as Elaine Showalter argues persuasively in "Tradition and the Individual Talent: *The Awakening* as a Solitary Book," the fact that Chopin's novel was not widely read for fifty years following its publication prevented it from exerting the influence on other writers that it might otherwise have had (Kate Chopin, *The Awakening*, pp. 169–189).

2. Annette Kolodny, "A Map for Rereading: Gender and the Interpretation of Literary Texts," pp. 46–62; Deanna L. Davis, "Feminist Critics and Literary Mothers: Daughters Reading Elizabeth Gaskell."

3. Henry T. Tuckerman, ed. *The Poetical Works of Elizabeth Barrett Browning*.

4. Our understanding of this story, of course, comes through numerous filters, including translations, centuries of interpretation, and countless pictoral renderings of the story. In recent decades, feminist biblical scholars have studied the account from the linguistic and the cultural standpoint in order to perform their own revision, that is, to read the story free from the assumption that it establishes woman's subordinate status. Phyllis Trible, for example, points out that in terms of narrative structure, the creation of Eve after the creation of Adam could well signal her greater importance—"not an afterthought; she is the culmination"—and that the Hebrew word for "helper" designates a beneficial rela-

tionship with no suggestion of subordination. See "Eve and Adam: Genesis 2–3 Reread." For an overview of the work of contemporary feminist biblical scholars who are attempting to reach back through centuries to understand women's original role in Christianity and in biblical narrative, see Cullen Murphy, "Women and the Bible."

5. A more recent novel that deals with these same themes and counterpoints *Housekeeping* in interesting ways is Jane Hamilton's *The Book of Ruth* (1988). Although the narrators share the biblical name Ruth, Hamilton's story is in many ways the obverse of Robinson's. Her Ruth is a victim of her mother's obsessive "housekeeping" (both mother and daughter, significantly, work at a dry cleaner's), and she cannot escape in either space or time. Early in the narrative, she rhetorically rejects the notion of a biblical past, even though biblical references continue to permeate the novel: "In the Bible it starts with the spirit of God moving upon the face of the water, but I don't buy those ideas. You couldn't pay me to take my story back that far" (2).

6. Thomas Foster reads *Housekeeping* against Julia Kristeva's essay "Women's Time," in which Kristeva posits historical movement from women's desire to "gain a place in linear time," to a preference for "a cyclic and monumental temporality," and finally to an insistence on radical difference within a historical continuum ("History, Critical Theory, and Women's Social Practices: 'Women's Time' and *Housekeeping*"). Scholarly appraisal of Robinson's novel, however, has more frequently focused on space than on time. See, e.g., Rosaria Champagne, "Women's History and *Housekeeping*: Memory, Representation, and Reinscription"; Elizabeth A. Meese, "A World of Women: Marilynne Robinson's *Housekeeping*"; Paula E. Geyh, "Burning Down the House? Domestic Space and Female Subjectivity in Marilynne Robinson's *Housekeeping*."

7. Martha Ravits has explored most fully the resonances between *Housekeeping* and the American (male, except for Emily Dickinson) literary tradition. She suggests that Robinson adapts "American literary romanticism and nineteenth-century prototypes to twentieth-century womanhood" ("Extending the American Range: Marilynne Robinson's *Housekeeping*"). Ravits, like others, notes the similarity between the opening line of *Housekeeping* and that of *Moby-Dick*, but even here there is a revision: "My name is Ruth" suggests a different sense of identity than does "Call me Ishmael." The former is a statement of fact; the latter is both a command and a suggestion that the speaker has assumed an identity for purposes of the story.

2. TWICE UPON A TIME

1. As Carter was well aware, of course, as long as such tales were part of an oral tradition, they were the shared and significant cultural property of both men and women. It was only when they became part of written literature (a process initiated in both France and Germany by men) that they were relegated to women

and children. See Jack Zipes, *Breaking the Magic Spell: Radical Theories of Folk and Fairy Tales*, and Nina Auerbach and U. C. Knoepflmacher, eds., introduction, *Forbidden Journeys: Fairy Tales and Fantasies by Victorian Women Writers*, pp. 1–10.

2. In recent years, increasing concern about the sexism of the earlier film versions of classic fairy tales has led the Disney studios to attempt to modify the sterotypes in such films as *Aladdin* and *Beauty and the Beast*.

3. Perhaps partly because of the work of Zipes and others, both scholarly and popular interest in fairy tales—traditional, revised, and new—has been particularly intense since the 1980s. Zipes translated and edited a new collection of the Grimm tales—including forty that had not been published in English before—for Bantam Books in 1987 (revised edition 1992) and is currently editing a collection of American Victorian fairy tales. Ellen Datlow and Terri Windling edited a collection of modern tales published in 1993 that use traditional themes and motifs but are intended for adults (*Snow White, Blood Red*, Avon Books). Also in 1993, Alison Lurie edited *The Oxford Book of Modern Fairy Tales*, which includes tales written between 1839 and 1989 by such authors as Nathaniel Hawthorne, Charles Dickens, Carl Sandburg, Sylvia Townsend Warner, Ursula Le Guin, and Louise Erdrich. The collection constitutes a companion piece to her 1990 study *Don't Tell the Grown-Ups: Subversive Children's Literature*.

4. For a study of this and other feminist music videos, see Robin Roberts, "Humor and Gender in Feminist Music Videos."

5. Karen E. Rowe, "Feminism and Fairy Tales."

6. As this list of authors suggests, the new or revised fairy tale is often intended for an adult audience. Two recent collections of new and revised tales are Tanith Lee, *Red as Blood; or Tales from the Sisters Grimmer*; and Ellen Datlow and Terri Windling, eds., *Snow White, Blood Red*.

7. One of these ways, used less often than others, is to write a sequel to a traditional tale. A case in point is Sylvia Townsend Warner's "Bluebeard's Daughter," in her 1940 collection *The Cat's Cradle-Book*. Warner imagines a daughter born to one of Bluebeard's wives, who died in childbirth. The daughter, named Djamileh, enjoys a blissful childhood, partly because "none of the stepmothers lasted long enough to outwear their good intentions" (158), and eventually inherits her father's estate, where she channels the natural curiosity that has led so many other women to grief into the study of astronomy. Although it is her husband who achieves fame as an astronomer, it is widely known that Djamileh's talents are largely responsible for his success.

8. In "Of Babylands and Babylons: E. Nesbit and the Reclamation of the Fairy Tale," U. C. Knoepflmacher points out that even female writers who wrote tales that seemed to give female characters greater agency than in the traditional tales remained somewhat guarded about overturning social conventions regarding women's destinies. Edith Nesbit's personal life—among other things, she helped to found the Fabian Society—would seem to set her apart from her Victorian peers, but Knoepflmacher argues that her fiction did not seek to subvert

patriarchal norms. I would argue that Nesbit's use of the comic mode in such stories as "The Last of the Dragons" and "Fortunatus Rex & Co." constitutes just such a subversion, in which an insistence on male authority is made to seem absurd.

9. Alan Wilde notes that "the two major mythic prototypes of the novel" are Satan and Dr. Frankenstein, because each has an obsessive desire for the transformation of the self. Wilde cites Ruth's statement that, whereas Lucifer, who was male, had failed in his attempt to usurp the power of God, "she thought she might do better, being female," but he does not follow up on the implications of this comment. See "'Bold, But Not Too Bold': Fay Weldon and the Limits of Poststructuralist Criticism," p. 413.

10. Duncker refers to Carter as a "self-styled moral pornographer" (3). Robin Ann Sheets, in "Pornography, Fairy Tales, and Feminism: Angela Carter's 'The Bloody Chamber,'" reads the title story of Carter's collection in the context of her book *The Sadeian Woman and the Ideology of Pornography* (1979), in which Carter applies the term to herself. In this controversial work, Carter commends the Marquis de Sade for granting women sexual natures, despite the misogyny of his work. Sheets contends that, despite Carter's significant alterations of the fairy tales in *The Bloody Chamber*, she has not altered the power relationships of the original stories. "Carter envisages women's sensuality simply as a response to male arousal. She has no conception of women's sexuality as autonomous desire" (7).

11. On the point of mirrors and images in *The Passion of New Eve*, see also Roberta Rubenstein, "Intersexions: Gender Metamorphosis in Angela Carter's *The Passion of New Eve* and Lois Gould's *A Sea-Change*."

3. RESISTING AMERICAN MYTHOLOGIES: INDIVIDUALISM AND SENTIMENT

1. Somewhat ironically, the term "blue-stocking" was originally applied not to women at all, but to the men of Oliver Cromwell's "Little Parliament" of 1653, who affected plain dress rather than wearing black silk stockings. According to the *Oxford English Dictionary* (1961 edition), even when the term was applied to the mid-eighteenth-century literary salons held by wealthy Englishwomen, it was selected because of the attire of one of the male participants, a Mr. Benjamin Stillingfleet, who wore "blue worsted" stockings. By the end of the eighteenth century, the term was abbreviated in slang to "blues" and was used to apply specifically to women.

2. For two studies of how female writers negotiated with the prejudice against "literary women," see Mary Kelley, *Private Woman, Public Stage: Literary Domesticity in Nineteenth-Century America*; and Susan Coultrap-McQuin, *Doing Literary Business: American Women Writers in the Nineteenth Century*.

3. There would have been opportunities for the two women to become acquainted. Kirkland moved from Michigan to New York City in 1843, and Fern moved there from Boston in 1856. Both had friends among the journalists, editors, and other writers who lived in the city, and Fanny Fern's brother, Nathaniel P. Willis, was an acquaintance of the Kirklands.

4. The major exception in *Rose Clark* is an extended discussion of the legally sanctioned abuses—both physical and financial—that her character Gertrude Dean suffers at the hands of her husband. This depiction is based on Fanny Fern's disastrous second marriage to Samuel Farrington and reflects contemporary debates about the legal rights of married women—debates that resulted in the passage, beginning in 1839, of Married Women's Property Acts in a number of states.

5. Kirkland's statement is remarkably similar to one made more than thirty years later by humorist Marietta Holley. In the preface to *My Opinions and Betsy Bobbet's*, Holley writes: "I cant write a book, I don't know no underground dungeons, I haint acquainted with no haunted houses, I never see a hero suspended over a abyss by his gallusses, I never beheld a heroine swoon away, I never see a Injun tommy hawked, nor a ghost; I never had any of these advantages; I cant write a book ' (v). Both authors announce in this tongue-in-cheek manner their rejection of a tradition of romantic fiction in favor of coming to terms with issues of pressing concern to them—in Holley's case, women's lack of equality.

6. Such roots were, however, not permanent; Kirkland and her family moved back to New York in 1843.

7. As the example of Twain shows, however, the stereotype persisted, and female writers continued to resist it, often through satire. A notable example is Marietta Holley's creation of Betsy Bobbet in her first book, *My Opinions and Betsy Bobbet's*.

8. I am indebted to Sandra Zagarell's endnotes to her introduction to *A New Home* for the identification of Ainsworth and James.

9. For a summary discussion of Kirkland's intentions in her biography of Washington, see Zagarell's introduction to *A New Home*, pp. xxiii–xxvi.

10. Reynolds's confusion is understandable in light of the fact that he obviously has not read *Ruth Hall*. He makes several statements about the novel that are factually inaccurate, such as his comment that Ruth watches Mary Leon being beaten to death in an insane asylum (405), whereas Mary Leon has died (and not of a beating) before Ruth visits the asylum. Reynolds's most telling inaccuracy is his statement that Ruth ultimately "settles down in a marriage of equality with an intelligent man" (405), which reverses the intentions of Fanny Fern's plot (Reynolds, *Beneath the American Renaissance*).

11. A selection of these columns is included in the edition of *Ruth Hall* published in 1986 and edited by Joyce W. Warren. For an analysis of the themes of Fanny Fern's columns and sketches, which were collected in six volumes published between 1853 and 1872, see Nancy A. Walker, *Fanny Fern*.

12. From an 1852 review of *The Sunny Side* in the *Christian Examiner,* quoted in Coultrap-McQuin, *Doing Literary Business,* p. 11.

13. Susan K. Harris, *19th-Century American Women's Novels: Interpretive Strategies,* p. 113. Naming her central character for a flower, as Fern does in *Rose Clark,* sent the same message, although there is far less need for masking subversion in this novel.

5. OF HESTER AND OFFRED

1. It is true that Offred, as an essentially apolitical young woman, has been to some extent complicit in the creation of the Republic of Gilead, but by the time the narrative begins, she has become subject to its authority and surveillance.

2. Margaret Atwood has, in correspondence with the author, acknowledged that, as Marilynne Robinson was "meditating" on the Bible when she wrote *Housekeeping,* Atwood was meditating on Hawthorne's romance in writing *The Handmaid's Tale.* "Of course," she writes, "in a book dedicated to Perry Miller and Mary Webster, Hester Prynne could not be far away" (note from Atwood in response to an earlier draft of this discussion, dated 13 March 1987).

3. See Michael J. Colacurcio, "'The Woman's Own Choice': Sex, Metaphor, and the Puritan 'Sources' of *The Scarlet Letter.*"

4. David Van Leer, for example, explores Hawthorne's use of the language and conceptual framework of transcendentalism in "Hester's Labyrinth: Transcendental Rhetoric in Puritan Boston."

5. Atwood interview.

6. Linda S. Kauffman points out that, as an author who uses the epistolary form to record the experiences of a woman living "in a state of siege," Offred has as predecessors Dido, Penelope, and Medea. The difference is that, whereas those "epistolary heroines" address a real or imagined *reader,* Offred addresses an imagined *listener.* As a "handmaid of history," Offred compulsively tells and retells her story, "revealing the monstrous shape of things to come" ("Twenty-first Century Epistolarity in *The Handmaid's Tale,*" pp. 223–226). Kauffman also notes that, in terms of genre, *The Handmaid's Tale* is part of a tradition that reaches back to *The Letters of a Portuguese Nun* (1669).

7. In one of the many instances in which the language of *The Handmaid's Tale* echoes that of *The Scarlet Letter,* the Handmaids are told by Aunt Lydia during their training: "Think of yourselves as pearls." Offred reflects: "I think of pearls. Pearls are congealed oyster spit" (145).

8. In a sense, Hester does become an "Unwoman." In yet another remarkable parallel with *The Handmaid's Tale,* Hawthorne speaks of the change in Hester caused by so many hours of isolation and thought:

> *Some attribute had departed from her, the permanence of*
> *which has been essential to keep her a woman. Such is fre-*

> *quently the fate, and such the stern development, of the*
> *feminine character and person, when the woman has en-*
> *countered, and lived through, an experience of particular*
> *severity. . . . She who has once been a woman, and has*
> ceased to be so, *might at any moment become a woman*
> *again, if there were only the magic touch to effect the*
> *transfiguration.*
> (158; EMPHASIS ADDED)

9. The manipulation of language to attempt to change history and control thought is the element that most closely links *The Handmaid's Tale* with Orwell's *1984.*

EPILOGUE

1. From *Close Connections: Caroline Gordon and the Southern Renaissance* (1987), quoted in Magee, *Friendship and Sympathy: Communities of Southern Women Writers*, xvi.

2. As Ruth Bottigheimer points out in *Grimms' Bad Girls and Bold Boys: The Moral and Social Vision of the Tales*, however, it is a mistake to look for precise correspondences between the tales and specific social realities: "The complexity of the relationship between fairy tales and society clearly vitiates a simple equation of fairy tale content with any single cultural entity, whether individual, institutional, or national" (13).

Works Cited

Adams, Timothy Dow. *Telling Lies in Modern Autobiography*. Chapel Hill: University of North Carolina Press, 1990.

Atwood, Margaret. "Bluebeard's Egg." *Bluebeard's Egg and Other Stories*. Boston: Houghton Mifflin, 1986.

———. "The Curse of Eve—Or, What I Learned in School." *Second Words: Selected Critical Prose*, pp. 215–228. Toronto: Anansi, 1982.

———. *The Handmaid's Tale*. 1986; New York: Ballantine, 1987.

———. Interview with Tom Vitale. American Audio Prose Library, 1986.

———. "Nine Beginnings." *The Writer on Her Work*, Vol. II, ed. Janet Sternburg, pp. 150–156. New York: W. W. Norton, 1991.

———. Note to the author dated 13 March 1987.

Auerbach, Nina, and U. C. Knoepflmacher, eds. *Forbidden Journeys: Fairy Tales and Fantasies by Victorian Women Writers*. Chicago: University of Chicago Press, 1992.

Awkward, Michael. *Inspiriting Influences: Tradition, Revision, and Afro-American Women's Novels*. New York: Columbia University Press, 1989.

Barzilai, Shuli. "Reading 'Snow White': The Mother's Story." *Signs* 15, no. 3 (1990): 515–594.

Baym, Nina. *Woman's Fiction*. Ithaca, N.Y.: Cornell University Press, 1978.

———. "From Enlightenment to Victorian: Toward a Narrative of American Women Writers Writing History." *Feminism and American Literary History*. New Brunswick, N.J.: Rutgers University Press, 1992.

Bell, Michael Davitt. "Acts of Deception: Hawthorne, 'Romance,' and *The Scarlet Letter*." *New Essays on The Scarlet Letter*, ed. Michael J. Colacurcio, pp. 29–56. New York: Cambridge University Press, 1985.

Bercovitch, Sacvan. *The Office of the Scarlet Letter*. Baltimore: Johns Hopkins University Press, 1991.

Bernikow, Louise. *Among Women*. New York: Harmony Books, 1980.

Bloom, Harold. *The Anxiety of Influence.* New York: Oxford University Press, 1979.

Booth, Wayne C. *A Rhetoric of Irony.* Chicago: University of Chicago Press, 1974.

Bottigheimer, Ruth B. *Grimms' Bad Girls and Bold Boys: The Moral and Social Vision of the Tales.* New Haven: Yale University Press, 1987.

Brodhead, Richard. *The School of Hawthorne.* New York: Oxford University Press, 1986.

Broumas, Olga. *Beginning with O.* New Haven: Yale University Press, 1977.

Brownstein, Rachel M. *Becoming a Heroine: Reading about Women in Novels.* New York: Viking, 1982.

Bryant, Sylvia. "Re-constructing Oedipus through 'Beauty and the Beast,' " *Criticism* 31, no. 4 (fall 1989): 439–453.

Carafiol, Peter. *The American Ideal: Literary History as a Worldly Activity.* New York: Oxford University Press, 1991.

Carter, Angela. *The Bloody Chamber.* 1979; New York: Penguin, 1993.

———. *The Sadeian Woman and the Ideology of Pornography.* London: Virago, 1979.

———. "Notes from the Front Line." *On Gender and Writing,* ed. Michelene Wandor, pp. 69–77. London: Pandora Press, 1983.

———. *The Passion of New Eve.* New York: Harcourt Brace Jovanovich, 1977.

———, ed. *The Virago Book of Fairy Tales.* London: Virago Press, 1990.

Champagne, Rosaria. "Women's History and *Housekeeping*: Memory, Representation, and Reinscription." *Women's Studies* 20 (1992): 321–329.

Chopin, Kate. *The Awakening.* Case Studies in Contemporary Criticism, ed. Nancy A. Walker. Boston: Bedford Books, 1992.

———. "Elizabeth Stock's One Story." *A Vocation and a Voice,* ed. Emily Toth, pp. 37–44. New York: Penguin, 1991.

Colacurcio, Michael J. "'The Woman's Own Choice': Sex, Metaphor, and the Puritan 'Sources' of *The Scarlet Letter.*" *New Essays on The Scarlet Letter,* ed. Michael J. Colacurcio, pp. 101–135. New York: Cambridge University Press, 1985.

Coultrap-McQuin, Susan. *Doing Literary Business: American Women Writers in the Nineteenth Century.* Chapel Hill: University of North Carolina Press, 1990.

Culley, Margo. "What a Piece of Work Is 'Woman'! An Introduction." *American Women's Autobiography: Fea(s)ts of Memory.* Madison: University of Wisconsin Press, 1992.

Datlow, Ellen, and Terri Windling, eds. *Snow White, Blood Red.* New York: William Morrow, 1993.

Davis, Deanna L. "Feminist Critics and Literary Mothers: Daughters Reading Elizabeth Gaskell." *Signs* 17, no. 3 (spring 1992): 507–532.

De Morgan, Mary. "A Toy Princess." *Victorian Fairy Tales: The Revolt of the Fairies and Elves,* ed. Jack Zipes, pp. 163–174. New York: Methuen, 1987.

Desy, Jeanne. "The Princess Who Stood on Her Own Two Feet." *Don't Bet on the Prince: Contemporary Feminist Fairy Tales in North America and England,* ed. Jack Zipes, pp. 39–47. New York: Routledge, 1989.

Dobson, Joanne. "The American Renaissance Reenvisioned." *The (Other) American Traditions: Nineteenth-Century Women Writers,* ed. Joyce W. Warren, pp. 164–182. New Brunswick, N.J.: Rutgers University Press, 1993.

Duncker, Patricia. "Re-imagining the Fairy Tales: Angela Carter's Bloody Chambers." *Literature and History* 10 (spring 1984): 3–14.

Fern, Fanny. *Fern Leaves from Fanny's Port-Folio.* Auburn, N.Y.: Derby and Miller, 1853.

———. *Ruth Hall* (1854), ed. Joyce W. Warren. New Brunswick, N.J.: Rutgers University Press, 1986.

Fetterley, Judith, ed. *Provisions: A Reader from 19th-Century American Women.* Bloomington: Indiana University Press, 1985.

Fetterley, Judith, and Marjorie Pryse, eds. *American Women Regionalists 1850–1910.* New York: W. W. Norton, 1992.

Foster, Thomas. "History, Critical Theory, and Women's Social Practices: 'Women's Time' and *Housekeeping. Signs* 14, no. 11 (1988): 73–99.

Franklin, Benjamin. *The Autobiography of Benjamin Franklin,* ed. Louis P. Masur. Boston: Bedford Books, 1993.

Fryer, Judith. *The Faces of Eve.* New York: Oxford University Press, 1976.

Furst, Lilian R. *Fictions of Romantic Irony.* Cambridge: Harvard University Press, 1984.

Geyh, Paula E. "Burning Down the House? Domestic Space and Female Subjectivity in Marilynne Robinson's *Housekeeping.*" *Contemporary Literature* 34, no 1 (1993): 103–122.

Gilbert, Sandra, and Susan Gubar. *The Madwoman in the Attic: The Woman Writer and the Nineteenth Century Literary Imagination.* New Haven: Yale University Press, 1979.

Godard, Barbara. "Tales within Tales: Margaret Atwood's Folk Narratives." *Canadian Literature* 109 (1986): 57–84.

Godwin, Gail. *Violet Clay.* New York: Warner Books, 1978.

Greene, Gayle. *Changing the Story: Feminist Fiction and the Tradition.* Bloomington: Indiana University Press, 1991.

Halsey, Margaret. *This Demi-Paradise: A Westchester Diary.* New York: Simon and Schuster, 1960.

———. *No Laughing Matter: The Autobiography of a WASP.* Philadelphia: Lippincott, 1977.

Hamilton, Gail. "My Garden." *Gail Hamilton: Selected Writings,* ed. Susan Coultrap-McQuin, pp. 31–54. New Brunswick, N.J.: Rutgers University Press, 1992.

Hamilton, Jane. *The Book of Ruth.* New York: Ticknor and Fields, 1988.

Harris, Susan K. *19th-Century American Women's Novels: Interpretive Strategies*. New York: Cambridge University Press, 1990.

Hawthorne, Nathaniel. *The Scarlet Letter*. 1850; New York: New American Library, 1959.

Heilbrun, Carolyn. *Writing a Woman's Life*. New York: W. W. Norton, 1988.

Herrmann, Claudine. *The Tongue-Snatchers*, trans. Nancy Kline. Lincoln: University of Nebraska Press, 1989.

Hite, Molly. *The Other Side of the Story: Structures and Strategies of Contemporary Feminist Narratives*. Ithaca, N.Y.: Cornell University Press, 1989.

Holley, Marietta. *My Opinions and Betsy Bobbet's*. Hartford, Conn.: American Publishing Co., 1873.

Homans, Margaret. "The Woman in the Cave: Recent Feminist Fictions and the Classical Underworld." *Contemporary Literature* 29, no. 3 (1988): 369–402.

Howe, Florence, ed. *Tradition and the Talents of Women*. Urbana: University of Illinois Press, 1991.

Howells, Coral Ann. *Private and Fictional Words: Canadian Women Novelists of the 1970s and 1980s*. London: Methuen, 1987.

Johnston, Jill. "Fictions of the Self in the Making." *New York Times Book Review* (25 April 1993): 1, 29, 31, 33.

Kauffman, Linda S. "Twenty-first Century Epistolarity in *The Handmaid's Tale*." *Special Delivery: Epistolary Modes in Modern Fiction*, pp. 221–262. Chicago: University of Chicago Press, 1992.

Kelley, Mary. *Private Woman, Public Stage: Literary Domesticity in Nineteenth-Century America*. New York: Oxford University Press, 1984.

Kirkby, Joan. "Is There Life after Art? The Metaphysics of Marilynne Robinson's *Housekeeping*." *Tulsa Studies in Women's Literature* 5, no. 2 (spring 1986): 91–109.

Kirkland, Caroline. "Literary Women." *A New Home, Who'll Follow?* ed. Sandra A. Zagarell, pp. 193–201. New Brunswick, N.J.: Rutgers University Press, 1990.

———. *A New Home, Who'll Follow? or Glimpses of Western Life*, ed. Sandra A. Zagarell. New Brunswick, N.J.: Rutgers University Press, 1990.

Knoepflmacher, U. C. "Of Babylands and Babylons: E. Nesbit and the Reclamation of the Fairy Tale." *Tulsa Studies in Women's Literature* 6, no. 2 (fall 1987): 299–325.

Kolodny, Annette. *The Land before Her: Fantasy and Experience of the American Frontiers, 1630–1860*. Chapel Hill: University of North Carolina Press, 1984.

———. "A Map for Rereading: Gender and the Interpretation of Literary Texts." *The New Feminist Criticism: Essays on Women, Literature, and Theory*, ed. Elaine Showalter, pp. 46–62. New York: Pantheon, 1985.

Lauter, Paul. *Canons and Contexts*. New York: Oxford University Press, 1991.

Lee, Tanith. *Red As Blood; or Tales from the Sisters Grimmer*. New York: Daw Books, 1983.

Le Guin, Ursula. "She Unnames Them." *Hear the Silence: Stories by Women of Myth, Magic, and Renewal*, ed. Irene Zahava, pp. 192–194. Trumansburg, N.Y.: The Crossing Press, 1986.

———. "The Writer on, and at, Her Work." *The Writer on Her Work*, Vol. II, ed. Janet Sternburg, pp. 210–222. New York: W. W. Norton, 1991.

Lieberman, Marcia K. "'Some Day My Prince Will Come': Female Acculturation through the Fairy Tale." *Don't Bet on the Prince: Contemporary Feminist Fairy Tales in North America and England*. ed. Jack Zipes, pp. 185–200. New York: Routledge, 1989.

Lindemann, Marilee. "'This Woman Can Cross Any Line': Power and Authority in Contemporary Women's Fiction." *Engendering the Word: Feminist Essays in Psychosexual Poetics*, ed. Temma F. Berg, pp. 105–124. Urbana: University of Illinois Press, 1989.

Lurie, Alison, ed. *Don't Tell the Grown-Ups: Subversive Children's Literature*. Boston: Little, Brown, 1990.

———. *The Oxford Book of Modern Fairy Tales*. New York: Oxford University Press, 1993.

McCorkle, Jill. "Sleeping Beauty, Revised." *Crash Diet*, pp. 196–214. Chapel Hill, N.C.: Algonquin Books, 1992.

Maddux, Rachel. *Communication: The Autobiography of Rachel Maddux*, ed. Nancy A. Walker. Knoxville: University of Tennessee Press, 1991.

Magee, Rosemary M., ed. *Friendship and Sympathy: Communities of Southern Women Writers*. Jackson: University Press of Mississippi, 1992.

"Marilynne Robinson." *Conversations with Contemporary American Writers*, ed. Sanford Pinsker, pp. 119–127. Amsterdam: Rodopi, 1985.

Meese, Elizabeth A. "A World of Women: Marilynne Robinson's *Housekeeping*." *Crossing the Double-Cross: The Practice of Feminist Criticism*, pp. 57–68. Chapel Hill: University of North Carolina Press, 1986.

Merish, Lori. "'The Hand of Refined Taste' in the Frontier Landscape: Caroline Kirkland's *A New Home, Who'll Follow?* and the Feminization of American Consumerism." *American Quarterly* 45, no. 4 (December 1993): 485–523.

Merseyside Fairy Story Collective. "Red Riding Hood." *The Trials and Tribulations of Little Red Riding Hood: Versions of the Tale in Sociocultural Context*, ed. Jack Zipes, pp. 239–244. South Hadley, Mass.: Bergin and Garvey, 1983.

Middlebrook, Diane Wood. *Anne Sexton: A Biography*. New York: Vintage, 1992.

Murphy, Cullen. "Women and the Bible." *The Atlantic Monthly* 272, no. 2 (August 1993): 39–64.

Nesbit, Edith. "The Last of the Dragons." *Victorian Fairy Tales: The Revolt of the Fairies and Elves*, ed. Jack Zipes, pp. 351–358. New York: Methuen, 1987.

Oates, Joyce Carol. *Black Water*. New York: Dutton, 1992.

O'Donnell, Patrick, and Robert Con Davis, eds. *Intertextuality and Contemporary American Fiction*. Baltimore: Johns Hopkins University Press, 1989.

Olsen, Tillie. *Silences*. New York: Delacorte, 1978.

Ostriker, Alicia Suskin. *Feminist Revision and the Bible*. Oxford: Blackwell, 1993.

———. *Stealing the Language: The Emergence of Women's Poetry in America*. Boston: Beacon Press, 1986.

Palmer, Paulina. *Contemporary Women's Fiction: Narrative Practice and Feminist Theory*. Jackson: University Press of Mississippi, 1989.

Pilzer, Kay Leslie Campbell. "'Contrary Possibilities': A Woman Reads Shakespeare's *King Lear* and Smiley's *A Thousand Acres*." M.A. thesis, University of Alabama in Huntsville, 1993.

Pinsker, Sanford. *Conversations with Contemporary American Writers*. Amsterdam: Rodopi, 1985.

Ravits, Martha. "Extending the American Range: Marilynne Robinson's *Housekeeping*." *American Literature* 61, no. 4 (December 1989): 644–666.

Reynolds, David. *Beneath the American Renaissance: The Subversive Imagination in the Age of Emerson and Melville*. New York: Knopf, 1988.

Rich, Adrienne. *On Lies, Secrets, and Silence: Selected Prose 1966–1978*. New York: W. W. Norton, 1979.

———. "Diving into the Wreck." *The Fact of a Doorframe: Poems, Selected and New 1950–84*. New York: W. W. Norton, 1984.

Roberts, Robin. "Humor and Gender in Feminist Music Videos." *Sexual Politics and Popular Culture*, ed. Diane Raymond, pp. 173–182. Bowling Green, Ohio: Popular Press, 1990.

Robinson, Marilynne. "Belles Lettres Interview." *Belles Lettres* 6, no. 1 (fall 1990): 36–39.

———. *Housekeeping*. 1981; New York: Bantam Books, 1982.

Rose, Ellen Cronan. "Through the Looking Glass: When Women Tell Fairy Tales." *The Voyage In: Fictions of Female Development*, ed. Elizabeth Abel, Marianne Hirsch, and Elizabeth Langland, pp. 209–227. Hanover, N.H.: University Press of New England, 1983.

Rowe, Karen E. "Feminism and Fairy Tales." *Women's Studies* 6, no. 3 (1979): 237–257.

Rubenstein, Roberta. "Intersexions: Gender Metamorphosis in Angela Carter's *The Passion of New Eve* and Lois Gould's *A Sea-Change*." *Tulsa Studies in Women's Literature* 12, no. 1 (spring 1993): 103–118.

Ruland, Richard, and Malcolm Bradbury. *From Puritanism to Postmodernism: A History of American Literature*. New York: Viking, 1991.

Russ, Joanna. *How to Suppress Women's Writing*. Austin: University of Texas Press, 1983.

Ryan, Maureen. "Marilynne Robinson's *Housekeeping*: The Subversive Narrative and the New American Eve." *South Atlantic Review* 56, no. 1 (January 1991): 79–86.

Sage, Lorna. *Women in the House of Fiction: Post-War Women Novelists.* London: Macmillan, 1992.

St. Laurent, Maureen E. "American Women's Travel Narratives: Gender and Genre." Ph.D. dissertation, Vanderbilt University, 1992.

Schwartz, Lynne Sharon. "Beyond the Garden." *Belles Lettres* 7 (spring 1991): 36–38.

Sexton, Anne. *Transformations.* Boston: Houghton Mifflin, 1971.

Sharp, Evelyn. "The Spell of the Magician's Daughter." *Victorian Fairy Tales: The Revolt of the Fairies and Elves*, ed. Jack Zipes, pp. 359–372. New York: Methuen, 1987.

Sheets, Robin Ann. "Pornography, Fairy Tales, and Feminism: Angela Carter's 'The Bloody Chamber.'" *Forbidden History: The State, Society, and the Regulation of Sexuality in Modern Europe*, ed. John C. Fout, pp. 335–359. Chicago: University of Chicago Press, 1992.

Showalter, Elaine. *Sister's Choice: Tradition and Change in American Women's Writing.* New York: Oxford University Press, 1991.

———. "Tradition and the Individual Talent: *The Awakening* as a Solitary Book." *The Awakening.* Case Studies in Contemporary Criticism, ed. Nancy A. Walker, pp. 169–189. Boston: Bedford Books, 1992.

Smart, Elizabeth. *By Grand Central Station I Sat Down and Wept.* 1945; London: Panther Books, 1966.

Smith, Martha Nell. *Rowing in Eden: Rereading Emily Dickinson.* Austin: University of Texas Press, 1992.

Smith, Sidonie. *A Poetics of Women's Autobiography: Marginality and the Fictions of Self-Representation.* Bloomington: Indiana University Press, 1987.

Spender, Dale. *The Writing or the Sex?; or Why You Don't Have to Read Women's Writing to Know It's No Good.* New York: Pergamon Press, 1989.

Sprengnether, Madelon. "(M)other Eve: Some Revisions of the Fall in Fiction by Contemporary Women Writers." *Feminism and Psychoanalysis*, ed. Richard Feldstein and Judith Roof, pp. 298–322. Ithaca, N.Y.: Cornell University Press, 1989.

Strout, Cushing. *Making American Tradition: Visions and Revisions from Ben Franklin to Alice Walker.* New Brunswick, N.J.: Rutgers University Press, 1990.

Todd, Janet. *The Sign of Angelica: Women, Writing, and Fiction, 1660–1800.* New York: Columbia University Press, 1989.

Tompkins, Jane. "Susanna Rowson, Father of the American Novel." *The (Other) American Traditions: Nineteenth-Century Women Writers*, ed. Joyce W. Warren, pp. 29–38. New Brunswick, N.J.: Rutgers University Press, 1993.

Trible, Phyllis. "Eve and Adam: Genesis 2–3 Reread." *Andover Newton Quarterly* 13 (March 1973): 74–83.

Trubowitz, Rachel. "The Reenchantment of Utopia and the Female Monarchical Self: Margaret Cavendish's Blazing World." *Tulsa Studies in Women's Literature* 11, no. 2 (fall 1992): 229–245.

Tuckerman, Henry T., ed. *The Poetical Works of Elizabeth Barrett Browning*, Vol. 1. pp. ix–xxii. New York: Worthington, 1890.

Twain, Mark. "The Diary of Adam and Eve." *The Complete Short Stories of Mark Twain*, ed. Charles Neider, pp. 272–294. Garden City, N.Y.: Doubleday.

Van Leer, David. "Hester's Labyrinth: Transcendental Rhetoric in Puritan Boston." *New Essays on The Scarlet Letter*, ed. Michael J. Colacurcio, pp. 57–100. New York: Cambridge University Press, 1985.

Walker, Nancy A. *Fanny Fern*. New York: Twayne, 1992.

Warner, Sylvia Townsend. "Bluebeard's Daughter." *The Cat's Cradle-Book*, pp. 157–180. New York: Viking, 1940.

Warren, Joyce W. *Fanny Fern: An Independent Woman*. New Brunswick, N.J.: Rutgers University Press, 1992.

———. "Subversion versus Celebration: The Aborted Friendship of Fanny Fern and Walt Whitman." *Patrons and Protégées: Gender, Friendship, and Writing in Nineteenth-Century America*, ed. Shirley Marchalonis, pp. 59–93. New Brunswick, N.J.: Rutgers University Press, 1988.

Weldon, Fay. *Down among the Women*. 1972; Chicago: Chicago Academy Press, 1984.

———. *Female Friends*. New York: St. Martin's Press, 1974.

———. *The Life and Loves of a She-Devil*. 1983; New York: Ballantine Books, 1985.

———. *Moon over Minneapolis*. 1991; New York: Penguin, 1992.

———. *The Rules of Life*. New York: Harper and Row, 1987.

———. *Words of Advice*. 1977; New York: Ballantine Books, 1978.

Wilde, Alan. "'Bold, But Not Too Bold': Fay Weldon and the Limits of Poststructuralist Criticism." *Contemporary Literature* 29, no. 3 (1988): 403–419.

Wilson, Sharon Rose. *Margaret Atwood's Fairy-Tale Sexual Politics*. Jackson: University Press of Mississippi, 1993.

Woolf, Virginia. *A Room of One's Own*. 1929; New York: Harcourt Brace Jovanovitch, 1957.

———. "A Sketch of the Past." *The Virginia Woolf Reader*, ed. Mitchell A. Leaska, pp. 3–40. New York: Harcourt Brace Jovanovitch, 1984.

Yolen, Jane. "America's Cinderella." *Cinderella: A Casebook*, ed. Alan Dundes, pp. 294–306. Madison: University of Wisconsin Press, 1982.

Zagarell, Sandra A. "Expanding 'America': Lydia Sigourney's *Sketch of Connecticut*, Catharine Sedgwick's *Hope Leslie*." *Tulsa Studies in Women's Literature* 6, no. 2 (fall 1987): 225–245.

Zipes, Jack. *Breaking the Magic Spell: Radical Theories of Folk and Fairy Tales*. Austin: University of Texas Press, 1979.

————. "Recent Trends in the Contemporary American Fairy Tale." *Journal of the Fantastic in the Arts* 5 (1992): 13–41.

————, ed. *Don't Bet on the Prince: Contemporary Feminist Fairy Tales in North America and England.* New York: Routledge, 1989.

————. *The Trials and Tribulations of Little Red Riding Hood: Versions of the Tale in Sociocultural Context.* South Hadley, Mass.: Bergin and Garvey, 1983.

————. *Victorian Fairy Tales: The Revolt of the Fairies and Elves.* New York: Methuen, 1987.

Index